Spiritual Sensations

Also available from Bloomsbury

Martin Scorsese's Divine Comedy, Catherine O'Brien
Science Fiction and the Imitation of the Sacred, Richard Grigg
Figurations and Sensations of the Unseen in Judaism, Christianity and Islam,
edited by Birgit Meyer and Terje Stordalen

Spiritual Sensations

*Cinematic Religious Experience and Evolving
Conceptions of the Sacred*

Sarah K. Balstrup

BLOOMSBURY ACADEMIC
LONDON • NEW YORK • OXFORD • NEW DELHI • SYDNEY

BLOOMSBURY ACADEMIC
Bloomsbury Publishing Plc
50 Bedford Square, London, WC1B 3DP, UK
1385 Broadway, New York, NY 10018, USA
29 Earlsfort Terrace, Dublin 2, Ireland

BLOOMSBURY, BLOOMSBURY ACADEMIC and the Diana logo are trademarks of
Bloomsbury Publishing Plc

First published in Great Britain 2021
This paperback edition published in 2022

Copyright © Sarah K. Balstrup, 2021

Sarah K. Balstrup has asserted her rights under the Copyright, Designs and Patents Act, 1988, to be identified as Author of this work.

For legal purposes the Acknowledgments on p. ix constitute an extension of this copyright page.

All rights reserved. No part of this publication may be reproduced or transmitted in any form or by any means, electronic or mechanical, including photocopying, recording, or any information storage or retrieval system, without prior permission in writing from the publishers.

Bloomsbury Publishing Plc does not have any control over, or responsibility for, any third-party websites referred to or in this book. All internet addresses given in this book were correct at the time of going to press. The author and publisher regret any inconvenience caused if addresses have changed or sites have ceased to exist, but can accept no responsibility for any such changes.

A catalogue record for this book is available from the British Library.

A catalog record for this book is available from the Library of Congress.

ISBN: HB: 978-1-3501-3017-3
PB: 978-1-3503-2776-4
ePDF: 978-1-3501-3018-0
eBook: 978-1-3501-3019-7

Typeset by Deanta Global Publishing Services, Chennai, India

To find out more about our authors and books, visit www.bloomsbury.com and sign up for our newsletters.

For Andrew, Elise, and Brendan

Contents

Acknowledgments		ix
Note on the Text		x
Introduction: Religious Experience in the Cinema		1
Religion, Film, and Cultural Change		2
Chapter Outline		4
1	Religion and Film	7
	The Transcendental Style in Film	10
	Religious Experience and the Ritual Function of Film	14
	Conclusion	20
2	Religious Experience	21
	Alternative Spirituality	21
	Religious Experience and Spiritual Authority	28
	The Easternization of the West	31
	Conclusion	35
3	*2001: A Space Odyssey*: Cosmos and Ethos	37
	Re-Imagining the Universe	38
	Mystery and Potentiality	45
	Conclusion	54
4	*2001: A Space Odyssey* and Meditative Perception	57
	Meditative Qualities of Sound, Composition, and Pace	59
	Transcendental Style: Structure and Stasis	70
	Meditative Practice and Focused Awareness	76
	Conclusion	80
5	*2001: A Space Odyssey*: Crossing the Perceptual Threshold	81
	Ineffability	81
	Noetic Quality	88
	Transiency	95
	Passivity	99
	Conclusion	105

6	*Enter the Void*: The Initiatory Moment	107
	The New Extremism in a Media-saturated Age	108
	Agency, Authority, and Epistemology	114
	The Initiation of a Director	117
	Conclusion	123
7	*Enter the Void*: Trauma, Psychedelics, and the Lightning-Bolt Path	125
	Sex, Stasis, and the Spiritual	125
	Sensory Possession	133
	Profane Paths to the Sacred: Cinematic Journeys of Realization	143
	Conclusion	149
8	*Melancholia*: In Dreadful Beauty and Trembling	151
	Frontality, Vibrations, and Inversions	153
	Mystical Experience	163
	Conclusion	167
9	*Melancholia*: Presence in Absence/The Long Withdrawing Roar	171
	Longing for Reality	172
	Searching the Darkness	177
	Conclusion	185
Conclusion: Spiritual Sensations		187
	Religion, Film, and the Transcendental Style	187
	The Many Paths	188
	Sacred Sensations and the Beholding of Truth	190
References		193
Index		217

Acknowledgments

My sincere appreciation goes to the editorial team at Bloomsbury for the opportunity to publish this research. *Spiritual Sensations* is a refinement of my doctoral thesis that has benefited from the considered feedback of both my examiners and reviewers. I warmly acknowledge my academic mentor, supervisor, and friend Professor Carole Cusack from the Department of Studies in Religion at the University of Sydney for her unfaltering support, practical advice, and wisdom. The many years I spent in the Department of Studies in Religion are filled with fond memories, and I consider myself privileged to have worked in an environment where freedom of thought and academic creativity were always encouraged.

The ideas presented in this book developed slowly over a ten-year period and during that time I met my husband Andrew with whom I now have two beautiful children, Elise and Brendan. The love that we share has enriched my life immeasurably and I am deeply thankful for my little family. Yet, as any parent knows, when caring for young children it can become a challenge to find the space and solitude necessary to work. To Andrew and my aunties Judy and Carole I owe special thanks for the precious gift of time. Without their generous assistance this book would not have come into being.

As this project emerged from my personal experiences of film I wish to thank the filmmakers whose work inspired the ideas explored herein. I am equally grateful to those who shared their experiences of film with me (in conversation and unwittingly in online reviews) demonstrating that film can touch us most profoundly and can reveal the shape of our inner world.

Note on the Text

This study incorporates viewer responses recorded in the *Internet Movie Database (IMDb)* database. Viewer testimony is an important and often overlooked resource in the study of religion and film. However, online reviews are an unruly mixture of profound insight and throwaway comments, replete with grammatical errors and more than a little hyperbole. Unlike interview data, clarification about the deeper meaning of comments cannot be obtained. With these limitations in mind, *IMDb* reviews nonetheless offer a candid, albeit impressionistic, insight into the reception of the films studied.

The anonymity of *IMDb* users means that a person's gender can only be guessed. To preserve sentence flow, this study employs "he" or "she" where names are suggestive of gender, and s/he, where no indication is given.

Reviews consulted fall within the following date ranges:

Stanley Kubrick, *2001: A Space Odyssey* (1968).
First *IMDb* user review July 30, 1998.
Last accessed on April 9, 2016 (most recent review at this time April 7, 2016).
Total reviews on this date: 1,712.

Gaspar Noé, *Enter the Void* (2009).
First *IMDb* user review September 13, 2009.
Last accessed April 9, 2016 (most recent review at this time April 2, 2016).
Total reviews on this date: 195.

Lars von Trier, *Melancholia* (2011).
First *IMDb* user review July 14, 2011.
Last accessed April 9, 2016 (most recent review at this time March 25, 2016).
Total reviews on this date: 548.

Introduction

Religious Experience in the Cinema

Religious experiences were once reserved for mystics, people with special dispositions (Hollenback 1996: 33), or aristocratic esotericists (Sutcliffe 2003: 215-16), but in the contemporary West, where religiosity has been de-institutionalized and subjectivized, spiritual truth can be accessed by anyone who seeks it (Demerath 2000: 3). This book is an exploration of spiritual experiences and the conditions that are necessary to bring them about. Outside of traditional religious contexts, film directors are particularly well equipped to engage the senses and to facilitate powerful viewing experiences. Stanley Kubrick, Gaspar Noé, and Lars von Trier are three directors that have developed distinctive film styles that produce strong audience responses. The films that will be considered here are Kubrick's *2001: A Space Odyssey* (1968), Noé's *Enter the Void* (2009), and von Trier's *Melancholia* (2011). The latter two films draw influence from *2001* and each of these films incorporate techniques that play on the religious emotions and encourage alternative states of perception, generating viewer responses that are reminiscent of traditional accounts of mystical experience. As Jess Hollenback has argued, "Religious experiences are never wholly spontaneous and are part of the cyclic interaction of religious understanding, contemplative techniques, post-experiential reflection and actions such as prayer" (1996: 1). As such, this study considers filmic experience in the context of interacting influences from the religious culture of the West.

The *Internet Movie Database* (*IMDb*) holds a rich repository of audience responses to film. Viewer responses from *IMDb* offer a candid insight into the religious function of film, remembering experiences of the late 1960s and reflecting on more immediate responses to these films up until early 2016. Considering these user reviews together, particular trends emerge, revealing the shape of the underlying religious culture of the West. Rather than being tied to a particular religious tradition or being linked to individuals' ostensible beliefs, the religious qualities that emerge in filmic experiences point to an epistemological mode that has become increasingly prominent in the Western psyche as structured and socially reinforced religious behaviors become less stable. It is linked to the inalienable veracity of personal experience and interpretation and to the desire to seek the truth while continually engaging in its deconstruction. The shifting nature of truth and the continual revelation of the inauthentic where truth holds its boldest claims disenfranchises institutions and places authority in the personal certainty of feeling. This powerful epistemological change was a part of the spiritual revolution of the late 1960s when *2001* was released, and has remained an integral part of the contemporary Western orientation toward truth. Tracing the development of this orientation half a century later, audience responses to *Enter the Void* and *Melancholia* reveal the increased importance of intense and abstract experiences as characteristic of an authentic encounter with truth.

Religion, Film, and Cultural Change

Writing from a religious studies perspective, *Spiritual Sensations* contributes to the study of religion and film, specifically building on the work of Paul Schrader (1972). Although film studies emerged as a discipline quite early in the history of cinema, the study of religion and film developed much later, with the majority of scholarship produced from the 1990s onward. As religion and film studies is a branch of religious studies or theology (in its different forms), it has not produced much work that considers film technique and largely ignores the various approaches to the study of the mise en scene found in film studies. Religion and film scholars are only just starting to move beyond a consideration of narrative and symbolism in their treatment of film. Yet film studies is equally uninterested in matters of religion. Film studies is deeply intertwined with major schools of continental philosophical thought, so the social reality of religion is of peripheral interest. Situated within religious studies, a full consideration of insights from film studies is not attempted here. However, film theorists such as Torben Grodal, Sheila Nayar, and Alison Griffiths offer useful perspectives on the viewing experience that are discussed in relation to viewer testimonies.

According to Kubrick *2001* was created to explore "the God concept" (Gelmis 1969: n.p.) but it is also a film with no overt religious references. *Enter the Void* and *Melancholia* are similarly free from explicit religious content, while being capable of triggering spiritual experiences. Although it could be argued that *Enter the Void* includes religious content in its reference to the *Tibetan Book of the Dead*, the overt themes of the film are in fact related to relationships, drugs, and the dark underbelly of Tokyo. Although my approach builds on Schrader, his argument that there is a universal transcendent reality that is accessed by filmmakers (and audiences via films made in this style) is an existential and essentialist claim that I do not endorse. Rather, viewer's film experiences are analyzed in relation to concepts, feelings, and sensations commonly understood to be religious. As a filmmaker himself, Schrader's methodology is meaningfully grounded in technique and a nuanced appreciation of the complexities of film form and structure. However, the film style explored here is not precisely the same as that described by Schrader in his analysis of directors Yasujiro Ozu, Robert Bresson, and Carl Dreyer. For this reason, I do not argue that *2001, Enter the Void*, and *Melancholia* are films made in the "transcendental style." Whereas Schrader's case studies involve slow, minimalist aesthetics, *2001, Enter the Void*, and *Melancholia* are films that also employ devices of richness and intensity that overwhelm the viewer's senses. These films are influenced not by a single religious tradition or a universal transcendent reality, but by the broad cultural movement of alternative spirituality. This term is used to indicate widespread resistance to adopting institutionally sanctioned religious beliefs in favor of personally determined approaches. Working in harmony with the dominant economic and governmental systems of Western society—consumerism and pluralist democracy—modern religious epistemology privileges individual free will where appeals are made to emotion and sensation rather than logic.

Colin Campbell has referred to the late 1960s as the "'hinge' of modern history" and a crucial transformation point in the worldview of the West (2008: 213), while Howard Brick refers to this time as the "point of origin" of contemporary trends in art, politics, and religion (2000: xi). These comments reveal a culture in radical reassessment of its core values. Kubrick's *2001* was conceived in collaboration with science fiction writer Arthur C. Clarke in this context and audiences who came to see it in 1968 were primed to discover the true potential of humanity. Focusing on the religious ideas that this generation was drawn to, and their development over time, I investigate the role played by the arts (specifically film) in generating spiritual experiences. Rejecting the social, artistic, and religious values of their parents, the youth who came of age during this period sought to revolutionize society by casting doubt on all apparent certainties and exploring the Big Questions of life firsthand. Nothing was sacred in the sense that nothing was beyond individual reevaluation. And yet, the potential to discover the sacred anew was ever present. This implicit religious attitude of antiauthoritarianism, individualism, personalized truth, and experiential epistemology that reached its height in the late 1960s continues to develop both overtly and diffusely in the mainstream twenty-first century Western worldview (Hanegraaff 1998: 97). Wouter Hanegraaff identifies the overt with "New Age religion"; however, this study is more concerned with the diffuse manifestation of this form of religiosity.

The possibility of having a spiritual experience in the cinema, in the broadest sense, comes as a result of the democratization of religious experience. This change accompanies the transference of functions previously performed by religious institutions to the arts and popular culture (Houtman and Aupers 2007: 315). In a secular culture where religion is a matter of personal choice, a film audience may be comprised of people with a wide range of religious views. However, the commonality among them is the pluralist and individualist culture that they are situated in. From the late 1960s onward, authenticity was reconfigured so that traditional religious intermediaries were no longer required in one's personal journey, and were not called upon to certify the authenticity of subjectively divined truth. With subjective experience at the heart of authenticity, individuals seek out the hidden knowledge of spiritual truth, rejecting the old binary of faith and reason (Hanegraaff 1998: 519). Emotions and sensations that arise spontaneously are felt to be trustworthy because they seem to operate independent of social imposition. If the individual can maintain the sense of encounter with this raw mystery, then they are on the frontier of discovery—not yet understanding but perceiving *something*—and this moment is at once an assertion of individual freedom, the rejection of social determinism, and the opening up of the possibilities of human potential. Couched in the dissociative feelings of trance, films like *2001*, *Enter the Void*, and *Melancholia* can bring about a moment of deconstruction that (like religious ritual) allows for subsequent reintegration. Mirroring the invocation of spiritual presence in religious practice, cinematic experiences become sacred where there is temporary submission to the higher power of irresolvable sensation (Wood 2007: 154–75).

Chapter Outline

Commencing with an introduction to the subdiscipline of religion and film, Chapter 1 situates this study in relation to Schrader's *Transcendental Style in Film: Ozu, Bresson, Dreyer* (1972) and more recent work that investigates the socioreligious significance of film experience. Chapter 2 details the significant cultural shift that occurred in the late 1960s that transformed the dominant Western worldview into what is referred to here as "alternative spirituality." In

Chapter 3, Kubrick's *2001* is introduced in relation to the cultural and religious context of this era. Chapter 4 explores the techniques that Kubrick has employed to engage his audience in a meditative cinematic experience that is capable of eliciting spiritual responses. Viewer commentary considered here demonstrates that such responses are widespread and recurrent. Chapter 5 reflects on viewer testimony in light of William James's attributes of mystical experience (2014: 206–7). This chapter outlines specific areas of correlation between cinematic and religious experience, revealing the unusual affective power of *2001*. The three chapters devoted to *2001* establish an approach to the study of religion and film that evaluates the impact of cinematic techniques in relation to audience responses, considering both film viewing and directorial design in light of their cultural context. This method of analysis is similarly applied to comparative examples, demonstrating the complex interrelationship between the creative work of filmmakers and film reception, as the culture changes. This is particularly important because religion does not exist as a static framework. Rather, the religious values and orientations of a culture determine how meaning comes to be embedded in the individual's life and how aesthetic experiences are understood.

Chapters 6 through 9 focus on more recent films that were specifically influenced by *2001* to reach a deeper understanding of the spiritual affect of film technique. Noé's *Enter the Void* and von Trier's *Melancholia* share a common approach in their appeal to dissociative sensations, despite differences in subject matter and narrative content. Including films that were made over forty years after *2001*'s release, it becomes possible to see how the underlying religio-cultural context of the West remains structurally similar to the late 1960s when alternative spirituality first became prolific. However, the mediatized early twenty-first century is marked by more extreme approaches to cinema, and both *Enter the Void* and *Melancholia* force the viewer to confront the darkness of the human spirit, treating this as an integral element of psychic revelation.

Chapter 6 explores the impact of new media and contemporary cultural developments in relation to the new extremism in cinema, situating filmic revelation in relation to Noé's childhood experience of *2001*. Chapter 7 focuses on the film techniques used in *Enter the Void* in consideration of audience responses, detailing Noé's "tantric" representation of sexuality and the influence of Buddhist concepts in the film. In Chapter 8, responses to von Trier's *Melancholia* are detailed in terms of their mystical qualities, and specific techniques are analyzed in comparison to Schrader's transcendental style. In Chapter 9, audience responses to *Melancholia* highlighting the decline of Western civilization are brought into dialogue with the experiential and epistemological, revealing the present conception of ultimate truth in alternative spirituality.

The differences in cinematic style and representation that emerge in these three films demonstrate underlying developments in the cultural conception of truth. It is also evident that film techniques can be more important in triggering spiritual responses than overt religious content. Together, these observations present a new perspective on religion and film that links social, experiential, and religious elements of film. Further, these case studies demonstrate that it is no longer reasonable to assume that Western films relate primarily to Christianity, or that films only contribute to a person's belief system through the dramatization of narrative meaning.

1

Religion and Film

The interaction between religion and film is complex and has attracted the interest of scholars from a variety of disciplines including sociology, cultural studies, and theology. Scholarly work on religion and film is also diverse due to the range of films that are open to study and the contested definition of "religion." The 1990s saw an increase in publications in the area of religion and film studies, yet it remains a subdiscipline characterized by methodological variety rather than an agreed "orthodoxy" (Kickasola et al. 2013: 4, 47, and 53). According to William L. Blizek, Michele Desmarais, and Ronald R. Burke, there are four common approaches to the study of religion and film (2011: 476–81). The first approach, "using religion to interpret film," refers to a religious reading of a film, for instance, undertaking a Gnostic reading of the Wachowski's *The Matrix* (1999). This position does not exhibit the theological investment of those writing about their own religious tradition (Blizek, Desmarais, and Burke 2011: 476; Blizek 2009: 29–38). In the second approach, "using film to interpret religion," theorists discuss the ways in which religion is presented in film and how film can encourage a reinterpretation of religion (Blizek, Desmarais, and Burke 2011: 478–9; Blizek 2009: 39–48). The third category, "the religious use of film," includes theological perspectives that seek to use film as a means of exploring religious faith from an insider's perspective (Blizek, Desmarais, and Burke 2011: 480; Marsh 2009: 59–69). The fourth category is the "cultural studies" approach that critiques the religious aspect of culture, and its inherent power relationships as they are represented through film (Wright 2009: 101–2). This category can include any film that the scholar identifies as containing religious content that is reflective of an aspect of culture (Blizek, Desmarais, and Burke 2011: 480–1). The authors also identify less common approaches to the study of religion and film, including "censorship, storytelling, psychoanalysis, film theories, propaganda, the transcendental style, critical religious film theory, and film as religion" (Blizek, Desmarais, and Burke 2011: 481).

Of these categories, this study is best placed under "transcendental style," an area of study that is based solely on Schrader's *Transcendental Style in Film: Ozu, Bresson, Dreyer* (1972). Situating Schrader's work within the context of religion and film studies is no simple task. As a director and a film critic writing before religion and film studies had taken shape as a discipline, Schrader's work is unique. In the 1990s, religion and film studies emerged out of theology and religious studies where film was a specific focal area within broader considerations of the link between religion and popular culture. In this context, few writers cited Schrader, as his approach did not cover the key areas of interest that had drawn scholars of religion to study film. Broadly speaking, theologians sought to find evidence in popular culture of the ongoing relevance of Christianity by identifying Christian themes in film or by producing theological readings of film that could engender a deepening of faith (Lyden 2003: 13). Religious studies scholars, on the other hand, sought to demonstrate that secularization did not amount to a decline in religiosity as elements of religion were being revived in a secular context (Landy and Saler 2009: 1). Popular culture was a primary site of investigation, and religion and film studies contributed to the argument for the continued relevance of religion. However, religion and film studies tended to limit itself to isolated observations of instances where film could be linked with religion. From a narrative or symbolic perspective scholars of religion identified the presence of concepts such as grace, sin, redemption, sacrifice (Bergesen and Greeley 2003: 1–2), and apocalypse (Ostwalt 1995: 62), or more commonly, those of God (Haunton 2009: 260) or the Christ-figure (Bergesen and Greeley 2003: 1–2). With the introduction of the *Journal of Religion and Film* in 1997, religion and film studies began to move beyond Christian concepts to consider the relationship between film and other religions such as Buddhism, Gnosticism, Native American religion, ancient Egyptian religion, witchcraft, American civil religion, and Judaism (*Journal of Religion and Film* 2014). Religious content from outside of the Christian tradition also began to become more prominent, and the Eastern religious concept of enlightenment became especially popular. For example, Sam Mendes's *American Beauty* (1999), David Fincher's *Fight Club* (1999), and the Wachowski's *The Matrix* (1999) have all been associated with Buddhist tropes (Cusack 2011: 311). Eastern religious concepts have also been identified in a range of articles where films do not overtly deal with religion (Ford 2000; Schwartz 2000; Smith 2005). Despite this broadening of the field, Douglas Cowan points out that there is still an issue of "sedimentary" scholarship in the study of religion and film where Christian interpretations dominate and build upon each other, often with little convincing evidence provided from the case studies themselves (2009: n.p.).

One of the principal criticisms of religion and film studies is the tendency to treat film as a narrative, or "visual story" (Nolan 2009: 21), without acknowledging the special qualities of cinema that have been recognized in film studies (Martin 1995: 2). However, it is also the case that film studies does not exhibit much interest in religion (Martin 1995: 2). While film studies has its roots in philosophy (Thomson-Jones 2008: vii–viii), the concerns of religion and film studies are often sociological, where the "conversion potential" of film is central. As Margaret Miles notes, because "religion and film *share* an interest in, an attention to, values," the cinema has become the place that people reflect on "moral quandaries" rather than in a church (1996: 25). Joel Martin and Conrad Ostwalt present a similar point of view, arguing that films are more than entertainment, because they "have the potential to reinforce, to challenge, to overturn, or to crystallize religious perspectives, ideological assumptions, and fundamental values" (1995: vii). Here, values as seemingly universal as love, sacrifice, forgiveness, and mercy are interpreted as being "Christian." It is quite shortsighted, however, to assume that Christianity remains the dominant symbolic system underlying Western secular culture when such dramatic changes have occurred in the religious landscape over the last century.

Tomas Axelson provides a more nuanced analysis of the way that film can contribute to the development of personal values by considering the religious background of interviewees in relation to their engagement with film. After separating 179 Swedish students into groups according to their level of religious socialization, Axelson interviewed participants asking what might be traditionally understood as the Big Questions of life, including the meaning of life, the nature of reality and the human, moral questions, the existence of God, and the definition of love. Those who had less religious socialization were found to use films in a more interested and creative manner to find meaning in their lives (Axelson 2008: n.p.). Axelson also found that individuals used films in the development and continual transformation of self that sometimes translated into "profound and long-lasting ideas of being part of a moral community" (2010: n.p.).

Further to this, Axelson has reflected on "spiritual meaning making" in film viewing, arguing that the cinematic experience engages audiences on multiple levels, involving affective cognition and higher-order processes, and plays an important role in the development of one's worldview (2017: 9). Axelson makes an important contribution to the study of religion and film by moving beyond the generic notion of values to a sociologically and psychologically grounded interpretation of film's role in the construction of individuals' worldviews.

While scholarship on the religious significance of film sometimes incorporates firsthand viewer responses, Christopher Deacy points out that studies of religion and film often speak for the audience by presuming their response (2005: 5–11). He therefore recommends the use of online viewer testimonies from websites such as *IMDb* (Deacy 2005: 11). Recognizing the importance of viewer testimony in determining the nature of religious experience in the cinema, this study takes up Deacy's recommendation by making extensive use of *IMDb* commentary. All viewer responses recorded in *IMBb* relating to Kubrick's *2001*, Noé's *Enter the Void*, and von Trier's *Melancholia* at April 9, 2016, were considered in this research, amounting to 2,455 reviews. As each review contains multiple perspectives, themes, and responses, it is an unwieldy task to provide a quantitative analysis of these sources. The act of categorizing their prose would also impose a false uniformity on viewer comments. Instead, audience responses have been used qualitatively to demonstrate the existence of spiritual reactions to film.

The Transcendental Style in Film

Unlike the approaches mentioned above, Schrader's *Transcendental Style* is not interested in organized religion, narrative, symbolism, or the ability of film to change a person's moral perspective. Schrader sees film as a means of accessing the Holy (1972: 3), wherein a director uses specific techniques to lead the viewer to a moment of "stasis" or an encounter with the transcendent (1972: 108). Schrader identifies Ozu, Bresson, and Dreyer as exemplary directors who employ the transcendental style. As a director himself, Schrader offers useful insights into the techniques employed by Ozu, Bresson, and Dreyer that enable an experience of what Schrader calls "the Transcendent." While it may be "ineffable or invisible," Schrader recognizes that the path to the transcendent is created using "camera angles, dialogue, [and] editing" (1972: 3–4).

Revealing the strong influence of Eastern religious concepts in his work, Schrader refers to the transcendental style as a practice, "a way (a tao, in the broadest sense of the term) to approach the Transcendent" (1972: 3). Steve Nolan has concerns about Schrader's approach, which he believes "expects too much of film" (2009: 13). Indeed, Schrader has very high expectations of film, but he has chosen specific examples through which to make his claims, and does not gear his analysis toward a general assessment of cinema. Similarly, this study of *2001*, *Enter the Void*, and *Melancholia* represents an unusual form of cinematic engagement, where audience members are more likely to be consumers of art films rather than mainstream cinema. While sharing structural similarities with Schrader's transcendental style, the content and mood of these films do not wholly conform to the quality of sparseness that is evident in the work of Ozu, Bresson, and Dreyer (1972: 159).

Making reference to Schrader's *Transcendental Style*, Nayar argues that the representation of religiosity in Western film reveals cultural associations between sparseness, silence, stillness, and the sacred (2012: 105–15). According to Nayar, critics and commentators like Schrader are "long conditioned by literacy-driven culture to search *beneath* texts; to pursue *multiple meanings*; to fill in the ever-widening *gaps* between signifier and signified," generating a "meditative beneath-ness or behind-ness vis-à-vis narrative" (2012: 117). The more oblique or ambiguous the symbol, the more one feels they are "stripping away artifice in order to reveal something more essential underneath" (2012: 118–19). The observation that transcendental experiences of film involve the activation of learned associations between particular stylistic and experiential features and the religious is relevant to this study as such associations are present in culture despite individual religious affiliation.

Schrader breaks the transcendental style down into three steps that relate to film techniques. The first is "the everyday" which he describes as "a meticulous representation of the dull, banal commonplaces of everyday living" (1972: 38–9). Recognizing the similarity with "realism" Schrader says that the everyday is distinct in its non-expressive forms: "coldness," "silence," and "stillness" (1972: 38–9). The viewer is offered no catharsis, but rather the monotonousness of the transcendental style builds to a single moment of "redemption, when ordinary reality is transcended" (Schrader 1972: 42). The everyday is not designed to teach the viewer to "see life in a certain way, but rather preventing him from seeing it as he is accustomed to" (Schrader 1972: 69–70). The viewer seeks "emotional and intellectual exits" in an attempt to avoid confrontation with "The Wholly Other" (Schrader 1972: 69–70). This technique is used to great effect in *2001*, *Enter the Void*, and *Melancholia*, and viewers either find themselves transfixed or they experience irritation, boredom, and disengagement. As I will argue, this polarization of experience is also common in meditative practice and in ritual contexts.

The second step is "disparity" wherein a sense of disunity between the characters and their environment is evoked to cast "suspicion on the non-emotional everyday" (Schrader 1972: 42). As Schrader explains, the viewer begins to feel the ineffectual nature of emotion, but at the same time, expectation builds that "there might be more to life than everyday existence" (1972: 42). This generates "a sense of emotional weight within an unfeeling environment," and there is a need for emotional release but no place for this to occur (Schrader 1972: 77). By simultaneously stimulating and repressing emotion, disparity works toward the sudden release of an immense and dissociated feeling (Schrader 1972: 77). The final step is stasis. Without warning, the viewer experiences "an inexplicable outpouring of human feeling that can have no adequate receptacle. This overwhelming compassion seems sui generis" and is experienced as "holy agony" (Schrader 1972: 43). In the film "there is a blast of music, an overt symbol, an open call for emotion" that triggers an experience of stasis in the immersed and focused viewer (Schrader 1972: 79). For viewers of *2001*, *Enter the Void*, and *Melancholia*, this moment is an experience of awe and noetic understanding.

Schrader notes other techniques, such as excessively slow or immobilized camerawork (1972: 22), and the de-emphasis of narrative and characterization that prevents an empathetic bond between the viewer and the hero (1972: 64). Actors embody "non-expressiveness" (Schrader 1972: 66); the composition is primarily "frontal," "static," and "flattened," and sound is used to subtly manipulate the viewer without raising their attention (1972: 67–9). The compositional technique that Schrader refers to as "hieratic frontality" involves the direct frontal gaze between viewer and screen generating "an I-Thou devotional attitude" (1972: 53). Frontality can "create a respectful, noncommitted attitude" of veneration resembling that inspired by the contemplation of a religious icon (Schrader 1972: 100). Each of these important aspects of film form will be explored in Chapters 4 through 9.

Schrader's work has been viewed as problematic due to his proposition that there is a universal transcendent that filmmakers "tap into." Schrader describes his own worldview as a belief in "spirituality" but not in "any sectarian notion of God" (2004: 28). Schrader's worldview is also based on the following notions about East and West:

> The East sought the Transcendent within the world, the West apart from it. . . . The Way of Unifying Vision leads to introspection and the Way of Introspection leads to Unifying Vision. The fusion is the necessary condition of mysticism; it engenders a common transcendental style in the East as well as the West, in film as well as all the arts. (2004: 54)

In line with this, Schrader explains that the transcendental style rejects "conventional interpretations of reality" and aims to "maximise the mystery of existence" (1972: 10). From Schrader's point of view, religion and art both seek to enable an experience of the transcendent (Schrader 1972: 7 and 17). Schrader agrees with Gerardus van der Leeuw in his statement: "Absolute religion is mysticism; it is without shape and without sound. Absolute art can be neither seen nor heard" (Schrader 1972: 7). As Nayar points out, "The sacred pertains less to religion than to an experience long identified *with* religion" (2012: 17). The experience that Schrader identifies with religion places the ineffable at the heart of spiritual reality, and viewer responses to *2001*, *Enter the Void*, and *Melancholia* similarly apply special value to experiences that possess the mystical quality of the ineffable. As will be discussed in Chapter 5, this type of experience accords with James's definition of religious experience (James 2014: 206–7).

While viewers may be left with a feeling that is "without shape and without sound" that feels as if it is beyond human comprehension, Kubrick, Noé, and von Trier guide their audiences into this state using a variety of techniques. The combination of Schrader's transcendental style with techniques designed to affect the viewer in an intense and embodied manner result in physical reactions among viewers including shivering, tears, and visceral sensations of awe. As will be discussed in the chapters that follow, the attribution of spiritual qualities comes as the result of such intense reactions. Viewer comments demonstrate the inextricable unity of affects that might be labeled emotional, visceral, transcendental, meditative, or existential. In fact, the attribution of spiritual descriptors often occurs where viewers feel confused about the origin of intense feelings.

Situated within religious studies and drawing insight from numerous disciplines, the aim here is not to classify experiences according to a particular theoretical model, but to retain a certain openness of terminology in order to capture the aspects of viewer responses that resemble religious behavior, experience, practice, or engagement. In film studies, scholars like Martine Beugnet have written about the affective and embodied qualities of what she calls the "cinema of sensation" (2007). *Spiritual Sensations* shares Beugnet's observation that directors who depart from a conventional focus on plot progression and character identification, foregrounding sensory engagement, engender new ways of "watching, sensing and thinking through film" (2007: 5 and 63). Such experiences can make the viewer feel as if they do not have full mastery of their perception. There may be a confusion of the senses that is not characteristic of conventional plot-driven film (Beugnet 2007: 74). This unusual mode of perception can then give rise to the impression that they are having a "prelogical" or unmediated experience (Beugnet 2007: 74). However, Beugnet interprets these experiences in political and philosophical terms, whereas this study is focused on religious and sociological implications. For instance, sensual cinema is deemed to be consequential to "questions of identity and difference we associate with globalization, immigration and colonial after-effects, work and exploitation, gender, desire and possession" (Beugnet 2007: 125). For Beugnet, conventional film viewing is associated with a Cartesian "vision-knowledge-mastery paradigm" typified by a rational and detached objectifying gaze where even the "establishment of a perspectival space and on the distinction between figure and ground" is viewed to be a form of "Western ocular-centrism and Cartesian subjectivity" (Beugnet 2007: 65–8). Citing theorists like Gilles Deleuze and Vivian Sobchack, Beugnet interprets films with heightened sensual focus to be active in the destabilization of "visual hierarchies" and the concept of self as an independent entity in a position of epistemological certainty and control (2007: 63). Despite occasional instances where such observations overlap with my own, they are nonetheless entrenched in a different discourse that would distract from the core questions that this book seeks answer. While the films discussed here can be said to affect the viewer and trigger bodily responses, these comments do not insinuate the complex political and epistemological connotations of the terms "affect" and "embodiment" as usually understood by film theorists.

Religious Experience and the Ritual Function of Film

The term "ritual" is sometimes used in the study of religion and film, but generally this word is used in a symbolic or limited sense. John Lyden's comparison between religious ritual and film viewing is based upon the idea that audiences connect with the meanings that are communicated through story in order to find meaning in their lives (2003: 94). As the title of his book suggests, "rituals" are linked with "myths" and "morals." Viewers of *2001*, *Enter the Void*, and *Melancholia* seldom mention morals in their online comments, as the type of "religious experience" that is relevant to them is of a mystical variety that is integrated at the level of feeling into a subjective worldview. *Spiritual Sensations* draws upon ritual and religious practice in terms of the state of mind and affective qualities of these experiences. This type of engagement is distinct from classical modes of viewing that are plot driven and rely on the development of empathy with the characters on screen. Miles refers to the "visual training" required of film viewers that is "at least as complex as that of religious devotion" (1996: 27). However, Miles too returns to a consideration of morals and values, and the special quality of film is not necessarily the ability to produce a religious experience but to lead the audience to temporarily forget that what they are seeing is not real (1996: 27). Thomas Martin sees film as a form of public storytelling that engages an audience for a long period of time, and on regular occasions, impacting on "the basic notion of oneself as it relates to one's sense of religious reality" (1991: 3 and 13). In this sense, film is considered ritualistic in its repetition.

The ritual aspect of cinema has received more thorough attention in relation to Christian examples such as Jill C. Stevenson's insightful analysis (2013: 70–97) of Mel Gibson's *The Passion of the Christ* (2004). Investigating the film's function as a devotional aid for evangelical Christians, Stevenson presents film experience alongside several other examples of performative religious engagement. Working from a theological perspective, Peter Fraser's *Images of the Passion: The Sacramental Mode in Film* (1998) also makes an important contribution to the study of cinematic religious experience. Fraser defines a genre of films that, he believes, replicate the liturgical pattern of the Passion, thus enacting an "incarnational moment," where the film is transformed into religious ritual (1998: 5). Fraser's work is reminiscent of Schrader's; however, Fraser is quick to disqualify the comparison (1998: 117–28). Working from very different points of view, Fraser and Stevenson both attempt to draw viewing experience into a meaningful relationship with the religious orientation of audiences. Despite some similarities between their approach and my own, their findings are very case specific, and do not easily translate to the examples considered here.

S. Brent Plate treats religion, ritual, and film as general terms, where the ritualized religiosity that he connects with film is that of world-building (2008: 4–5). This term is borrowed from sociologist Peter Berger who argues that human beings project meaning onto the world around them by seeking to create meaningful equivalences between the social and metaphysical orders of existence, with religion being the most notable example (Plate 2008: 4–5). Plate posits that "film production borrows millennia-old aesthetic tactics from religions" (2008: 3) and that film and religion are the means by which myth is reimagined and reinvented throughout time (2008: 70). Perceptively, Plate writes that film and ritual engage the viewer on a primal level that precedes rational thought, where it is "the body that believes" (2008: 16 and 66). He explains that religion is not a matter of intellectual belief, but of being persuaded by what *feels* real (Plate 2008: 15). While Plate speaks of the importance of this aspect of film, he does so in a generic manner. The audience responses considered in this study provide examples of experiences characterized by feelings of preconscious cognition and direct bodily apprehension that Plate alludes to. That is, viewers feel as though they are experiencing the film on a nonrational level. This study does not make any particular claims about the order in which the brain processes what is seen and heard in the cinema. This filmic quality makes such films persuasive in a way that feels religious. As anthropologist Harvey Whitehouse has observed in his study of religious ritual, listening to a dry sermon requires regular repetition to maintain a tradition, while theatrical forms of ritual that engage strong emotions have a more lasting impact (1996: 710). In this sense, certain mainstream films that convey a moral message through narrative can be considered similar to Whitehouse's "sermon" example, while *Spiritual Sensations* is concerned with a form of filmmaking that seeks to affect the viewer viscerally and emotionally without necessarily conveying a clear moral message.

Taking a slightly different approach, Griffiths investigates embodied viewing using case studies that involve a particular spatial environment: the medieval cathedral, panorama, planetarium, and IMAX theatre. These spaces overwhelm the senses as they envelop the viewer to the full extent of their peripheral vision. Griffiths recognizes the aesthetic features that enable immersive viewing in these spaces are used to evoke "a religious experience" (2008: 18) particularly in relation to the cathedral and planetarium. In her discussion of religious immersion, Griffiths draws upon Abraham Maslow's concept of "peak experience" where "emotions of 'wonder, awe, reverence, humility, surrender, and even worship before the greatness of the experience' are reported" (2008: 32). While Griffiths is writing from a film studies perspective, her comparison of religious and secular forms of immersion is pertinent to the study of religion and film. Unlike many religion and film scholars who recognize only the "church-like" aspect of the cinema, or the influential qualities that film can possess, Griffith points out that immersive environments like the cinema can enable a transcendent and "sense-altering experience" (2008: 36). Here, feelings of grandeur and excess contribute to the religious qualities of the experience and it is the "shivers down one's spine" that generate a spiritual interpretation as much the content presented. In Griffiths's examples, the viewer is overwhelmed by visual scale and intensity of sound, while films like *2001*, *Enter the Void*, and *Melancholia* employ multiple devices to ensure sensory overload, so that they are able to draw the viewer into deep perceptual immersion even in the home.

Art theorist James Elkins has taken a particular interest in both emotional and religious responses to art. In *Pictures & Tears: A History of People Who Have Cried in Front of Paintings* Elkins seeks to account for the fact that for some, art brings about "no emotional effect," while a small but significant number of people have profound experiences that bring them to tears (2004b: 51). Elkins focuses on the Rothko Chapel in Texas as his principal case study. This chapel is an interfaith church that is used for worship, but is also a space set up for the contemplation of Mark Rothko's (1903–70) art (Elkins 2004b: 5). In the chapel guest book, Elkins discovers repeated instances where visitors wept during their experience of the space who could not explain the reason for their tears (2004b: 20–1). Mirroring Griffith's observations, Elkins speaks of the immersive qualities of Rothko's art and associated spiritual feelings that can be enhanced by standing at a particular distance from the work and through extending the duration of contemplative viewing (2004b: 18). Elkins seeks to challenge the cool intellectualized approach that he feels is dominant in the art world by arguing that intense and emotional experiences of art are valid. To encourage emotive experiences, Elkins provides a detailed list of instructions that will enable the viewer to be absorbed and affected by art (2004b: 210–12). His advice involves an ideal perceptual foundation and aesthetic considerations relating to the viewing environment. It is evident that the affect of art and film is not automatic and the viewer must be engaged in a particular way if they are to be receptive to the experience. Like religious ritual or practice, spiritualized experiences of film require a perceptive shift that is generated through a particular mode of viewing.

As I will argue, films like *2001*, *Enter the Void*, and *Melancholia* effectively guide viewers into a "meditative" state. Francisca Cho has made a similar claim in relation to the film *Why Has Bodhi-Dharma Left for the East?* (1989); however, that film is about Buddhism and the overt religious themes of this film distinguish her reading from my own. *Why Has Bodhi-Dharma Left for the East?*, she says, is an example of the "cultic mode of signification" where the film's "ideological content is subservient to its significance as ritual function" (Cho 1999: 177). Cho identifies religious significance in the sense of "presence" that is enacted by the film (1999: 177–8). Like Schrader, Cho looks to Mircea Eliade to explain how art can be experienced as hierophany (1999: 178). Employing Chan Buddhism as a methodological tool to interpret her case study (Cho 1999: 179–80), Cho observes that the pace of the film leads the viewer into a contemplative state of stillness, as meditation also does (1999: 172). Focusing on the contemplative experience or practice of film viewing, Cho consciously moves away from a reading of the film that focuses on symbolic references to Chan Buddhism (1999: 175). In addition to meditative experience, Cho argues that the opening shots of *Why Has Bodhi-Dharma Left for the East?* function like a "visual *koan*" that disrupts narrative logic (1999: 187). In the Buddhist context, *koans* force the mind to a logical impasse (Streng 2005: 9376; Ogata 1959: 71–2), an experience that Cho identifies in this scene. Importantly, she notes that this can be "experienced as either frustrating or enlightening" (1999: 187).

Although I do not employ Zen/Chan Buddhism as a methodological framework to analyze film, all three of the case studies featured in this volume involve a meditative mode of viewing that culminates in sensations of spiritual awakening. Buddhist concepts appear to be relevant to viewing experiences of *2001*, *Enter the Void*, and *Melancholia*. These include approaching film as a site of open-minded contemplation that is free from expectation and attempting to attain emptiness of mind while simultaneously experiencing the vision, textures, sounds, and movements of the film. Following these rhythms in the right state of mind can bring about a sense of unmediated encounter with the truth of existence that is described by some as a moment of revelation. It is possible to account for this when one considers the context of *2001*'s release, at a time when Eastern religious ideas were taken up by counter-culturalists.

Schrader, Nayar, and Cho adopt an approach to religion and film that moves beyond Christian concepts, focusing on film technique and viewer experience. However, the nature of the techniques and associated experiences are specific to their case studies and are not directly applicable to mine. Schrader is concerned with transcendental experiences of the Holy achieved through "sparse" filmic techniques; Nayar focuses on religious experiences that embrace the color, narrative, and spectacle typical of Indian epics; and Cho explores the meditative cinematography of a film that is also a narrative about Buddhism. Their examples are as varied as religious experience itself and tied to different types of films that each forge a path—not to a common experience—but to a set of experiences that are commonly deemed religious. Handling films that are of yet another style, and that generate different religious experiences than those considered by Schrader, Nayar, and Cho, this study will detail far more intense, and at times traumatic, spiritualized cinematic experiences. The cultural influences that enable these experiences are important as they account for both the mode of experience and the attribution of spiritual meaning. *2001*, *Enter the Void*, and *Melancholia* all share the characteristics of art film, and this contributes to their ability to trigger spiritual responses in a way that classical Hollywood cinema is unlikely to.

In 1979, David Bordwell defined "art cinema" as a mode of film practice tracing a historical lineage from German Expressionism and French Impressionism, becoming a distinct mode in the postwar period, and continuing in Neorealist and New Wave cinema (56). Bordwell cites examples from different cultures and time periods drawing them together based on their common stylistic conventions and associated modes of viewing. Principally, art film is defined against classical Hollywood cinema where the artist-director infuses the film with the presence of their authorship each time they challenge a classical convention. Characterizing

Hollywood film as narrative-driven, goal-oriented, and operating in accordance with the laws of cause and effect, art film adopts the opposite tendency, creating loose logical connections and maintaining a strong sense of ambiguity (Bordwell 1979: 59–60). Bordwell argues that art film maintains cohesion instead through realism and the overarching presence of the author's vision. Realism here includes new depictions of sexuality, shooting in real locations, psychologically complex characters, and the portrayal of subjective reality (Bordwell 1979: 59–60). This focus on subjective reality reflects the value of interior experiences in both religion and the arts in the modern West. Insofar as art film stands in contradistinction to classical cinema, it can also be considered countercultural or alternative in spirit, even if such films achieve commercial success.

Building on Bordwell's initial observations, Grodal links makers of art films (or *auteurs*) to the romantic understanding of artistic genius as "the source of new (as well as eternal) insights into man and world" (2009: 206). Grodal observes that "transcendental values" used to be "worshipped" via religion, but in the romantic period, this became the task of the artist (2009: 206). The existential tenor of art film has developed out of this conceptualization of the artist, where they function in part as a spiritual intermediary. As a result, art films are expected to act as an "inexhaustible source" of meaning (Grodal 2009: 206–7). To this day, *2001* sparks passionate conversations about its ungraspable or manifold meanings. Adding greater specificity to Bordwell's observation that ambiguity is an essential feature of art film, Grodal describes the "lyrical-associative" techniques that directors employ to develop a cognitively satisfying experience of the ambiguous (2009: 224). In short, art films present experienced viewers with stimuli that are linked by tenuous associations, and the viewer engages with the film by attempting to resolve layers of inconclusive meaning. The question of how directors achieve this and Grodal's hypotheses about the way that film techniques interact with the architecture of the brain shed much light on the viewer responses that are considered in subsequent chapters.

In his work on the ritual function of film, Plate singles out "avant-garde" film as being particularly well suited to the task of affecting viewers religiously. As a genre that creates alternative representations of reality that do not adhere to Hollywood conventions, such films are able to engender new ways of seeing (Plate 2008: 67–9). Plate notes that avant-garde filmmakers "work on an abstract, even mythical level" that is akin to artistic movements like Minimalism or "the Buddhist orientation towards 'mindfulness'" (2008: 69–72). These passing observations are central to my argument, as spiritual responses to *2001*, *Enter the Void*, and *Melancholia* bear evidence of the interrelationship between

Eastern religiosity, abstraction, and art film that will be later discussed. Plate also sees avant-garde film as a form of re-enchantment where directors seek to facilitate "a transcendent experience in and through media" thus reawakening "magical" modes of perception in a post-Enlightenment context (2008: 71). Plate's observations lend support to Grodal's in terms of art film's heightened ability to generate transcendent experiences through the use of unconventional cinematic techniques. These films tend toward the abstract and ambiguous but maintain the viewer's attention by encouraging a mode of focus resembling mindfulness meditation.

Conclusion

Recognizing the paucity of work on religious experience in religion and film studies, this chapter has identified value of reviving Schrader's *Transcendental Style* in light of the significant developments that have occurred in religious studies and film studies since the publication of this work in 1972. In Chapter 2, the cultural context of the late 1960s will be discussed in order to properly situate viewer responses to *2001*. Religious thinking during this period contributes to viewer reception in complex ways, framing viewer experience, and subsequent interpretations of what the film might mean. As both *Enter the Void* and *Melancholia* draw from Kubrick's 1968 classic, responses to these later films pick up on various trends found in responses to *2001*. Some of these similarities can be attributed to the stylistic link with *2001*, but there are also parallels that are related to religious change in the West. During the period from the late 1960s to the present, the cosmology, epistemology, and religious practices of the West have changed significantly. This dramatic cultural shift and the way that it manifests in films like *2001*, *Enter the Void*, and *Melancholia* demonstrate the need for more careful investigations of the "religion" aspect of religion and film studies.

2

Religious Experience

Although initially dominated by Christian readings, the study of religion and film has now come to include other religions, spiritualities, and alternative representations of the sacred. This can be attributed in part to the increasing tendency for directors to represent the sacred in an abstract manner that lends itself to personal interpretation. Christian epics are still produced and attract large audiences, especially in the United States, but they appeal to a niche market. Owing to the influence of globalization and the wide scope for the distribution of films through the internet and streaming services, inclusive filmmaking that allows for pluralistic responses is an effective means of capturing diverse viewer markets. These changes mirror trends in Western culture that have seen Christianity recede in public prominence to be succeeded by personalized religiosity and seekership (Wuthnow 1998: 1–18). The rise of alternative spirituality roughly coincides with *2001*'s release and has become quietly pervasive in Western culture. Characterized by its eclecticism and resistance to forming stable institutional structures (Chandler 2010: 69) alternative spirituality is often elusive, yet can still be successfully identified and defined. This chapter will determine a working definition of alternative spirituality, and will outline how this religious position shapes experiences in the cinema.

Alternative Spirituality

The late 1960s was not only a time of political unrest and social change, but of religious transformation (Campbell 2008: 213) that has been referred to as "the spiritual turn in late modernity" (Houtman and Aupers 2007: 310). Those coming of age in the late 1960s and early 1970s were increasingly seeking out alternative ways of thinking, living, and being, in an attempt to bring about radical change. While church attendance and formal religious affiliation would decline steadily from this period, the religious desire to ascribe meaning and purpose to one's life (and to human existence) continued in new forms. Religious affiliation and belief were succeeded by spiritual seekership, where individuals embark on an autonomous journey to discover religious truth and achieve personal transformation using tools from both secular and religious sources (Campbell 2002: 15–16). It is for this reason that David Lyon suggests that scholars "think of religion today more as a cultural resource than as a social institution" (2000: 88). Seekership presumes dissatisfaction with inherited systems of belief (Campbell 2002: 15–16), yet it also avoids permanent affiliation with alternative systems, as Steven Sutcliffe explains: "By definition, seekers do not join institutions; they leave them. Seekers are seceders and their participation in institutions of any kind is likely to be enthusiastic but temporary" (2003: 99). Rather, the self is conceived a free agent of limitless potential. The ability to reimagine and transform can also be seen as the result of spiritual uncertainty, where religious reality is focused on the present (and present lifetime). Uncertainty is generated through the creative and selective adoption of religious content and the reconfiguration of truth from a singular position to a hierarchical system of layers that correspond to one's degree of spiritual progress. Privileging interior experiences as reliable evidence for the formation of a subjective worldview, alternative spirituality values mystical modes of religiosity and is also highly compatible with modern pluralism (Campbell 2002: 15–16).

While some theorists have argued that secularization would eventually eradicate religion, it is now widely recognized in religious studies that religious behaviors and beliefs have not disappeared; rather, they have been relocated to new contexts (Houtman and Aupers 2007: 315). In particular, modernity has witnessed aspects of religious belief and practice move from institutional settings into the subjective realm where they are transformed into a meaning-making personal narrative (Demerath III 2000: 3). Taking this into account, N. J. Demerath III argues that scholars of religion should consider "religion" substantively, but should study "the sacred" functionally (2000: 1–3), as "there are religious phenomena that have lost their power and are no longer sacred. Just as surely as there are sacred entities and symbols that have compelling power without being religious" (2000: 3). Demerath's recommendations here separate institutional religion (typified by a clear set of doctrines, practices, and expectations) from a personal and emotionally vibrant connection with the sacred. In a sense, this methodological approach replicates actual changes in religious orientation that are regularly identified by religious studies scholars. In this study, the sacred is associated with concepts like ultimate truth, reality, and the divine, and in a cinematic setting, it is most certainly separated from the context of institutional religion. As it is understood here, sacredness carries traces of traditional religious meaning drawn from Western culture and continues to function as a category of special significance. The reification of experiences associated with the sacred is considered religious in the sense that religions share a sacred orientation.

Many different terms have been coined to describe the predominant trends in Western religious culture stemming from the late 1960s, each with their own set of associations. In this study, I use the term "alternative spirituality" to characterize a shift toward personalized spirituality that is asserted in resistance to perceived cultural norms. In line with Demerath's separation of religion from the sacred, alternative spirituality holds that personal experiences of the sacred constitute authentic religiosity, while religions are human institutions that are capable of distorting truth to serve the interests of religious authorities. Broadly speaking, this is an epistemological position rather than a set of particular beliefs or practices. However, in a narrower sense, alternative spirituality is characterized by a familiar set of concepts, principals, orientations, and appropriated beliefs and practices.

Alternative spirituality, as Hanegraaff explains, sees the individual transcend the dichotomy between "faith" and "reason," in the adoption of "gnosis" (1998: 519). Although few would describe their epistemological orientation as "gnostic," it is clear that for modern individuals, "truth can only be found by personal, inner revelation, insight, or 'enlightenment'" where there is "no other authority than personal inner experience" (Hanegraaff 1998: 519). This "gnostic" approach could also be considered esoteric in the sense that esoteric knowledge is attained "only by a personal effort of progressive elucidation through several successive levels" (Faivre 1994: 5). Esoteric knowledge can be passed to initiates secretly, yet the gnostic epistemology of alternative spirituality is more commonly associated with freely available knowledge where deeper, hidden meaning is divined (Faivre 1994: 32–3). While human impressions of the sacred can be communicated through analogy and explanation, the ultimate source of religious truth remains beyond "human language and conceptual frameworks," where it can only be directly experienced (Hanegraaff 1998: 186).

The importance of unmediated access to truth is tied to a mistrust of authority. As Dick Houtman and Stef Aupers observe, "Mainstream values amount to a form of indoctrination that alienates the individual from their true Self" (2007: 307). Conceived as a "divine spark," as in ancient Gnosticism, the true self is "still smoldering, waiting to be stirred up, and succeed the socialized self" (Houtman and Aupers 2007: 307). Ancient Gnosticism as it is characterized here and by other modern thinkers is often used as an analogy for a more recent conception of an ongoing alternative spiritual tradition that can be traced back to the ancient world. In contrast to the modern symbolic application of Gnosticism, Dylan M. Burns, for example, presents Gnosticism in the second and third centuries as a complex dialogue between Jewish, Christian, Gnostic, Manichaean, Platonic, and Hellenic thought that does not hinge upon the concept of the Self as a divine spark overcoming socialization (2014: 1–5 and 141–8). This analogy reflects the sentiment that something has gone wrong in the relationship between humanity and divinity, but that there is hope for this to be remedied. In alternative spirituality, there is a widespread belief that religion obscures and prevents an authentic connection with the sacred, so it is up to the individual to personally rediscover the divine. Hanegraaff notes that there is a strong focus on the need to "unlearn" what one has been socialized to believe (1998: 237; Farber 2002: 15). The individual can only become their true self and re-integrate with the fullness of reality (where all things are interconnected) through experience, intuition, and introspection (Houtman and Aupers 2007: 309; Hanegraaff 1998: 119–20 and 230).

The active role that the individual adopts in relation to their own spiritual development involves a strong sense of personal responsibility that comes with the realization that they create their own reality through their thoughts and actions (Hanegraaff 1998: 230). Connected with the ostensible primacy of freedom and autonomy in the modern West, the power and agency of the individual is amplified beyond all measure through a spiritual understanding of the universe. However, this extreme position is tempered through psychological adjustments that relativize seemingly undesirable or incorrect outcomes. For example, as Findhorn's Peter Caddy explains, if a prophecy divined by a medium does not eventuate, "it would seem that they have tuned in to planes of illusion created by man's fears and thoughts and in some cases, subconscious desires" (Sutcliffe 2003: 101). As Caddy's comment shows, one's degree of spiritual development is believed to determine their clear and accurate understanding of reality, and unconscious intentions have their own effects independent of conscious will. In alternative spirituality the individual is comprised of a conscious self and a Higher Self that orchestrates lessons for the individual's personal growth, and in this way, difficult or undesirable outcomes can be reinterpreted in a pragmatic and positive light (Hanegraaff 1998: 211–13).

The influence of psychological thinking in alternative spirituality cannot be overstated. As Hanegraaff has argued, the "psychologizing of religion" and "sacralization of psychology" have been essential to the development of alternative spirituality (1998: 197). Prominent figures in early psychology such as James (1842–1910), Sigmund Freud (1856–1939), and Carl Jung (1875–1961) have all contributed to the trend that Hanegraaff describes. However, other prominent thinkers also contributed to this generational shift with Friedrich Nietzsche's declaration of the Death of God in 1882 (1974: 181–2), and Max Weber's theory of the "disenchantment of the world" in 1905 (2003) being particularly stark examples. Janet Oppenheim neatly encapsulates the pervasive sentiment of late-nineteenth-century intellectuals in the following statement:

> Whether their loss of faith was part of the ethical revolt against the punitive rigidity of Christian dogma, a response to the persuasiveness of evidence from science and biblical scholarship, or a reaction against an orthodoxy that seemed at first unwilling to listen to the voices of modernity, the final result was the rejection of formal religion. (1988: 118)

While institutional religion was indeed rejected, James explored the psychological usefulness of belief in the face of doubt (1956b: 25–9). For James, the practical outcome of the loss of belief in God is the realization that evil is a matter of human responsibility, a view that has contributed in part to the strong focus on personal responsibility in alternative spirituality (1956a: 47). According to James's "pragmatic method," individuals should use their own powers of reflection to decide what is true based on the psychological usefulness of beliefs (Meyers 1997: 21), contributing to the development of the concept of relativized truth. James's work developed in resistance to both the theological perspective and the rigidity of the scientific method that claimed to be objective and to be privy to absolute truths (1956b: 51). In fact, he viewed the scientific method to be akin to religious fundamentalism (Rorty 1997: 92–3), both of which stunted human progress by discouraging the individual from exploring and experiencing possibilities for themselves. Demonstrating that the individual has within them all they need to move toward knowledge, create meaning, and make value judgments, he advised that the subjective faculties should not be discounted, stating that "no man should dare speak meanly of these instincts which are our nature's best equipment, and to which religion herself must in the last resort address her own particular appeals" (James 1956b: 48). As this last comment makes clear, James views religion not as something that exerts its authority over the individual, but as a belief system that must answer the subconscious demands of the individual (James 2014: 25–9).

As a key member of the Society for Psychical Research (SPR), James was interested in using the tools of science to study paranormal phenomena and the nature of consciousness. According to Oppenheim, the SPR *Proceedings* privileged the study of paranormal phenomena linked to the human mind and to subjective experience, including mediumship, automatic writing, telepathy, and hypnotism (1988: 120). SPR research was simultaneously interested in evidence of the supernatural as it might manifest through a human medium, and in evidence that might prove the supernatural to be a product of psychological processes. Departing from the strictures of the scientific method, the SPR gave unprecedented weight to personal testimony and processes of self-reflection, leading individual researchers to form varied theories about the nature and significance of (human experiences of) the supernatural. James's exploration of consciousness also involved the use of perception-altering drugs, contributing to his personal understanding of mystical states (Nicotra 2008: 199–213). By extension, this research was applied to theories about religion itself, contributing to a relativized understanding of religion.

For Freud, who was an honorary member of the SPR, religious belief was as a marker of psychological immaturity and neurosis (Palmer 1997: 8–10). Freud's characterization of religion as a form of "infantilism" that must be overcome aligns with the belief in alternative spirituality that those who continue to believe in religious authorities are spiritually underdeveloped (1989: 72). Freud's theory that the unconscious mind could exert agency over the individual in spite of their conscious will was also influential in the sacralization of psychology. According to Freud, the unconscious mind revealed itself through slips of the tongue and nonrational outbursts (2002), yet the psychoanalyst could unveil and exorcise that which was repressed by the conscious mind (Palmer 1997: 90–2). This simultaneously placed an unknowable and mysterious power within the self and elevated the role of the therapist as a psychic intermediary.

It is here that Jung's characterization of the collective unconscious becomes prominent. Jung described this subliminal realm to be the source of deep wisdom that connected all of humanity with the Ultimate (1960: 229–30; 1981). The collective unconscious presented itself to the human mind in the form of archetypes, which accounted for the gods of world religions, yet "the divinity of the gods can only be experienced spiritually, in the illumination of an *idea*, by direct revelation" (Jung 1951: 147). Jung's approach effectively legitimizes the truth of religious revelation, but removes the authority that any tradition can hold over the particulars of that insight. Most importantly, he stresses that spiritual truth is only accessible by the individual through unmediated experience. The combination of this Jungian view, Freud's understanding of traditional Christian faith as infantile, and James's pragmatic approach to belief are all present in the epistemological mode that is dominant in alternative spirituality. The legitimacy of personal religious experiences and the high regard for mysticism in alternative spirituality also owes much to James's influential definition of mystical experience, which is the focus of Chapter 5.

While late-nineteenth-century and early-twentieth-century intellectuals may have felt themselves to be at a crossroads between a traditional Christian worldview and a series of dimly lit paths that lay before them, by the late 1960s, an increasing proportion of the general population walked these paths with relative confidence. Becoming popular and widespread during this period, the divide between alternative and mainstream begins to break down (Sutcliffe 2003: 111-12). As Campbell asserts, "Now it is only a minority of people in the West who hold to traditional Christian teachings, these having been largely replaced by belief in a diffuse spirituality, one that centers on the self and nature" (2008: 141; Schofield Clarke 2002: 7-8). Despite the apparent contradiction that exists when the alternative becomes mainstream, the important point to remember is that the individual must feel that they are resisting socialization and freely choosing their unique path through life, accessing truth through personal experience. This self-perception is also the driver of consumer culture where individuals continually recalibrate themselves in relation to an ideal (Campbell 1989: 72). This ideal is associated with the possibility that if "undertaken in the right manner" one can access "the fundamental pleasure which 'exists' in life itself" (Campbell 1989: 69). This constant relativistic reassessment of the ideal is perfectly aligned with the notion of progressive spiritual awakening through the revelation of esoteric knowledge. What is felt to be spiritually revolutionary at one point may eventually become redundant as marginal ideas are absorbed and assimilated into mainstream culture. This cyclic relationship of reevaluation feeds alternative ideas into the mainstream, resulting in the widespread acceptance of concepts that may have once been radical (Campbell 2002: 15-16).

Flourishing in popular culture during the late 1960s, alternative spirituality crystalized a range of cultural trends associated with modernity. Visibly, this was most apparent among the countercultural youth who sought radical social and spiritual change through the exploration of practices drawn from non-Christian traditions including Buddhism, Hinduism, paganism, and shamanism. Aspects of these traditions have been assimilated into Western culture, and in this sense the religious repertoire of the West has changed and is now remarkably diverse. However, appropriated teachings and practices have always been selectively adopted, serving an existing need. Those needs are driven by the core values of the West including freedom, democracy, social mobility (capitalism), liberalism, pluralism, individualism, and consumerism. From the perspective of the individual, however, alternative spirituality is practiced through rejection of social expectations in favor of autonomously chosen paths. In order to "find out for oneself," and have unmediated access to divine truth, the individual makes use of a range of views and practices drawn from religion and secular culture. As a democratized and de-institutionalized religious position, alternative spirituality holds the promise that the individual can divine insight into the meaning of existence and experience the sacred first hand, in the ordinary processes of everyday life.

Religious Experience and Spiritual Authority

As outlined above, the epistemological mode of alternative spirituality is often associated with the esoteric, mystical, and gnostic. It is, however, worth explaining how modern religious experiences are generally understood in the study of religion. Ann Taves argues that in the twentieth century, the term "religious experience" has been used in three senses that are derived from cultural shifts in the modern era. First, the term is "linked with the rise of individualism and the democratization of religious authority" (Taves 2005: 7737). Secondly, it refers to the "common core" of all religions, arising out the universalizing trends of globalization and early research into comparative religion (Taves 2005: 7737). Thirdly, it has been used in an epistemological sense where it is used as a means to claim religious authority in light of "enlightenment critiques of traditional sources of religious knowledge and social scientific explanations of the origins of religion" (Taves 2005: 7737). As is evident here, the question of authority is central to religious experience, as the claim that the individual can experience the divine directly removes the legitimizing function of traditional religious authorities and intermediaries. However, democratization does not necessarily equate to the triumph of individual agency, as will be discussed in Chapter 6.

In line with Taves's observations, Arthur Versluis draws a connection between a universalist view of religion (or "perennial philosophy") and the privileging of unmediated spiritual experiences that do not rely on religious affiliation or training (2014: 2). Versluis employs the term "immediatism" to describe the privileging of direct and spontaneous mystical experiences, which he identifies as being central to contemporary alternative spirituality, whose roots can traced as far back as the seventeenth century in the religious history of the West (2014: 2). Following the Enlightenment, personal religious experience was granted a higher value, as can be found, for example, in the theological writings of Friedrich Schleiermacher (1768–1834) and Rudolf Otto (1869–1937). Influenced by Immanuel Kant's *Critique of Pure Reason* (1781), both Schleiermacher and Otto conceived of religious feelings as being something qualitatively unique and set apart. Religious feelings are conceived as being sui generis and incomparable to other feelings that may relate to the world of the profane (Marina 2007: 458). Schleiermacher and Otto have had a lasting impact on folk understandings of religious experience that achieved currency in the 1960s and that remain prevalent in secular culture. One could even identify Schrader's transcendental style as an example of this. Otto's work is particularly evocative in the description of what religious experience feels like. Otto describes it as a feeling of *mysterium tremendum et fascinans*—a sense of trembling awe, as if one were held in the thrall of a vital and majestic force, at once terrifyingly powerful and infinitely strange (1958: 12–40). Such sensations are "wholly other" and excessive by nature, conveying "more than the intellect can conceive in them" (1958: 25–33).

While Otto provides a useful set of descriptors for religious experience, James's four attributes of mystical experience provide a clearer typology when studying accounts occurring outside of religious traditions. Developing his definition, James creates correlations between his personal experiences of revelation with accounts from a wide range of individuals from religious and nonreligious contexts (2014: 206–33), linking the variety of accounts back to the following attributes: ineffability, a noetic quality, transiency, and passivity (2014: 206–7). The ineffable nature of mystical experiences makes them impossible to adequately describe (James 2014: 206), yet their simultaneous noetic quality leaves the individual with the sense that they have received "insight into depths of truth unplumbed by the discursive intellect" (James 2014: 206). James acknowledges the use of preparatory practices such as "fixing the attention" but the mystical experience itself is temporary, lasting thirty minutes to an hour or so, where the individual's will is overwhelmed by "a superior power" (2014: 207). These experiences are initially vivid and infused with "a curious sense of authority for after-time" (James 2014: 206). Where such experiences are repeated, their faded quality in memory is returned to clarity, leading to "continuous development in what is felt as inner richness and importance" (James 2014: 207). Each of these attributes can be found in audience responses to *2001*, *Enter the Void*, and *Melancholia*, making it reasonable to refer to these experiences as spiritual. As will be discussed in subsequent chapters, the intensity and extraordinary character of viewer experiences is evident in their cognitive impact. Viewers report sensations of being overpowered, made privy to profound and ineffable knowledge, and to being haunted by the film long afterward. These affective properties come about as the result of carefully designed film techniques but can also be attributed to the viewing attitude adopted during the experience.

Resembling James's approach in his use of cross-cultural examples (including those of mediums and clairvoyants) Hollenback draws attention to the practices that surround religious experience (1996: ix). According to Hollenback, the individual's cultural context and religious preconceptions subconsciously determine the type of experience that they have, including the content of visions, revelations, and emotional states (1996: ix). While James recognizes the importance of "fixing the attention" (2014: 207) Hollenback sees this as an essential precursor to mystical experience (1996: 21 and 47). Achieving single-pointed focus of the "mind, will and imagination" and "quieting the mind" (Hollenback 1996: vii and 1)

> eventually shuts down the incessant mental chattering that is normally present as a kind of background noise behind all our activities in the waking state. Once mystics stop this process of silently talking to themselves, they transform their mode of consciousness and begin to have their first tangible encounters with that spiritual world that otherwise remains imperceptible to the five senses. (Hollenback 1996: 94–5)

Reflecting a definitive shift in perception, the mystic's inner visions may arise from still silence, unlike film viewers, whose visions are supplied by the film itself. However, viewers of *2001*, *Enter the Void*, and *Melancholia* do engage in a specific mode of viewing conducive to deep focus and openness of mind while watching these films. Being able to calm "mental chatter" is crucial in facilitating the perceptual shift that transforms film viewing into spiritual experience. One may note that the language Hollenback employs to describe the focus that precedes mystical experience is reminiscent of meditative concepts commonly found in Western Buddhism. It is also worth drawing attention to the fact that Otto, James, and Hollenback consulted examples of mystical states of mind drawn from Eastern religious traditions like Buddhism and Hinduism when formulating their definitions. The interweaving of these concepts into the category of mysticism is in itself evidence of the cultural shift that reached its height in the late 1960s.

In the first section of this chapter, religious experience was identified as one of the defining features of alternative spirituality, alongside the rejection of religious authority. Matthew Wood is critical of the conception of the freely choosing "self" that is commonly used to characterize alternative spirituality and the New Age

(2007: 12, 14, and 27–33, and 45–6). Wood remarks, "Rather than dominating individuals' lives, and thus imposing external authority, [religions] are seen as resources from which individuals draw by exercising self-authority" (2007: 45). Wood contends that in their association with eclectic spiritual sources individuals are in fact deferring to a range of authorities. These authorities contribute to the individual's religiosity in a relativized manner and are "nonformative" in the sense that no single religious authority has total influence (2007: 14 and 21–2). Religious authority is not necessarily characterized by competing traditions in the spiritual marketplace but by instances where the individual defers personal authority to spiritual forces. Examples of such experiences include channeling, meditation, Reiki or crystal healing, and divination. According to Wood, "These religious experiences function to legitimize the individual's worldview (and other more secular practices) as religious" (2007: 21). While *Spiritual Sensations* highlights the antiauthoritarian ethos of alternative spirituality and the centrality of self-perceived spiritual autonomy, deferral to a higher power is absolutely central in raising filmic experience to the level of the spiritual. This can be explained through the importance of having a direct experience of spiritual truth. Earthly authorities are rejected, in order to open up the possibility of unmediated access to divine truth, which is considered to be a superior authority (Sutcliffe 2003: 11–12 and 216–18). This truth is conceived as being unknown, undetermined, and indescribable, so it can only be recognized through the intuitive faculties. While the individual charts their own course, they regularly defer power to alternate authorities that communicate via intuition to provide guidance. In the sense that the individual becomes passive to the reception of guidance from their Higher Self or subconscious, these aspects of the self can be considered functionally external and comparable to practices like divination. These practices are interspersed by periods of psychologized or rationalized reflection that contribute to the impression of seamless self-authorship and authority. In terms of viewer responses to *2001*, *Enter the Void*, and *Melancholia*, the film experience can be seen as a transient spiritual experience that reverberates with a lasting sensation of profound meaning, and may be but one in a series of similar experiences arising from other contexts in the viewer's life.

The Easternization of the West

Religious traditions from the East, particularly Buddhism, are integral to the development of alternative spirituality. References to Buddhism and meditation are woven through audience responses to *2001*, *Enter the Void*, and *Melancholia*, revealing the pervasiveness of what Campbell refers to as the "Easternization of the West" (2008). The attraction of Buddhism and the way it has been adapted reveal an existing trajectory of cultural change that illuminates the deeper meanings of viewer comments. According to Campbell, in the postwar period, the basic beliefs "concerning the nature of reality and truth" in the West changed so much that they began to resemble those of the East (2008: 15). Campbell treats both terms as "ideal types" in the Weberian sense with an understanding that the categories of East and West are both Western constructs (2008: 11–15). The "West" is traditionally characterized by "materialistic dualism," belief in a personal God, and the Christian concepts of sin and salvation, while the "East" is associated with "metaphysical monism," a belief in an "impersonal divine force," and the goal of attaining self-knowledge or enlightenment by overcoming "ignorance and error" (Campbell 2008: 141–2). Evidence of this fundamental shift can be found in alternative spirituality and associated movements from environmentalism to the human potential movement (Campbell 2008: 142). Epistemologically speaking, intuition and mysticism are favored over rationalism, analysis and empiricism, and cosmologically, dualism is replaced by a holistic view of human beings, nature, mind, body, spirit, and the divine (Campbell 2008: 141–2). Importantly, there is a shift from divinely bestowed salvation to self-spirituality, where the individual has the ability to effect change and to experience the divine without deferring to spiritual intermediaries (Campbell 2008: 124).

The Easternization thesis demonstrates that the religious eclecticism that is commonly associated with alternative spirituality does not treat all religious traditions equally and that Buddhism has had a particularly strong influence in the modern West. Campbell's *Romantic Ethic* (1989) argues that romantic thinking underpins Western values linked to the imaginative work implicit in individualism and consumerism, existing alongside Weber's "protestant ethic" of capitalism but not necessarily replacing it. Similarly, Campbell's "Eastern" category refers to a development of Western culture, not a conflict between Eastern and Western philosophies. Insofar as Western culture is characterized by "materialistic dualism," where Enlightenment rationalism and Christianity coexist as dominant discourses claiming the singularity of truth (Streng 2005: 9374), modes of thinking develop to counter what is seen as outdated and repressive. Resisting institutionalization is a part of the impetus toward the new or unknown that gives this worldview its cutting edge. It is for reasons such as this that the term "*alternative* spirituality" is a most fitting descriptor as it alludes to the dynamic between past and present worldviews. Romanticism and the Eastern turn are both examples of thinking that aimed to counter Enlightenment rationalism without returning to the previously dominant Christian faith. These movements laid the foundation of what would eventually emerge as alternative spirituality in the late 1960s.

Buddhism's influence in the West first became significant in the Victorian period when aspects of Eastern cosmology, epistemology, and ontology sparked reevaluations of the traditional Western worldview that were already the subject of dissatisfaction and critique (Kay 2007: 5). Events like the 1893 World Parliament of Religions, held in Chicago, had a particularly strong impact where charismatic leaders like Anagarika Dharmapala (1864–1933) and Shaku Sōen (1860–1919) presented their religion as amenable to contemporary values (Cusack 2011: 305). As such, Buddhism was understood to be a nonhierarchical, nondogmatic, and intellectually rigorous tradition that worked in harmony with science and emerging psychological thought (Kay 2007: 5–7). Due to the focus on meditative practice and personal reflection, the religion was viewed to be democratic and supportive of individualism (Kay 2007: 6). The transcendental poets and Theosophists were influential during this period in propagating Buddhist thought through their sympathetic writings about Buddhism (Cusack 2011: 297–8; Versluis 1993: 8; *The Theosophical Society* 2017: n.p.). Both groups held the view that all religions sprung from a common source so Eastern religious concepts were an aspect of universal wisdom as much as they were a cultural interpretation of that wisdom (Versluis 1993: 12; *The Theosophical Society* 2017: n.p.) This meant that they were critical of certain aspects of Buddhism, while adopting and transforming others. One of the common critiques of Buddhism in this period was the charge that it was a pessimistic tradition due to the negative Western interpretation of concepts like no-self and voidness (Prebish 1999: 7). However, this apparent negativity was somewhat suited to the disenchanted Western mind that looked to the future with the dual visions of millennialism, where creation and destruction were both imminent (Versluis 1993: 3).

Unlike earlier forays into Eastern spirituality undertaken in nineteenth century, the level of interest in Buddhism in the 1960s was comparatively monumental (Prebish 1999: 7; Campbell 2008: 25–6). As Jan Nattier observes, the youth of 1960s and 1970s counterculture came to establish the most prominent Buddhist organizations that now exist in the United States (1997: 80). Zen Buddhism, Tibetan Buddhism, and Hinduism achieved great popularity, facilitated by charismatic monks and gurus such as Daisetz T. Suzuki (1870–

1966), Chögyam Trungpa Rinpoche (1939–87), and Maharishi Mahesh Yogi (1918–2008) (Campbell 2008: 24). Initially, yogis and Buddhist monks brought their ideas to the West, but soon Westerners began to see themselves as authentic practitioners of Eastern traditions (Campbell 2008: 24). However, the influence of Eastern religion is not just felt in terms of an increase in converts but in the transformation of Western thought in areas such as art, music, philosophy, psychology, and ecology (Kay 2007: 4; Park 2011: xvi). Many of these seekers were artists and musicians whose works spread the influence of Eastern religions further still (Cusack 2011: 307). As the primary aspects of Buddhism that come through to the West are concerned with perception, it is not surprising that artists, filmmakers, and poets have found these new ways of seeing inspirational. Carole Cusack notes that the religious influences flowed both ways and Suzuki's presentation of Zen bore the influence of his research into romanticism and transcendentalism, movements that were themselves influenced by Eastern religious philosophies (Cusack 2011: 306).

The character of Buddhism as it has been adopted in the West since the 1960s is distinct enough to be considered a new religious movement (Prebish 1999: 243). In the Western context, meditation is viewed as the authentic core of Buddhism, and other aspects of the religion like devotional practice and ethical codes are superfluous by comparison (Nattier 1997: 75; Prebish 1999: 253–4). Western Buddhism is typically nonsectarian, amenable to the values of democracy, feminism, and peace movements, and is socially engaged, taking part in interfaith dialogue (Prebish 1999: 253–4). Rather than being a belief-oriented tradition, it is inquiry based and experimental (Prebish 1999: 265). Western practitioners rarely adopt monasticism and instead use Buddhist meditation to enrich their experience of life and to understand their place in the universe (Nattier 1997: 75). Reflective practices often take on a therapeutic focus linked with psychology (Prebish 1999: 265). As an antidote to the toxic culture of modernity, meditative practice stills the mind and frees the individual from desire, emancipating them from the carousel of consumer capitalism (Schmidt and Walach 2014: 4). Unlike those who grow up in a Buddhist culture, Western converts access Buddhist teachings through the printed works of a thriving book industry (Nattier 1997: 80; Prebish 1999: 18) and through the vast resources now available on the internet. This means that teachings can be cognized in solitary reflection, leading to highly subjective interpretations. The present character of Buddhism reflects the many ways in which religious teachings were interpreted as they came to the West. For instance, Peggy Teresa Nancy Kennett's (1924–96) characterization of Zen reflected Protestant critiques of Catholicism stressing the centrality of personal intuitive experiences, while the Beat poets emphasized the "anti-structural ideas of spontaneity, experience and freedom" (Kay 2007: 6–7 and 141). Interpretations such as these led to the common belief that Zen Buddhism is a "mystical" tradition about "private ineffable experiences" (Kay 2007: 145–7).

As can be seen, Buddhism and its associated meditative traditions have developed in concert with various streams of Western thought from the late nineteenth century to the present day. Viewed as being compatible with modernity, rationality, science, romanticism, art, democracy, feminism, individualism, philosophical deconstruction, antiestablishment thinking, psychology, and environmentalism, it is evident that the worldview of alternative spirituality underpins the impetus and style of engagement with the Buddhist tradition. Understanding the ways in which Eastern religious ideas have come to the West is important when considering viewer responses as the presence of Buddhist (and occasionally, Hindu) references may at first seem out of place. It is evident, however, that Eastern ideas and religious practices have been molded and translated to suit particular existing needs in the Western psyche. The principals of meditative practice, enlightenment, and an Eastern-inspired understanding of identity are frequently interwoven into viewers' responses demonstrating the integration of these concepts into Western conceptions of the sacred. Each of these elements has taken on a distinct significance in Western culture as a part of the broader trend of alternative spirituality, which itself was born from the thinking of generations of artists, writers, musicians, poets, and scholars who saw in the East a solution to the problems of the modernizing West.

Conclusion

Recognizing that Christianity no longer defines the worldview of the West this chapter prepares the ground for an analysis of religious experience in the cinema. This consideration of cultural change is necessary to contextualize the type of experiences that viewers report. As will be discussed in the following chapters, viewers of *2001*, *Enter the Void*, and *Melancholia* regularly refer to the physical and mental preparations that they have undertaken in order to experience the film in the "right way." Stating that *2001* is "more than a movie," viewers treat the film with a degree of reverence that might be reserved for religious practice. One of the features of religious experience is the sense that one is being affected by a spiritual entity or force. Spiritually toned cinematic experiences, however, leave the ultimate source of spiritual sensation undefined. As just one example, David G. Hoch (writing from a scholarly perspective) interprets the monolith from *2001* to be "the faceless Uncreated Uncreating of the cabala or, in Paul Tillich's terminology, the God beyond God" (1971: 961). The nonconformist attitude that directors like Kubrick, Noé, and von Trier express through their unconventional film styles is compatible with the epistemological mode of alternative spirituality, and these directors share a common desire to push their audiences beyond their perceptual comfort-zone. In turn, their films provide the viewer with the opportunity to enter a state of otherness where correlations with mysticism are easily found.

3

2001: A Space Odyssey
Cosmos and Ethos

Kubrick's *2001* has gone down in history as one of the most important films of all time. To understand how *2001* stirred the imagination of a generation, it is helpful to briefly consider the cultural significance of outer space during the period. While the institutions of society continued to manipulate and oppress, endangering the existence of life on Earth through the threat of atomic warfare and the despoliation of the natural environment, counterculturalists were attracted to the imaginative uncharted territories of space, foreign spiritualties, and unconventional forms of creation and perception in art, music, and film. As a collaborative project undertaken with science fiction writer Arthur C. Clarke, Kubrick's film stands alongside Clarke's novel of the same name. In their respective authorial processes, Kubrick and Clarke engaged in personal journeys of discovery as they questioned religious leaders, anthropologists, cosmologists, and scientists about the possibilities of nonhuman intelligence. As works of science fiction, both Kubrick and Clarke's *2001* touched on questions as pivotal to the Western religious worldview as the origin of intelligence, evolution, future travels beyond Earth, and the transformation of the human into pure consciousness. The spiritual relevance of Kubrick's *2001* has been widely recognized (Bergesen and Greeley 2003: 129; Krämer 2010: 40; Agel 1970: 252) along with its depiction of pseudo-religious concepts like "the sublime" (Pezzotta 2013: 17; Gonzalez 2009: n.p.) and "transcended intelligence" (Walker, Taylor, and Ruchti 1999: 193). As will be discussed below, Kubrick and Clarke's comments about *2001* show that they were influenced by streams of thinking relevant to alternative spirituality. The salience of the film can be garnered from its immediate impact with audiences of the late 1960s and, as the *IMDb* reviews featured in the final section of this chapter show, spiritual responses to the themes of the film have continued through to the present day.

Re-Imagining the Universe

In 1964, Kubrick approached Clarke to see if he would be interested in creating a science fiction film (Krämer 2010: 18). Their projects developed collaboratively and in tandem, but the finished products have distinct stylistic features and should be considered separate and unique works. Following early discussions, Kubrick and Clarke decided to model the plot of *2001* on Clarke's short story "The Sentinel" (1951). Clarke's 1953 novel *Childhood's End* was also a major influence on the development of *2001*. Kubrick's final creation utilized narrative to a limited extent and left many things unexplained, and for this reason, some have turned to Clarke's novel to fill in the gaps. While the film and novel may seem compatible in this way, Clarke's novel was not necessarily designed to explain Kubrick's film. Adopting a different style and medium to Clarke, Kubrick engages the viewer in an experiential manner (Poole 2001: 44) triggering spiritual responses that are not associated with the novel.

The film can be summarized as follows. *2001* opens with an extended period of blackness accompanied by eerie music, followed by a dramatic image of aligned planets, heralded by the triumphant notes of Richard Strauss's famed 1896 tone poem, *Thus Spoke Zarathustra* (1896). The film then turns to "The Dawn of Man" sequence involving a tribe of humanoid apes in a prehistoric desert setting. The man-apes are shown going about their daily business, eating, grooming each other, and gathering at night in the shelter of the caves. The unexplained appearance of a black monolith rouses the man-apes to approach in curiosity, as the monolith emits bizarre noises. One man-ape touches the monolith and in a subsequent scene discovers the power of violence, using a large bone to kill a rival from another tribe. Throwing this primitive tool in the air, cinema's most famous jump-cut transforms the bone into a similarly shaped spaceship and the narrative is cast thousands years forward, into humanity's future.

In the future, technology has advanced to allow human beings to travel in space and a trip to the moon is depicted to be as unremarkable as an airplane flight. In a zero gravity setting, the ship has been designed with various quirks to accommodate eating, walking, and visits to the lavatory. Following the discovery of a mysterious monolith on the moon, a team of astronauts led by Mission Commander David Bowman and Deputy Commander Frank Poole are sent on a deep space mission shrouded in secrecy. The ship is equipped with the latest technology, including a computer, HAL9000, who speaks and interprets information like a human. As the mission proceeds, HAL kills those members of the crew who were being kept in a hibernation state, along with Poole, leaving only Bowman alive. While disabling HAL's higher functions in order to fight for his own survival, Bowman discovers that HAL was programmed to follow a higher mission that he and the crew were unaware of. HAL is successfully shut down and Bowman remains on the ship as it moves toward Jupiter. Here Bowman transcends time and space, and is transported through a vortex of psychedelic colors to arrive in a strange Louis XVI-styled room. In a series of shot-reverse-shots Bowman is transformed, seemingly by the presence of the monolith, into an elderly man, and finally, into a glowing fetus known as the Starchild. Floating in space, the Starchild gazes toward Earth (and directly at the viewer) before the film plunges into darkness again.

Referred to as one of the "biggest hits" of the late 1960s, Kubrick's *2001* has also been recognized as one of the greatest films of all time, and remains one of the most frequently analyzed films in cinema history (Krämer 2010: 10; Agel 1970: 315). While it has been commonly associated with the countercultural youth of the late 1960s, in reality, *2001* reached a very large audience and has continued to be considered a classic despite its art film style (Krämer 2010: 11–12 and 34–5). This big budget film changed dramatically from the time of its inception to the final product that cost Metro Goldwyn Mayer (MGM) between ten and eleven million dollars (R. B. Palmer 2006: 18; Krämer 2010: 40). Originally known as *Journey Beyond the Stars*, Kubrick planned to open the film with a ten-minute prologue featuring interviews from prominent scientists, cosmologists, and religious leaders amenable to the idea of extraterrestrial life. However, this section was cut along with other instances of explanatory dialogue, increasing the film's ambiguity with a greater focus on visual and aural elements (Agel 1970: 27–57; Poole 2001: 43). *2001* has been credited as the film that redefined science fiction (and perhaps film itself) through its nonconventional cinematic approach (Schmidt 2010: 22) and has had a formidable impact on Western thought in terms of the mythology of space.

Kubrick and Clarke undertook extensive research in the development of their complementary versions of *2001*, which included scientific, philosophical, and religious investigations into the origin of life on Earth and human potential in light of scientific and technological advances. Their research included watching every available science fiction film, reading hypotheses on the nature of religion and mythology like Joseph Campbell's *The Hero with a Thousand Faces* (1949), and studying writings concerned with evolutionary development such as Louis Leakey's *Adam's Ancestors* (1934) and Robert Ardrey's *African Genesis* (1961) which formed the inspiration for the "Dawn of Man" sequence (Poole

2001: 42; Schwam 2010: 35). Dr. Harry Shapiro, Head of Anthropology at the Natural History Museum New York, was also consulted regarding early human development for that scene (Schwam 2010: 36). The spaceships and planetary sets used in the film were designed with such fastidious attention to realism that *2001* has been likened to a "miniature space project" (Poole 2001: 43). Clarke was more closely aligned with the scientific community, but Kubrick also became quite obsessed with the accurate depiction of space, and under guidance from his chief scientific adviser, The National Aeronautics and Space Administration's (NASA's) Dr. Frederick Ordway III, was able to create such a tangible rendition of space travel that the Apollo 8 astronauts viewed the film in preparation for their historic mission to the moon (Poole 2001: 42). While the image "Earthrise" taken by the Apollo 8 astronauts in 1968 has been credited as forever changing human self-perception by revealing the first image of planet Earth taken from space, the powerful imagery from *2001* became associated with this in the imaginations of thousands. The underlying religious significance of these parallel journeys into the unknown is underscored by the fact that the image of "Earthrise" was first televised on Christmas Eve as the astronauts read the biblical account of creation from Genesis (Poole 2001: 45). Although many big budget films consult experts from different fields to advise the director on the plausibility of their fictional creations, *2001* was a unique project in its close relationship with the US space program and the extent to which it engaged with the scientific and religious thinking of the era.

On the whole, *2001* came to contribute to the mythology of space, and Kubrick's version was particularly effective in this as it made audiences feel like they had traveled there. Jeremy Bernstein from *The New Yorker* reported that Kubrick and Clarke believed space to be "a source of endless knowledge, which may transform our civilization in the same way that the voyages of the Renaissance transformed the Dark Ages" (Poole 2001: 42). The possibility that advanced extraterrestrials existed in space was of particular importance to both Kubrick and Clarke. In an interview with Joseph Gelmis, Kubrick spoke passionately about the immensity of the universe and the likelihood that intelligent life exists beyond humankind (1969: n.p.). From Clarke's perspective, Kubrick's principal aim was to make a film "about Man's relation to the universe" rather than the "simpleminded" space films that currently existed that were "concerned more with the schoolboy excitement of space flight than its profound implications to society, philosophy, and religion" (Schwam 2010: 31). Clarke's comment here demonstrates that the spiritual significance of *2001* is bound up with the symbolic potential of space and its ability to signify the unknown. Furthermore, Cowan argues that "science fiction is the genre of possibility, a principal cultural canvas on which writers, artists, and filmmakers have sketched their visions of transcendent potential" (2010: 11).

Kubrick's aim with *2001* was to create a film that "directly penetrates the subconscious with an emotional and philosophic content" (Turnock 2014: 251). However, as Kubrick discovered during early press screenings of the film, it is not easy to engage the viewer in this way. Kubrick recalled, "I will never forget my irritation at watching the sight of the Star Child's enormous eyes gazing at their backs as they headed up the aisles towards the exit" (Poole 2001: 43). At this point, Kubrick rapidly edited the film, removing around twenty minutes of footage that amounted to "almost all the remaining dialogue and explanation" (Poole 2001: 43). Kubrick also previously decided to omit the music that composer Alex North had prepared for the film, opting for a selection of strategically edited classical pieces, including compositions by György Ligeti and Johann Strauss II, that were not originally designed for film (Krämer 2010: 51). Such creative decisions ensured that *2001* broke with the conventions of classical cinema and expected features of the science fiction genre and, in its final form, was unconventional enough to be compared to avant-garde cinema (Agel 1970: 254). Kubrick's shift away from plot-driven narrative and characterization in favor of visual and aural excess influenced later filmmakers to adopt increasingly visual modes of communication aimed to evoke visceral or sensual responses (Turnock 2014: 111). While Clarke and Kubrick were equally interested in investigating the Big Questions of existence that took them into traditionally religious territory, Kubrick's film has a stronger reputation for generating religious feelings. This may be because Clarke's writing is speculative and rationalistic in style, while Kubrick's more abstract approach affects the viewer in a nonrational manner (Poole 2001: 44).

Set in space, thirty-three years in the future, MGM counted on a level of fascination from audiences who were already looking to the heavens in fear and hopeful expectation as the Cold War space race unfolded. President John F. Kennedy's promise to put man on the moon in 1961 along with other groundbreaking and widely publicized "firsts" in space ensured keen public interest in extraterrestrial subjects. As the increase in new religious movements associated with alien beings and outer space attest, the space race did not simply capture people's interest on a scientific and political level, but also at the level of human aspirations and religious belief. Bryan Sentes and Susan Palmer make some insightful observations about the cultural context of the era that encouraged the development of a range of religious movements inspired by science, technology, and UFO's, including the Aetherius Society, Unarius

Academy of Science, Human Individual Metamorphosis (Heaven's Gate), and the Raëlians (2000: 86–105). UFO-inspired new religious movements of the late 1960s through to the mid-1970s built upon a general fascination with the potentialities of outer space that had developed in the previous decade. However, the desire to find scientific explanations for the paranormal that is evident in the new religious movements of this period is also a part of a broader attitude to religious claims following the Enlightenment. As Sentes and Palmer argue, the late 1960s and early 1970s stand "within the horizon of the death of God" and by this, the authors mean that a natural scientific worldview, and not a theological one, is taken for granted (2000: 87–8). Because all things are understood to be "natural or immanent rather than supernatural or transcendent" (Sentes and Palmer 2000: 87) scientific explanations for all phenomena will eventually be found. According to this logic, the Raëlians recast gods as advanced alien beings and effectively reinterpreted the biblical narrative as an elaborate scientific experiment (Sentes and Palmer 2000: 90). These alien beings are of the same species as present human beings but are far more advanced. Interestingly, Clarke had an idea during the process of writing *2001* that he deemed "crucial" to the book's development; that the aliens that humans meet are in fact humans "who were collected from Earth a hundred thousand years ago, and hence are virtually identical with us" (Schwam 2010: 35).

While the particular claims of UFO religions of this period may not be considered strictly scientific, they nonetheless criticize religion for fostering ignorance, seeking to break down the mythology of religion into scientifically plausible postulations. Benjamin Zeller explains that the epistemology and associated worldview of science had become so influential by this time that "all religions had to respond to it." However, "new religions reacted to science with a clarity and alacrity that more established religions could not" (2010: 2 and 4). The traditional dichotomy between religion and science (or perhaps more specifically, Christianity and rationalism) was transformed in an era of alternative religiosity where the language of science and technology was used to reinterpret and justify spiritual concepts. At the same time, the subjective turn evident in alternative spirituality involved a certain disregard for authoritative discourse, including that of the scientific community, making all evidence malleable and open to personal reconfiguration (Sutcliffe 2003: 218).

The idea that humanity is becoming increasingly enlightened following the trajectory of scientific and technological advancements serves to idealize the dominant cultural practice of the modern West (Sentes and Palmer 2000: 89). The complexity of modern religiosity is found in the simultaneous "affirmation, critique, and transcendence" of both science and religion as the irresponsible adoption of either system can lead to disaster. Religion can immure humanity in primitive ignorance, while science can potentially destroy life on Earth, as is evident in the environmental crises of the period and the nuclear threat (Sentes and Palmer 2000: 87). Typically new religious movements of this type contain eschatological warnings, and human beings are positioned at a crossroads between destruction and salvation. The active role of the individual in determining their fate is characteristic of religious movements in the modern West.

The creators of *2001* were clearly influenced by such thinking as they developed their vision of *2001*. The same can be said about a number of their advisers and consultants, including prominent astronomer Dr. Carl Sagan and biologist J. B. S. Haldane, who was to be quoted in the original opening scenes of *2001* (Bjørnvig 2012: 131). These figures may not consider themselves to have anything in common with the religious movements mentioned above, but they are similarly engaged in the sacralization of space, science, and technology paired with highly speculative cosmological and existential thinking.

Historian of religion Thore Bjørnvig highlights the vital role that figures like Clarke and Sagan played in promoting space exploration in the public sphere (2012: 127). Notably these figures sacralized space, imbuing the dark frontier with spiritual potential (Bjørnvig 2012: 128). Clarke was not just a writer of science fiction, but played an influential role in space lobby organizations such as the British Interplanetary Society, where he served as chairman on two occasions (Bjørnvig 2012: 127). Clarke has been referred to as "one of the most influential advocates in the twentieth century for the exploration and colonization of space," and the "prophet of the Space Age" (Bjørnvig 2012: 127 and 132). As Bjørnvig explains, while Clarke was skeptical of supernatural religious claims and a strong advocate for scientific inquiry, "religious ideas and longings ran deep in his thinking about the human future in space" (2012: 127). Like the UFO religious movements mentioned above, Clarke's speculative fiction made use of concepts and symbolism from religion, re-casting the unknown as the yet-to-be-known, imbuing the scientific realm of space with an aura of sacredness and ultimate meaning. Bjørnvig offers numerous examples of religious content in Clarke's writings, most notably his fascination with the expulsion of Adam and Eve from Eden and apocalyptic visions of future utopian transcendence (2012: 132–3). However, Clarke's references to religious concepts are not limited to Christianity. The group mind of Clarke's 1953 novel *Childhood's End* is reminiscent of Jung's collective unconscious (1990: 168) and terms like "the Transcendental Drive" (Bjørnvig 2012: 136) in his work reveal an interest in emergent Western adaptations of Eastern religious practices like meditation. Maharishi Mahesh Yogi's Transcendental Meditation (TM), for example, was conceived as a method to bring about perfect health, well-being, and "an expansion of consciousness to unimagined states" that would, in turn, bring about the improvement of society (Olson 2005: 9291). Clarke kept company with the likes of Allen Ginsberg and William Burroughs (McAleer 1992: 184) who were also advocates of Eastern religion (Cusack 2011: 306). Bjørnvig observes numerous examples of "curious coincidences" and "uncanny predictions" in Clarke's autobiography *Astounding Days* (1989) demonstrating Clarke's general fascination with unseen powers or forces (2012: 132). Clarke's approach to science fiction was "technological realism with a sense of wonder and what he called 'a search for ultimate values'" (Poole 2001: 44). Overall, Clarke saw science as the path toward those advanced goals that humans had previously defined as religious (Bjørnvig 2012: 140). Clarke's interests are important to consider to the extent that he worked as a co-creator with Kubrick.

Kubrick's own comments confirm that "the God concept is at the heart of [*2001*]" (Gelmis 1969: n.p.). Kubrick also reportedly said that "MGM don't know it yet, but they've just footed the bill for the first six-million dollar religious film" (Poole 2001: 44). This overt declaration of religious meaning is not, however, drawn from Christianity but from a type of alternative spirituality that embraces the potentialities of science. In the interview from which this quote was taken, Kubrick evokes the story of evolution in the language of scientific wonder. The essence of this is that human history is minuscule in the vast story of the universe and that intelligent life is likely to exist beyond humankind (Gelmis 1969: n.p.). This inverts the Judeo-Christian worldview where human beings are placed front and center in the story of the universe. It is Kubrick's view that "the ultimate destiny of humankind is to become 'pure energy,' or 'pure spirit'" and that is the "ultimate form that intelligence would seek" (Kloman 1968: n.p.). Kubrick's comments demonstrate a form of religiosity that is typical of 1960s counterculture, rejecting traditional prescriptive religious ideas and reformulating concepts of God and ultimate meaning. Clarke shared this approach as is evident in his comment that "any path to knowledge is a path to God—or to Reality, whichever word one prefers to use" (Poole 2001: 44). The interchangeable terminology that Clarke adopts, equating God with Reality, indicates the dexterity of religious concepts when they are understood in a functional sense that is relevant to the individual.

The influence of Jung on Kubrick's personal philosophy and filmmaking is well recognized, especially in relation to *2001* (Rice 2008: 26; Kuberski 2008: 51–73). Kubrick explains that the monolith was depicted as an opaque black rectangular slab because it embodied the "unimaginable" (Gelmis 1969: n.p.). Referring to the monolith as a "Jungian archetype," Kubrick indicates that like Minimalist art this symbol is primal and elemental to human consciousness (Gelmis 1969: n.p.). Jung's exploration of the "God concept" surely influenced Kubrick's use of the term in reference to *2001*. As outlined in the previous chapter, Jung was an influential figure in the development of alternative spirituality. His approach to psychology blended the religious with new understandings about human subjectivity. As a prime example of the "psychologizing of religion" and the "sacralization of psychology" that is characteristic of alternative spirituality (Hanegraaff 1998: 197), the Jungian God-concept retains the functional spirituality of "God" while removing any requirement to prove God's existence (Kuberski 2008: 65).

It is Philip Kuberski's view that in being influenced by Jung, Kubrick picks up on the psychologist's deep fascination with historical Gnosticism (2008: 61). Kuberski describes gnosis as

> an embodied knowing, the transcendence of verbal or conceptual cognition, and the recognition of immanence. It is to see though the local conventions, past even the known God, to the eternal unblemished; the unknown or alien god who has never been revealed but can only be encountered through a momentous fragmentation of expectation and definition of society and self. (2008: 61)

This epistemological orientation harmonizes with Hanegraaff's "gnostic" truth (1998: 519) that privileges esoteric forms of knowledge and can be considered typical of alternative spirituality. Such a conception of "God" is clearly evident in Kubrick's *2001*, yet it is not the traditional Judeo-Christian God. In fact, it can seem almost atheist in its "momentous fragmentation" (Kuberski 2008: 61) and rejection of social and religious conventions. However, the God-concept remains "spiritual" in the terminology of this study as it is oriented toward the sacred, and its function and attributes are clearly drawn from religion.

At this point the discussion will turn to a consideration of viewer responses. The following section explores the existential and cosmological themes present in *IMDb* commentary, while the affective dimensions of the cinematic experience will be analyzed in Chapters 4 and 5.

Mystery and Potentiality

The mysteries that *2001* would impart to its audiences were foreshadowed by MGM's promotional material, which included Haldane's famous quotation,

"The Universe is not only stranger than we imagine; it is stranger than we *can* imagine" (Krämer 2010: 36). Echoing this statement, *IMDb* viewer mfb138 posits that *2001* is about "unanswerable mysteries" that fill the viewer with awe. Like the presence of God, this viewer says, the monolith in Kubrick's film is "always there" but "never responds to our inquiries," as humans are not ready to attain this type of awareness (September 27, 2003, user review of *2001*). Here the unresponsiveness and impenetrability of the sacred, or even its seeming absence, is taken as evidence of authentic divinity because spiritual truth is beyond human comprehension. For seanwilson556, *2001* deals directly with the question of God; after watching the film, the viewer hypothesizes that God could be "a metaphysical creation" or "the cosmos itself" where humans "look up at the night skies and see a vast and wonderful array of stars, planets, suns and galaxies" and one could be "staring at God everyday without knowing it" (July 17, 2011, user review of *2001*). This comment refers to the immanence of the divine that is hidden from human awareness until the individual experiences a moment of realization. Spiritual truth is esoteric and hidden in plain sight, revealed to the individual as they become ready and willing to know. Viewers such as lost2you2002 report that Kubrick creates expectancy in the audience, making them "wish to peek behind the curtain" and discover the unknown (June 26, 2003, user review of *2001*). Similarly, Andrews Benatar Luque feels a sense of "discovery" while watching *2001* and says that the film is "spiritual and Godly in its essence." This viewer clarifies that he does not mean a sentient being, but rather a manifestation of God as the continuing realization of divine knowledge. This encounter with universal wisdom is felt rather than cognized in a "poetic feeling of the beautiful and mysterious cosmos we still hope to understand in our gradual evolutionary development" (October 30, 2013, user review of *2001*). This evolutionary parallel highlights the layered nature of truth that is successively revealed to the individual. As Elisa Pezzotta points out, Kubrick creates "levels of meaning" or a "density of meaning" that is challenging for the viewer to process and can lead to feelings of the sublime (2013: 34–5).

Using the symbolism of the film, viewers like txk02 have likened the ability to appreciate *2001* to a superior level of consciousness while those who do not understand the film "can only screech, jump around and flail their arms" at the enigma presented to them (May 18, 2008, user review of *2001*). Mypharmcon links the monolith with the black screen that Kubrick presents in the "Pre-Credit" and "Intermission" sequences, saying that "it is easy to envisage that we, the audience, were being 'educated' by the black monolith before us as represented by the seemingly void, imageless screen" (February 16, 2014, user review of

2001). Such comments demonstrate that the development of consciousness and perception is not simply a theme from the film, but is something that viewers feel they are participating in first hand.

As a rejection of the authority of institutional religion and their claim to knowledge, an esoteric approach to truth is an affirmation of the awesome power of the divine and the individual's natural connection with the eternal wisdom of the universe. According to polos are minty, *2001* demonstrates how "God can be explained as a part of the universe, and not outside it" where God is "a natural as opposed to a supernatural phenomenon" (April 7, 2010, user review of *2001*). While the sacralized universe is considered to be natural, it is also thought to be beyond human comprehension, as opposed to the confidence of scientific empiricism. That which is beyond knowledge or difficult for scientists to explain can therefore take on mystical qualities. Because outer space lies at the very limit of scientific knowledge, it is the perfect site for the contemplation of the unknown.

For many viewers, the esoteric nature of *2001* is linked with the process of evolution (jonathandoe se7en, September 6, 2001, user review of *2001*; Lechuguilla, February 6, 2005, user review of *2001*; mameeshkamowskwoz, December 6, 2012, user review of *2001*). However, this does not necessarily equate with the scientific definition of evolution that is concerned with biological change mediated by natural selection (Salthe 2013: 793–8). Instead, these viewers imagine themselves as participants in the evolution of consciousness that is portrayed in *2001* as the film traces human development from a primitive state to one that transcends the human altogether. According to mfb138, "Human evolution is the gradual awakening of consciousness. It's like slowly opening your eyes and realizing the true nature of things." This viewer sees evolution as progressing from "pure instinctual existence" to "self-awareness" and then to "the understanding that we are all one consciousness, the same pulsing, vibrating energy that makes up everything in the universe." This final stage sees the dissolution of life and death and the freeing of consciousness from matter (mfb138, September 27, 2003, user review of *2001*) Echoing the Buddhist philosophy that suffering is caused by an attachment to identity, the viewer draws on Alice Bailey's vision of the New Age in the belief that a sudden apocalyptic event will inevitably bring about mass realization and change (Sutcliffe 2003: 51). This concept, while salient for viewers like mfb138, is not necessarily the unifying feature of what is commonly referred to as New Age religion. As Sutcliffe has argued, post–First World War esotericists like Bailey used the term as a symbol for apocalyptic renewal, at the level of civilization

(2003: 51). However, by the 1970s the term "New Age" was somewhat artificially applied from an etic standpoint to refer to a form of religiosity that was more concerned with subjective experiences of inner awakening (Sutcliffe 2003: 107).

Despite mfb138's comments about collective realization, *2001* only depicts the awakening of consciousness on an individual level. The film may infer that Bowman's transformation has cosmic significance, but this only occurs at a symbolic level. Others who exist in the world of the film do not factor into the moment of enlightenment. In fact, they are all but forgotten. According to Sutcliffe, from the 1970s, the focus on "'private' gnosis" or "self-realization" supplants any literal expectation of apocalypse (Sutcliffe 2003: 107) while the psychologizing of religion recasts "reality" in terms of perception. Self-realization can be understood as the attainment of unclouded perception and deep insight, where the subjective apprehension of reality is unmediated by desire, attachments, beliefs, and preconceived concepts. This state is a transitory religious experience that can give rise to subsequent reflections in daily life. Alternative spirituality privileges such moments of interior apocalypse, and they are extraordinary enough to be rare occurrences. The life affirming and therapeutic dimensions of alternative spirituality that Sutcliffe mentions apply to the total picture of this religious position characterized as a "humanistic project of spiritual growth and self-realisation in the here-and-now" (Sutcliffe 2003: 117). In this discussion, peak moments of realization are the primary focus, yet these states are not permanent. Rather, they are felt to be experiences of radical deconstruction that dissolve the self, freeing perception in a moment of revelation. Wood's view that "spirit possession" is central to alternative spirituality is of crucial importance here (2007: 154–75). The temporary sensation of direct insight involves the implicit submission of ordinary perception and feelings of self-mastery. In this moment, the individual is open to the unmediated experience of reality and becomes the medium for mystical truth.

As mfb138 reflects, contact with the monolith enacts a "full force unmediated confrontation" with the unknown (September 27, 2003, user review of *2001*). The inference here is that an experience of the divine is less authentic if it is mediated, understood cognitively, or experienced with a sense of self-control. The encounter between the man-apes and the monolith is one where the apes are acted upon by something that changes them irrevocably, and it also seems that *2001* is able to exert this power over audiences. While this type of interaction with the holy is experienced by the individual (doing away with religious intermediaries), it is also depersonalized. By depersonalizing God and transforming the Judeo-Christian Deity into a primal force of nature and consciousness, the individual who experiences an encounter with the divine is also depersonalized, as they are awakened to the realization that they are one with the universe. For anthonymueller the individual who "insists on knowing without restraint, the revelation may be too much to bare [sic]" (October 12, 2000, user review of *2001*) As such, the confrontation with truth that *2001* presents challenges the viewer to let go of all restraint in a powerful and potentially traumatic process of awakening. Ironically or paradoxically, the modern Western value of self-determination here is articulated in the individual's rejection of institutional authority and their openness and submission to the will of the universe, which is capable of erasing the significance of the individual in a moment of enlightenment.

For mfb138, the "Stargate" sequence is a faithful representation of the final stage of evolution where human beings become one with the universe. Regardless of what humans think or want, evolution continues and "the monolith is coming anyway" (September 27, 2003, user review of *2001*). Mfb138's comments provide an interesting insight into the evolutionary theme of *2001* as there is a distinct sense that natural and uncontrollable forces will awaken human beings, effectively removing their individual agency, but at the same time, people who experience early awakening through their perceptive insights are ahead of the pack. Those who attain esoteric knowledge or awakening of consciousness are evolutionary leaders and at the apex of human potential, yet because this is a natural process, they are not special so much as in tune. Importantly, the revelation of truth often involves the inversion of the traditional Christian worldview that places human beings at center stage in God's plan.

Reflecting a worldview that is frequently associated with *2001*, The Ebullient One explains that humans are not subservient to God in a Christian sense, but rather they come to realize their utter irrelevance in the face of the awesome power of the universe. This power does not distinguish between good and evil but works through nature and consciousness in ceaseless evolutionary progression toward an endpoint of pure abstraction and mystery. The Ebullient One describes a desire to transcend dichotomies in order to rise above an attachment to opinion and current events (December 14, 2002, user review of *2001*). Numerous viewers characterize the universe as being indifferent to human existence, a concept that sits in an interesting relationship with the associated narrative of spiritual progress. ShibanPD notes that in *2001* humans "wait to be converted into—to be replaced by—a better species" (November 12, 2012, user review of *2001*). There is a distinct ambivalence about whether anything personal or human will survive this process. It is, however, viewed positively or at least with equanimity. Viewers such as John Novarina have adopted the notion that humanity can evolve beyond matter and become "pure energy" with a positive understanding of this transition (July 30, 1998, user review of *2001*). The acceptance of this radical deconstruction of the human, and the individual, is captured in comments that refer to the true nature of human beings in highly abstract terms. For instance, dunmore ego refers to Sagan's expression that human beings are comprised of "star stuff" (June 1, 2006, user review of *2001*). Dunmore ego interprets this type of cosmology as being atheist despite a persistent and diffuse sense of the sacred or spiritual that remains in the concept of consciousness. According to this viewer, *2001* offers atheist transcendence by freeing the mind, without resorting to an interaction with traditional religion (June 1, 2006, user review of *2001*).

The notion that the universe is vast and unknowable, which is one of the core themes of *2001*, is something that is, in fact, shared by religion, spirituality, and atheism. What is often rejected is a traditional, personal monotheistic God like that of the Abrahamic faiths. In terms of Kubrick's self-professed religious position, he says, "I don't believe in any of Earth's monotheistic religions, but I do believe that one can construct an intriguing scientific definition of God" that arises out of evolutionary thinking and a strong focus on human potential (Kloman 1968: n.p.). In alternative spirituality, science and the mystical are compatible, and the same truth can be understood on different levels. StarCastle99 echoes Clarke's sentiment that humans would view more advanced civilizations as being magical or Godly because they are beyond present understanding (May 29, 2002, user review of *2001*). The rejection of traditional religion in favor of individualized spirituality is captured in Peter Henderson's comment that the film brings about a sense of being "'born again,' not in the debauched meaning given to that term by evangelical 'Christians,' but in some purer, more aesthetic, more ethical way" (October 2, 2013, user review of *2001*). Such spiritualized interpretations of *2001* are characteristically nondeterministic, remaining in a state of speculation, and not knowing, gesturing toward truth because this is more authentic than making definitive truth claims. This nondeterministic approach to knowledge is in part influenced by the pluralist culture of the West and the eclectic nature of alternative spirituality where different truths point to an immanent universal truth that cannot be encompassed by any one interpretation. The ultimate power and wisdom of universal truth are acknowledged in comments that remove individual agency by overriding the value of self-determination. Joebobs talks about the transcendence of "flesh and bone" that requires one to allow "consciousness to achieve its great ambition" (February 15, 2014, user review of *2001*). Here it is as if consciousness has a will of its own that is indifferent to human desires, beliefs, or requirements.

The overall meaning of *2001* has been judged optimistic or pessimistic, depending on one's interpretation of the final scene of the film, where the Starchild gazes upon the Earth. Esteban Esq. sees *2001* as a vision of hope for humanity (January 15, 2013, user review of *2001*), while others like Evolzzzz see it as a warning that society is in danger of destroying itself through the misuse of technological power. As this viewer comments, *2001* "warns us for the future: we MUST control science carefully. And the world doesn't end after death" (Evolzzzz, December 30, 1999, user review of *2001*). Optimistic conclusions are drawn when the Starchild is understood to be the next stage in human evolution—the new and enlightened version of humanity. Negative conclusions, on the other hand, are generally influenced by the additional detail that is included in Clarke's novel that describes the Starchild's destruction of the Earth through the detonation of nuclear warheads:

> There before him, a glittering toy no Star-Child could resist, floated the planet Earth with all its peoples ... history as men knew it would be drawing to a close. A thousand miles below, he became aware that a slumbering cargo of death had awoken, and was stirring sluggishly in its orbit. The feeble energies it contained were no possible menace to him; but he preferred a cleaner sky. He put forth his will, and the circling megatons flowered in a silent detonation that brought a brief, false dawn to the half sleeping globe. (Clarke 2000: 252)

Responding to viewers and critics, Kubrick and Clarke have tended to confirm both interpretations. Clarke denies that he depicted the annihilation of the Earth in his novel, but reflects, "Now, I am not so sure. . . . We have wasted and defiled . . . the beautiful planet Earth. Why should we expect any mercy from a returning Star Child?" Clarke states that the Starchild "triggered the orbiting nuclear bombs harmlessly," and according to Krämer, Kubrick shared this view (2010: 8–9). Kubrick has resisted political readings of *2001* linked to the nuclear arms race, seeking to push audiences toward a more mythological interpretation of perennial significance (Kloman 1968: n.p.). However, Kubrick expresses his personal concern about the nuclear threat to life on Earth (Kloman 1968: n.p.) indicating that the mythological nonetheless touches on burning issues of the day. While the meaning of *2001* may be open to interpretation, these comments from Kubrick and Clarke reveal a strong authorial focus on human responsibility in determining the trajectory that humanity will take moving into the future. For Kubrick, the nuclear threat is first and foremost a "moral" and "spiritual" problem and "perhaps even an evolutionary one rather than a technical one" (Kloman 1968: n.p.). This statement from Kubrick indicates that the current human (presumably rationalist) approach to the nuclear threat is not sufficient and that moral and spiritual systems of thought are required to address the threat of total human annihilation. Kubrick's view that this is also an evolutionary problem could be interpreted as a comment on whether humans should have a place in the universe if they are unable to responsibly and ethically manage the power of nuclear energy.

Viewers like ackstasis have made connections between *2001* and the vulnerability of the human race in the face of environmental threats. Ackstasis refers to the symbolic mirroring of the "Earth's razor-thin atmosphere" and the image of the Starchild that glows with an atmospheric halo around its body. For this viewer, the image of the Starchild conveys "the fragility, preciousness, and vulnerability of the planet on which we dwell" (December 6, 2007, user review of *2001*). Cantrell sam believes that *2001* forces people to realize that "we're alone in the universe. We are at the mercy of fate" and "to see *2001* is to be reminded of our humble station in existence" (August 14, 2003, user review of *2001*). For grrrr97, human aspiration is a "wonderfully natural, ever-evolving, manifestation of the universe" that is "devoid of any divine intervention" (January 24, 2003, user review of *2001*). These comments touch on the shift in focus from a human-centric universe and associated religious concepts about the inviolable nature of the human soul to a worldview where humanity hangs in the balance in a universe that evolves and progresses irrespective of the individual. However, recognition of humanity's vulnerability and lesser significance in the grand scheme of things does not necessarily equate to atheism. This worldview involves human humility and the acknowledgment of more powerful forces, a dynamic that can also be found in the history of Christian thought. However, the influence of Eastern philosophy is also present in such thinking as the humbled self is subject to radical deconstruction in order to be reimagined as a part of nature and the forces of consciousness. This Western interpretation of Eastern philosophy conceives of the annihilation of the self (and the world) with equanimity, and the humanist call to responsibility, where there is no savior to come to the rescue.

It is important to notice the influences above when considering the place of Nietzsche's philosophy in *2001*. Audience members have recognized the use of Strauss's *Thus Spoke Zarathustra* in *2001*'s soundtrack as a reference to Nietzsche's book of the same name (1883). In light of Nietzsche's philosophy, Dalibor Andric sees *2001* as revelation that "we are creators, we make all, our deeds, our minds, we are the GODS" (October 14, 2013, user review of *2001*). This statement reflects the belief typical of alternative spirituality that the individual actively creates reality through their thoughts and actions, which makes them responsible for their own fate. For ghosthawk5, the human creation of God prevents them from realizing their full potential, so the next stage of development necessitates the relinquishment of traditional religion. Stating that Kubrick laid the seeds of awakening in *2001* for those who were ready to draw these conclusions, this viewer examines the numerological messages contained in the film concluding, "*2001* IS the monolith" meaning that "forbidden (hidden) knowledge awaits us when we view the movie" (ghosthawk5, May 3, 2001, user review of *2001*). Josephclarkedunning believes the Starchild is a representation of the Superman who provides "the great hope of mankind in the absence of the living God" (November 12, 2012, user review of *2001*). Rejection of religious authority associated with the Judeo-Christian God is already evident in many of the readings considered thus far. The Nietzschean concept of the Death of God and the Superman adds to this by supplying a plausible interpretation of the Starchild's significance (Nietzsche 1999). By overcoming the concept of God, human beings take on an active, creative, and responsible role in the universe. For humans to become Gods they must be awakened to their true potential by overcoming ignorance and becoming receptive to the esoteric truth of existence that was previously hidden. However, in the case of *2001*, the power that the individual now holds still appears to be derived from mysterious forces. In this sense, human beings do not possess power so much as access the forces of the universe through enlightened understanding.

While *2001* is concerned with human potential, it is also a film that is rooted in Western culture where the ultimate destiny of humanity is really the next chapter in the story of the West. Michael sees *2001* as "a metaphor for the progressive ambitions and boundless dreams of Western man" (July 20, 2013, user review of *2001*), Brendan Sheehan agrees, saying that Western progress is portrayed in an "almost religious" manner (August 26, 2010, user review of *2001*). Other viewers, however, understand the film to be about the decline of the West. It is the opinion of Ezekiel Zeke Steiner that *2001* reveals the decline of Western civilization where "there is no energy, no purpose, no creative intelligence. Each individual is merely a bored, faceless cog in a technological system." This viewer sees *2001* as being "essentially a religious movie" wherein the "God of world religions" is reimagined as "cosmic intelligence" that is responsible for evolutionary progress (Ezekiel Zeke Steiner, November 4, 2005, user review of *2001*). Rather than being a film about the progress *or* decline of the West, it can be about both. Alternative spirituality is deeply pessimistic about the future of Western culture, while retaining a strong focus on progress and development that is instead tied to individual consciousness. From an emic point of view, this is a universalized perspective, but from an etic one, it is a Western point of view. As has been discussed, modernity has transformed the West into a culture that is eclectic, multicultural, and pluralistic. Because Western modernity has involved a trend toward universalization, it may seem that the West is becoming a globalized culture, but it is also recognizably distinct as a cultural and political conglomerate. As such, where the term "humanity" is used in this book, it refers to a conceptual ideal of future universalism. *2001* is then a film about the transformation of the West where traditional institutions such as Christianity, rigid scientific empiricism, and unquestioning obedience to the state are rejected in favor of that which the individual intuits to be true.

As the viewer comments above demonstrate, *2001* presents personal subjectivity as being of peripheral importance, while the realization of human potential is represented by the dramatic deconstruction of self as Bowman travels through the Stargate and transforms into the Starchild. Those aspects of Western culture that would reduce the individual into a "faceless cog" fall away as the individual awakens to their true purpose and place in the universe. As Kubrick has hypothesized, intelligent life will eventually "emerge from the chrysalis of matter transformed into beings of pure energy and spirit" (Ezekiel Zeke Steiner, November 4, 2005, user review of *2001*; Nordern 2001: 50). Transformation into an unimaginable state of being provides a powerful symbol where the individual is absolutely free from determinism. In line with the Western narrative of progress, this maximizes the sense of limitless potentiality.

In the interpretations included above, a distinctive set of ideas are repeated that reflect the changing view of the relationship between the self and universe arising out of the late-1960s countercultural shift. These include meditations on the ultimate mystery of the universe, the theme of awakening consciousness, spiritual progression, and the decline of the West. As Kubrick suggests, this involves an overarching "reaction to the stifling limitations of rationalism" (Kloman 1968: n.p.). However, *2001* is not just about the mysteries of the universe *of the film*; it also opens up contemplation of the viewer's universe, triggering existential questioning.

Conclusion

This chapter has outlined important influences arising out of the cultural context of the late 1960s that contributed to Kubrick and Clarke's authorial approaches and that have shaped the reception of the film. Kubrick and Clarke were shown to hold views that are compatible with the broad principals of alternative spirituality in the sense that they reject traditional forms of religious authority but are amenable to imagining human progress in terms of evolved consciousness. Like the term "evolution," "consciousness" takes on spiritual significance, as *2001* forges a new mythology for humankind. Tapping into the preexisting fascination with space and UFOs that arose out of the Cold War space race, *2001* was created in an unusually close collaboration with prominent scientists, members of US space program, and experts from a range of fields, including religious leaders. As will be argued in the following chapter, Kubrick's filmic style draws heavily on the experiential elements of religious practice, making the already mythic story of *2001* particularly salient to the spiritual seekers of the counterculture. As a religious film, *2001* captured a moment of spiritual transformation reflective of changes that were occurring in Western culture. As the credibility of religious institutions faltered, individuals realized that they were able to intuit the truth of existence directly and spontaneously. For many viewers, *2001* offered the opportunity to glimpse this truth and to strengthen their (perhaps preexisting) worldview about the ultimate destiny of humanity.

4

2001: A Space Odyssey and Meditative Perception

One of the principal qualities of *2001*, as a religious film, is that it operates at the level of experience. Many viewers have specifically recognized the relationship between *2001* and "religious experience" (brenda1028, March 31, 2002, user review of *2001*; woodpecker99, December 22, 2005, user review of *2001*; ShootingShark, March 15, 2008, user review of *2001*; Brendan Sheehan, August 26, 2010, user review of *2001*; eddie olsen, June 8, 2009, user review of *2001*). As Kubrick explains, *2001*'s "meaning has to be found on a sort of visceral, psychological level rather than in a specific literal explanation" (Kloman 1968: n.p.). This meaning is linked to "cosmic truth" located "somewhere in the mysterious, unknowable aspects of thought and life and experience" that can be accessed through religion and the arts (Kloman 1968: n.p.). Schrader makes this same observation in his adoption of Clive Bell's view that "art and Religion are the two roads by which men escape from circumstance to ecstasy. Art and Religion are means to similar states of mind" (Schrader 1972: 7). While the experiences considered here do not occur in a religious context, they can be considered paths to a state of mind that is commonly understood to be religious (Taves 2009: 13–15 and 26). In terms of directorial intent, Kubrick confirms that he aimed to create a film experience that "stirs the emotions and penetrates the subconscious of the viewer," stimulating the "mythological and religious yearnings and impulses" (Gelmis 1969: n.p.). It appears that Kubrick succeeded in this aim. However, it is not enough to say that this has been achieved merely through the incorporation of psychedelic imagery or narrative postulations about human origins. As such, various techniques are identified that Kubrick employs to subtly guide the viewer into a meditative state of perception increasing the likelihood of revelatory feelings.

When identifying the meditative attributes of *2001*, the term "meditation" is used in a generic sense to refer to techniques employed to attain a state of mind that is awake and focused, but is not engaged in "discursive ruminating thought" (Schmidt 2014: 142). In meditative practice, a practitioner's expectations can act as a barrier to experiencing meditative states (Schmidt 2014: 142). Expectations can bring about a range of subtle emotional and cognitive reactions that keep the practitioner thinking about what they want to experience rather than sinking into meditation. Stefan Schmidt identifies "logic relaxation" as an important feature of meditation that he defines as "a practice without analyzing, judging or expecting anything from the process" (2014: 139). In a meditative state of mind, and in waking mindfulness, the meditator is calm, focused, and awake to the subtleties of their thoughts and senses (Hanh 2016: 6–8, 14–15, and 84–5). As the practitioner lets go of thoughts, feelings, and sensations, they may eventually reach a subjective state of unity where there is "a sense of no space, no time, and no thought" (Newberg and Iversen 2003: 282).

Such states of mind are brought about thorough techniques such as applying single-pointed focus to a mantra, physical object, or mental image in order to attain "absorption with the object of focus" (Newberg and Iversen 2003: 282). This type of technique involves a very narrow range of focus (Schmidt 2014: 143). Alternatively, the practitioner can maintain sustained awareness that is "unfocused and inclusive" where "involuntary modes of bottom-up processing" and experiences of intuitive insight can occur (Austin 2014: 24). Schmidt refers to this type of practice as "open monitoring" where the practitioner observes "all phenomena coming into his or her mental space" with detachment (2014: 143–4). Mindfulness practices that involve open and focused awareness of the senses, actions, and emotions, enable meditative states of mind to be maintained in the presence of complex stimuli. Mindfulness is particularly suited to the appreciation of the arts, where the practitioner becomes sensitive to the subtleties of the work without seeking to analyze them.

Both Schrader (1972: 3) and Cho (1999: 179–80) have recognized film's capacity to encourage transcendent or meditative experiences. Cho argues that a director can challenge the viewer to adopt the "stillness of meditation" by employing a "contemplative pace" and can use disrupted narrative logic in order to trigger an experience of enlightenment in a similar manner to a Zen *koan* (1999: 172 and 187). *2001* viewers make similar observations, mentioning Buddhism explicitly. For example, Brando647 says that the film enabled a reflective state of mind through its slow pace. This quality reminded the viewer "of Buddhist philosophy, where enlightenment is achieved just by living in the moment, something we have lost touch with in this modern world." For this viewer, the film conveys something that is beyond understanding that relates to "a dissolved notion of self and our concrete place in space-time, where we can become more at one with the universe and each other, and away from the ideas we have of such a limited scope to life and consciousness" (brando647, January 17, 2011, user review of *2001*).

Hollenback (1996: 21 and 47) and James (2014: 207) highlight the importance of achieving a focused state of mind in order to experience mystical states. Meditative experience is included in the cross-cultural definitions of mysticism employed by James and Hollenback, and this study also acknowledges the close relationship between experiences that are variously described in meditative, mystical, spiritual, or religious terms. However, the preponderance of meditative concepts in audience responses to *2001* in comparison to Judeo-Christian terminology, provide evidence of "Easternization" in Western conceptions of the sacred (Campbell 2008). In the sections below, the meditative elements of *2001* will be analyzed in three stages. The first familiarizes the reader with the film, tracking the meditative attributes of Kubrick's directorial design. The second details the cultivation of a particular state of mind that viewers deem necessary for a positive experience of the film, and this viewing approach is compared with other forms of aesthetic-religious reception. Finally, the structure and techniques of *2001* are revisited in light of Schrader's transcendental style.

Meditative Qualities of Sound, Composition, and Pace

2001 begins with a black screen. Eerie strings offer sound, but there is no image for several minutes. Here Kubrick adapts the traditional features of overture and intermission from theatre, epics, and silent film to fulfill dramatic purposes (Paulus 2009: 104–6). To come to terms with unyielding blackness, the viewer must either perceive a blank screen and become impatient or see it as a black void and begin to move into its stillness. The music emitting from the void is taken from Hungarian composer and avant-garde pioneer György Ligeti's (1923–2006) 1961 orchestral piece, *Atmosphères*. This work was his first using the compositional technique dubbed "micropolyphony." As scholars like Mike Searby (1997: 9) and Owe Nordwall (1969: 22) have pointed out, Ligeti's work obliterates the possibility of perceiving the traditional elements of music such as harmony, rhythm, or melody, through the dense enmeshment of sound, urging the listener to find new qualities of sound, in texture, timbre, and sound color. Ligeti himself describes his micropolyphonic style as being inspired by a highly evocative dream that he had as a child where his room was filled with a "finely spun but dense and extremely tangled web" in which he and numerous insects were entangled and immobilized (Ligeti and Bernard 1993: 164). As the insects attempted to free themselves, the vibration of this movement shuddered through the web. This movement

> gradually altered the internal structure of the web, which became ever more tangled. In places impenetrable knots formed; in others, caverns opened up where shreds of the original web were floating about like gossamer. These transformations were irreversible and no earlier state could ever recur. (Ligeti and Bernard 1993: 165)

It has been referred to as an "esoteric" style of music that brings "a feeling of disquieting stillness" and "limitless emptiness" (Konzett 2010: 103; Prendergast 2000: 63–4).

Enveloped in this uncanny sonic space, frequencies merge and creep in curious developments, like processes of chemical reaction. As this mysterious shifting hum whispers and lingers, the viewer remains blind to anything but the black screen. Abruptly, the MGM logo appears, signaling the commencement of the film proper. Music continues to dominate as three ascending notes sound in dramatic sustained succession. This musical phrase is taken from the opening of Strauss's tone poem *Thus Spoke Zarathustra* entitled "Sunrise." The triumphant tones of Strauss accompany the enigmatic revelation of the symmetrically aligned sun, moon, and Earth before the screen turns black again. As Kubrick explains:

> The idea of the magical alignment of the sun, the Earth, and the Moon, or of Jupiter and its moons, was used throughout the film to represent something magical and important was about to happen. I suppose the idea had something to do with the strange sensation one has when the alignment of the sun takes places at Stone Henge. (Agel 1970: 80)

The design of this opening sequence shocks the viewer out of their reliance on the predictable cues of typical mainstream cinema. As Grodal explains, mainstream cinema privileges the efficient development of narrative along lines of cause and effect (2004: 133). From the moment the film begins with this "Pre-Credit" sequence, Kubrick is making unusual demands of the viewer, asking them to sit in pitch darkness and simply listen. Turning off the viewer's primary orienting sense—their sight—Kubrick plunges them immediately into a foreign space, isolating another sense that they will need to pay close attention to during the course of the film—their hearing. The selective focus on one sense at a time is commonly used in meditative practice to develop a heightened awareness of the present (Brahmasamhara 2008: 262–72). The "Pre-Credit" sequence also imitates mediation in its resemblance to the experience of having one's eyes closed in contemplative stillness.

Overall, *2001* uses a collection of techniques that establish, renew, and maintain contemplative perception. *2001*'s "Pre-Credit" sequence is crucial in encouraging this immersive mode of viewing; however, it is necessary for the viewer to follow this cue. If audience members chatter and move about during this sequence, or if the viewing environment is not sufficiently dark, it may not be effective. A pitch-dark cinema can heighten the affect of blackness, granting the screen powers of sense deprivation, or at least sense isolation. Kubrick immerses the viewer in visual absence for just under five minutes, heightening the affective qualities of the music and challenging the viewer to remain in the cinematic setting without seeing. By depriving the viewer of sight in the "Pre-Credit" sequence and "Intermission" of *2001*, Kubrick is able to lead the viewer into an unusually focused, yet suggestive state of mind in preparation for the highly hallucinogenic final scenes of the film.

The "Dawn of Man" sequence begins following the image of planetary alignment. This sequence is shot using a series of frames depicting a desert landscape at dawn. In a photographic style, Kubrick's camera holds still on the landscape before blinking to another similar frame, creating a slideshow of this prehistoric environment. Minimal panning is used in this sequence, and the predominance of static framing lends a primitive simplicity to these scenes. Man-apes live here among other herbivores, and a cheetah is shown devouring a man-ape who is helpless to defend himself. These scenes employ seven minutes of uninterrupted sparse natural sound including the soft rush of the wind, the rhythm of crickets chirruping, and the occasional grunts and screeches of the man-apes. Dusk falls and the man-apes huddle in their caves for the night. As morning comes, a strange sound emerges from the native aural landscape. As the sound builds, the viewer notices the unusualness of these noises, yet they are also familiar, as they are from Ligeti's *Lux Aeterna* ("Eternal Light") a piece that is intimately related to *Atmosphères* in its compositional style. This iconic piece features a sixteen-part choir whose voices are synthesized in a static mass that pulsates and hums like an unstable electric charge. Viewers refer to these sounds as "chilling" (BeardedVillain, June 9, 2014, user review of *2001*), inexplicably frightening, "powerful and moving," "hair raising" (Justin Watson, January 22, 2013, user review of *2001*), and capable of triggering goose bumps (BeardedVillain, June 9, 2014, user review of *2001*). The music is at once "fascinating," "visceral" (antonjsw1,

May 9, 2010, user review of *2001*), and anxiety-inducing (doveniki, November 21, 2011, user review of *2001*).

The desert landscape now includes a foreign object, a large black monolith that appears to be the source of the sound. The man-apes approach the monolith in theatrical hesitance and curiosity, reaching out to touch its black surface as if in fear of receiving a shock. The man-apes shriek and withdraw, one after the other, before returning with greater confidence. The seemingly esoteric significance of this moment is heralded by a sharp cut to the image of a semi-eclipsed crescent moon and sun aligned with the monolith. Soon the familiar phrase from *Thus Spoke Zarathustra* returns as a newly enlightened man-ape discovers that a skeletal bone can be used as a killing tool. Musically, this is a triumph, but visually and narratively, this is somewhat horrifying as the first step in the evolution of humanity is shown to be one of violence. After eating his first meat and subsequently killing a man-ape from another clan, the man-ape (known as Moonwatcher in Clarke's novel) tosses the killing bone skyward where it spins through slow rotations, and in a seamless transition through time, Kubrick takes us into the future as the bone is matched in jump-cut with the image of an elongated space ship against a starlit sky. A waltz begins and the viewer journeys into an entirely different mode of seeing and hearing.

In the "Dance of the Planets" sequence, Johann Strauss's waltz *The Blue Danube* (1866) provides an elegant and whimsical glorification of the beauty of movement in space. The song itself is about a flowing river, and the planets and mechanical structures that appear on screen rotate in such a way that they seem to twirl and flow in an ebullient dance. *The Blue Danube* is a well-known piece that is synonymous with the romantic era (Paulus 2009: 118) and it has been noted that some older viewers who saw the film at the time of its release were negatively disposed to this scene, while younger viewers did not have preexisting associations with the music and experienced it afresh (Patterson 2004: 453–4; Agel 1970: 88). There is nothing eerie about these scenes and viewers have commented on the beauty and grandeur of this sequence. As the scene progresses in dynamic style, Kubrick develops a strong sense of rotation and flow where objects appear to be moving slower or faster in line with the tempo and energy of the music. The rhythmic quality of movement takes on its own meditative qualities, gesturing the gaze toward the center to observe the simple beauty of geometric forms in motion. This sequence submerges the viewer in an environment of rhythmic movement and orchestral flourish for five minutes, in the complete absence of dialogue. Extended duration teaches the viewer to shift their mode of perception to observe symbolic and gestural cues and to become attentive to the language of sound. As previously mentioned, meditative practice often involves focus isolation and the quieting of discursive mental chatter (Schmidt 2014: 142), a process that can initially bring about an increased level of activity in the mind where images, feelings, and sensations appear to the practitioner, subjectively experienced as arising independent of their own will (Suzuki 2010: 18; Chopra 2017: n.p.). It is possible that viewers who are deeply immersed could experience something of this effect, leading them to feel complex or unattributed sensations during scenes in the film where little is happening in a narrative sense.

The continued use of techniques that isolate the senses and draw prolonged focus to particular aspects of filmic experience are responsible for generating the strong meditative mood of *2001*. Unlike popular genres of film where the director's focalizing powers are used to draw the viewer quickly from one point of narrative action to the next, providing information or meaning in each of these instances, Kubrick draws focus into localized abstract areas that encourage contemplation but do not necessarily (or merely) progress the narrative. A single shot of machines in space with a voice-over detailing the technical achievements of humankind would convey the same information as the "Dance of the Planets" sequence but would not affect the viewer in the same way. BeardedVillain attributes feelings of awe to Kubrick's technique of prolonging each scene beyond narrative requirements (June 9, 2014, user review of *2001*). Mameeshkamowskwoz says that the film is deliberately slow in order to "allow the film to breathe" and to evoke "the atmosphere of space" (mameeshkamowskwoz, December 6, 2012, review of *2001*) conveying the sparseness of the film's composition. Kubrick is careful to allow time for immersion to develop before moving to the next scene. Unlike the mobility of conventional cinema where scenes unfold in a variety of spaces, intercut with footage from other times and locations, *2001* isolates action in specific spaces. Often separated by a cut-to-black or intertitles, these discrete blocks are self-contained, featuring distinct stylistic features. Considerable narrative ellipses are concealed through editing in jump-cuts or the cut-to-black, a technique often used in Kubrick's oeuvre (Pezzotta 2013: 34–55). The task of making sense of the entire composition of the film requires the viewer to forge symbolic links between the film's parts.

Following the "Dance of the Planets," a more conventional narrative cinematic style is adopted through the introduction of dialogue. After the discovery of a mysterious black monolith buried under the lunar surface, a crew of astronauts is assembled to fly to Jupiter. The crew (some of whom are in hibernation-mode) is not provided with any information about why they have been sent to Jupiter, but the audience is aware that an energetic pulse was found to be emitting from the monolith and that the mission is somehow related to this mysterious discovery. The next seventeen minutes are set within the spacecraft, and are occasionally interspersed with images of the exceedingly slow progression of the ship through space. Aside from the members of the crew who are sedated in hibernation-mode, there are two astronauts, Mission Commander David Bowman and Deputy Commander Frank Poole, and the computer HAL 9000, who is capable of cognitive actions beyond the limit of the human brain and who converses with the other astronauts as if he were the third member of the crew. Narrative information is provided through dialogue in this portion of the film, but in an emotively dull manner. Recognizing the "highly meditative" qualities of the film, viewer Torgo Approves attributes them to "long periods of near-complete silence, the low-key dialogue, HAL's monotonous voice" and "the scattered pieces of classical music [that] set you in a state of complete relaxation" (Torgo Approves, August 19, 2006, user review of *2001*). The voice of HAL has become iconic due to its simultaneously pacifying calmness and the hint of independent will that viewers perceive in relation to the supercomputer's sinister actions. After reporting a fault in an external portion of the ship, HAL conspires to murder the entire crew, but is not able to succeed with Bowman.

If *2001* were a typical space film, the murder of the crew would be dramatized through emotionally charged struggles between man and machine, replete with suspenseful sequences, explosions, and near-misses. Instead, Kubrick keeps the spell of focalization unbroken. Music is absent from this portion of the film and once the audience has received the narrative information provided by the initial televised interview with members of the crew, conversations are predominantly simple one-on-one communications. A mechanical fault reported by HAL is attended to first by Bowman, who takes seven minutes to enter the pod, exit the ship, maneuver to the correct section of the outer hull, and inspect the fault. Bowman undertakes this work in a dispassionate and methodical manner despite the element of risk involved. Kubrick uses this time to deepen focalization through repetitious sound (e.g., the beeping pulse of the landing monitor) and excessively slow movements. In this scene, Bowman's breathing is heard throughout. Unlike horror or action films that typically use the sound of the breath to indicate exertion or fear, Bowman's breath is slow and even. Amplifying the sound of the breath through the astronaut's mask creates an artificial closeness that is in itself anxiety-inducing; however, the unsettling sound of the breath is transformed through its apparent calmness and monotonous repetition.

Meditative practice often begins with focus on the breath (Suzuki 2010: 11-13) and the foregrounding of breathing sounds evokes this aspect of meditative experience. Becoming deeply aware of the breath is a means of achieving mental focus, and in this context, it is Bowman's breath that is the point of focus rather than the viewers' own. The disconnection between embodied breathing and foreign, mechanically amplified breath highlights the fact that this correlation can only be applied in a limited sense, yet there is some evidence that this device has had a focalizing affect on audiences. For instance, Richard Pollard (HAL8000) recalls coming home after watching the film, sitting at the window and staring at the moon "for hours," indicating that the film was able to guide him into a deep state of contemplation. During the film, the repeated sound of Bowman's inhalation and exhalation gave him "shivers," highlighting the contribution that this technique had in the production of this affective state (Richard Pollard (HAL8000), October 27, 1999, user review of *2001*).

There is a subtle sense of anxiety generated through the doubt that Bowman appears to feel about the cause of the fault that HAL has identified. Evidence of this doubt cannot be obviously detected in his facial expression, the words he uses, or through his breathing, but the viewer still suspects that something is not quite right. This scene and many others in the film thus succeed in generating a mood of low-level anxiety, or a sense of the uncanny beneath the dominant frequency of calm, mundane, or hypnotic action. Following a "private" conversation between Poole and Bowman where they express their doubts about HAL, and their plan to turn off his higher functions, the word "INTERMISSION" appears on the screen and the viewer is again immersed in that same black void that they found themselves in during the "Pre-Credit" sequence. Ligeti's *Atmosphères* creates a foreboding sense of the unknown, and reminds the viewer of the film's opening scenes. The viewer's mind may come to imagine how the enigmatic monolith, the man-apes, the moon, and the ultimate destination of the mission are related. For some, these thoughts exist at the forefront of the mind, while others may simply sit there and observe the uncanny frequencies that emit from the darkness without forming clear conscious thoughts about the film's meaning. In either case, the viewer who watches the film in an unbroken stretch is submerged in a deep experience of sense isolation and focalization.

Visually, the sequence building up to the intermission includes a striking preponderance of symmetrical shots, many of which include a rounded or oval frame at the center of the image. Luis Mainar notes that Kubrick constructs "perfectly balanced or symmetrical shots" which generate "focalization" in many of his films (2000: 21). Mainar argues that this technique is used in Kubrick's

Barry Lyndon (1975) to create a sense of "artificiality" that blocks an emotional connection with the characters on screen (2000: 21). In *2001*, it is Mainer's view that symmetrical shots are used "as a symbol of tradition—one that must be transcended," in order to confront the unknown in the "Stargate" sequence (2000: 48–9). In *2001* Kubrick's camera observes objects, scenes, and people dispassionately. Emotive expression and dramatic modulation are noticeably absent. Rather than being something that the viewer should overcome or reject in order to experience the unstructured states of the "Stargate" sequence, I would argue that still, symmetrical shots, and slow camera work are essential in first harnessing the viewer's attention so that they are single-pointedly focused, relaxed, and expectant when the "Stargate" sequence begins—a technique that is linked to meditative practice (Austin 2014: 24).

Throughout *2001*, Kubrick uses unusual curved compositions and rounded movements that defy the Earthly experience of gravity. These scenes create an ungrounded and disembodied feeling linked to the expectation of falling; inverting everyday embodiment. In *2001*, orbiting objects roll clockwise, anticlockwise, upward, and away at obscure angles. Without a properly grounded bodily perspective, such movement does not narrate so much as flow in a disorienting manner. During the voyage to Jupiter, Bowman and Poole often walk upside down, and the dizzying sensation of orbit is present during Dr. Heywood R. Floyd's phone call to Earth where the moon revolves behind his head. This technique contributes to overall feelings of physical disparity. However, this sense of movement is generally slow, and in many scenes, the frame is still. Frontal circularity can be considered to be the "archetypal" composition of the film, performing several simultaneous functions. Principally, the focal power generated by such symmetry brings to mind a religious altar, a gateway, or mandala. It is possible that Kubrick's interest in Jung led him to appreciate the spiritual significance of the mandala. Jung became deeply fascinated by the power of the mandala and believed that it was an archetypal symbol of "psychic wholeness" that arose from the collective unconscious (rather than the Buddhist tradition). In this case, however, the potential symbolic function of a mandala-like composition is less important than its focalizing and associative function (Davis 2016: 248–9).

As Kubrick guides the eye to the center, the viewer is encouraged not to "read" the image, but to move into it and transcend it. Frontal compositions create a sense of expectation that evokes the intimacy of Schrader's "I-Thou" connection (1972: 53). Except in this case, the "Thou" position is utterly abstract. Kubrick employs close-ups of Bowman's eye, contrasting it with HAL's radiating red "pupil" and black "iris." The image of HAL's "eye," which appears repeatedly throughout the film, is a symmetrical circular composition held with static framing. In terms of compositional gesture, the respective human and mechanical eyes mimic ancient Platonic theories of vision that involve the intromission and emission of light, as beams moving in and out of the eye. Kubrick draws on this relation in scenes where the inner distance is left blank, or it seems that there is nothing to see, such as centrally framed doorways and portholes that are empty or closed. For example, when the camera looks out of the symmetrically framed porthole as Bowman searches for Poole's body in space, the dark interior of the pod almost blends with the black expanse outside, and there is very little to see in this lingering shot. Poole's body finally appears as the tiniest dot in the distance that is barely distinguishable from a star. The viewer is encouraged to gaze at this point in the extreme distance and be drawn into the sense of absence that this image evokes. In another instance, the viewer is drawn to focus on the symmetrical oval composition of a closed door, surrounded by the strong perspective lines of the hallway. Moments later, Bowman's body shoots through the door toward the viewer, foreshadowing the compositional movement of the Stargate.

This subtle dynamic between absence and oncoming movement creates an eerie feeling of presence, as the viewer looks expectantly into the image, without yet seeing what will eventually emerge. While expectation is involved, these centrally framed frontal compositions also encourage stillness or confinement of the gaze. In a well-known scene, a spaceship hostess enters a circular doorway wearing special grip shoes that allow her to walk the circumference of the door, until she is upside down. This frontal, circular composition remains still as the hostess steps like the ticking hand of a clock (moving anticlockwise). In the aforementioned scene where Bowman and Poole converse in the pod regarding HAL's recent behavior, the image is composed of a circular inner focal point and figural framing mimicking a symmetrical, elongated hexagon. As the astronauts talk, their heads move minimally in the frame. At the center of the composition, HAL's eye is present. The viewer is encouraged to gaze into the eye of this distant, motionless voyeur who, it is soon revealed, is learning the nature of their discussion by lip-reading. Frontal hexagonal framing also dominates an earlier scene where a space pod is slowly lowered to the landing pad in painstaking unidirectional movement from top to bottom. Planetary alignment scenes are notably still and symmetrical, occasionally including a single moving element in the center of the frame. In one scene, the monolith floats horizontally in vertical alignment with planets and moons, transforming the ascending elements into a cross. The monolith glows softly with reflected light, capturing the viewer's focus, and then disappears into shadow. Adding to this, images of concentric circles and converging lines (particularly in the monitoring tools within the ship) pulse and beep, evoking this motion toward the center in a hypnotic rhythm facilitated by sound.

Following the intermission, the viewer is brought back to the ship to observe Poole performing the same sequence of actions that Bowman had just done when he initially checked the reported fault. Repetition of this sequence asks the viewer to look again and see more. Deepening the detail and quality of sensory perception is a technique common to meditative practice (Brahmasamhara 2008: 262–72). As HAL cuts Poole loose from his umbilical connection with the ship while he is in the process of double-checking the fault, the moment is not met with a scream or with images of Poole's anguished asphyxiation. Instead the viewer is suddenly shocked out of the sound of Poole's rhythmic breathing and submerged in silence as they watch the distant image of his body floating and spinning in space. Viewers like Lostman_815 report that such dramatic silence is used to "chilling" effect (May 21, 2014, user review of *2001*). This viewer comment reveals the powerful emotional response that can be elicited through experiences of absence.

Bowman's triumphant victory over HAL—that leaves him the lone survivor of the mission—is presented in a procedural, rather than dramatic fashion. As will be discussed below, Schrader's transcendental style similarly employs the monotony of the everyday in order to slowly build an unsettling sensation of disparity. A slight furrow of the brow and tightness of the voice are all the emotion that Bowman expresses as he fights for his life against the will of the mutinous computer. Bowman does not show grief for his lost crew members nor fear that he will not return home. Presenting emotional equilibrium in the face of danger further depersonalizes Bowman, preparing the audiences for his radical transformation into a state beyond all human concerns. When Bowman finally reaches the control center where HAL's brain functions are stored (in blocks that fit into slots across the wall) HAL tries to convince Bowman to allow him to continue to operate despite his recent malpractices. Bowman does not respond to HAL's reasoning and begins to unplug each block of HAL's higher functions one by one. Here Kubrick provides an analogy for the mind that aligns with a functional, psychologized understanding of self found in alternative spirituality and Western Buddhism. As with meditative practice, HAL's complex and busy mind is turned off one part at a time. In practical terms within the narrative, this leaves only HAL's automatic functions. Symbolically, however, the progressive deconstruction of HAL's faculties raises the following questions: What is it about HAL that seemed human? In which cell did his personality and identity lie? According to Steven Collins, Buddhism "denies the existence of any continuing self or soul, holding that the process of rebirth . . . involves an individual but ever-changing continuum of impermanent and impersonal elements" (1992: 216). The teaching of "dependent co-arising" presents self and reality as *processes* of "radical relativity" and "interdependence," rejecting the notion of an enduring identity (Macy 1979: 38). Just as meditative practice interrogates the nature of self as a step on the path to enlightenment, Kubrick presents this symbolic deconstruction and questioning of self prior to Bowman's journey into the Stargate.

The words "JUPITER AND BEYOND THE INFINITE" appear on screen and the sounds of Ligeti's *Requiem* and *Atmosphères* are heard. Strange choirs wail in the darkness arising from the floating monolith. Mirroring earlier scenes of planetary alignment, the symmetrical image of the planets now sees the monolith slot into place in a seemingly magical configuration. The camera gazes into the blackness and colors begin to emit from a distant vanishing point, forming a central seam from which perspectival beams of light emerge. The colors stream faster in psychedelic configurations creating a strong sensation of flying forward though space (Agel 1970: 143 and 150). Interspersed in the flowing torrent of abstract colors and shapes, Bowman's face flicks into focus in a brief shot-reverse-shot image where his features are contorted in a frozen scream that we cannot hear. The experience of rapidly pulsating color is intense for the viewer who must watch this for over ten minutes straight (the musical element of the journey into the Stargate lasts approximately fifteen minutes, with intense colors slowly introduced early in the sequence) and Bowman's reaction is impactful due to its uncharacteristic expressiveness. The abstract moving imagery that the viewer is confronted with make it almost impossible to think (except perhaps in an associational manner) while the full effect of Ligeti's micropolyphonic style comes into its own in a mentally blinding mass of sound textures. In these abstract visions, the birth and infinite progression of the universe appear before the audience. For buckdharwin this scene "demands rigorous, unfaltering attention for an extended time," conveying "the discipline that would be demanded . . . by someone actually experiencing forcible Enlightenment" (May 2, 2009, user review of *2001*). Here again one finds a meditative parallel.

As the vibrations, pulses, and impressions of the "Stargate" sequence fade, the eye blinks back into focus and a disoriented Bowman enters a wordless sequence set in a Louis XVI interior. Again, Kubrick introduces the sound of Bowman's slow breathing as a hypnotic rhythm. Bowman looks and sees himself as an older man and in a series of shot-reverse-shots the younger Bowman is replaced by an older version, then an even older one who lies frail in his chamber, reaching toward the monolith that looms silently at the foot of his bed. Bowman looks to the monolith and when the shot returns to the place where he lay, a small glowing fetus (the Starchild) floats in his place in a sphere of blue light. The triumphant notes of *Thus Spoke Zarathustra* sound as the camera focuses on the Starchild who is now floating in space—a moment often interpreted in terms of the birth of the Nietzschean Superman (Nietzsche 1999). The peaceful child glows in soft focus, gazing upon the Earth and then slowly turns its gaze directly toward the viewer in time with the musical crescendo. This strange, compelling, and enigmatic image constitutes the film's final frame as the credits commence abruptly with the jovial return of the *Blue Danube*.

The "Louis XVI" sequence (used here to refer to the scenes commencing at the end of the "Stargate" sequence and concluding with the appearance of the Star Child) conveys a deconstruction of perception and identity that builds upon HAL's cognitive disassembly. The "Stargate" sequence may trigger a form of enlightenment, yet this sequence is a depiction of the Stargate's effect on Bowman, providing a stilted transmission of noesis inherent in his psychedelic journey. If time can be considered the ordering principal of the universe, this sequence presents a radical transgression of universal laws through Bowman's rapid evolution and the abstraction of cause and effect. It also involves a schizophrenic duplication of selves that erase each other at the moment of beholding. Conveying dissociative qualities and the shock of progressive revelation, this sequence evokes the enlightening realization of the nature of self as Bowman is stripped of all identifying features in his transformation into the Starchild. Rather than becoming a different person, Bowman becomes an archetype, embodying the symbolic potentiality of a yet unborn child.

Transcendental Style: Structure and Stasis

The three-step dynamic of the transcendental style, described by Schrader as moving from the everyday, to disparity, and culminating in stasis is usefully applied to *2001*. As previously outlined, in the transcendental style, the everyday is evoked through "non-expressive forms," creating a monotonous feeling of "coldness," "silence," and "stillness" that is both "dull" and "banal" (Schrader

1972: 38–9). In *2001*, this impression is developed through the slow and extended pace of the scenes. This can be found in the "Dawn of Man" sequence as the audience is made to observe the man-apes going about their business for extended periods of time where little new narrative information is conveyed. Once the film proceeds into space, the mundane day-to-day life of the astronauts comes across in the endless rotation of the ship and the insipid caged life that the astronauts lead, where there is limited opportunity for anything new or spontaneous to occur. For the majority of the film it appears that nothing happens, or will ever happen, in space. Mechanical maintenance and simulated chess games are the most exciting events that are capable of occurring. "Coldness," "silence," and "stillness" are everywhere (Schrader 1972: 38–9).

The second step of the transcendental style—disparity—plays with this sense of nonemotion and non-expression by introducing the suspicion that there is something "more" (Schrader 1972: 42). Stirring the viewer to feel "a sense of emotional weight within an unfeeling environment" they accumulate the suspicion that there is more to be known and begin to crave emotional release (Schrader 1972: 77). By simultaneously stimulating and repressing emotion, disparity works toward the sudden release of an immense and dissociated feeling (Schrader 1972: 77). This technique that Schrader identifies could be explained from a cognitive point of view as the viewer is stimulated (literally in their nervous system) but not provided the opportunity for release (for instance, through narrative resolution). Grodal has developed a model that he calls "PECMA (perception, emotion, cognition, and motor action) flow" to describe the cycle that viewers experience when they watch narrative-based films, such as Hollywood movies. These films are "linked to cause-effect or goal-means" (Grodal 2004: 133) where emotive energy can be released through a culminating narrative event, the provision of a rest period, or through devices that bring about laughter or tears (Grodal 2009: 151). As Grodal argues, art films block PECMA flow by employing "lyrical-associative" toning, bringing about intense and complex experiences (Grodal 2009: 224). As the dynamics of art films are applicable to *2001*, Grodal's insights will be considered further below. For now, it is worth noting that there are marked similarities between Schrader's assertion that simultaneous filmic stimulation and repression generate an emotional charge and Grodal's description of the lyrical-associative dynamics of art films.

In *2001*, disparity is generated through numerous mechanisms. An example of this can be found in Kubrick's use of rousing orchestral music to create intense emotional stimulation, while presenting distinctly nonemotional or ambiguous imagery. Such images may be abstract and obscure in significance such as that of aligned planets, where the viewer must actively develop an explanation for the connection between sound and image. Kubrick encourages the viewer to suspect that there is something "more" to know or feel through the use of ambiguity paired with clearly signposted moments of meaning (Schrader 1972: 42). For instance, the presence of the monolith is consistently marked as significant through the lingering gaze of the camera and the strangely evocative sounds of Ligeti as well as the repetition of this sign. The use of on-screen scene titles serve to signpost narrative blocks, guiding the viewer to structure the abstract content of that sequence into a meaningful progression. Kubrick also uses a host of other devices to create disparity, including extremely slow camera movement that contributes to a simultaneous sense of apparent emotional gravity and blocked action. By employing markers or hints of significance in an "unfeeling environment," Kubrick develops a strong sense of disparity that is vital in setting the viewer up for the powerful emotional experience at the film's conclusion (Schrader 1972: 77).

The final step in Schrader's typology of the transcendental style is stasis, the dramatic culmination of the energetic force of disparity (1972: 43). Without warning, the viewer experiences "an inexplicable outpouring of human feeling that can have no adequate receptacle. This overwhelming compassion seems sui generis" and is experienced as "holy agony" (Schrader 1972: 43). At this point "there is a blast of music, an overt symbol, an open call for emotion. The act demands commitment by the viewer" and "without commitment there can be no stasis" (Schrader 1972: 79). For viewers of *2001* this moment can be experienced as awe, something akin to esoteric understanding or enlightenment. In *2001* the "Stargate" sequence is the "overt symbol" and "open call for emotion" that Schrader describes. The force of this sequence is strong enough to flow into the final scenes of the film. The shot-reverse-shot progression that sees Bowman age and be reborn in the form of the Starchild involves a series of logical leaps that have generated viewer reactions as diverse as profound wonder (Gross Ryder, May 21, 2012, user review of *2001*) and derisive hilarity (billreynolds, July 6, 2005, user review of *2001*). Although it may be relatively easy to understand that Bowman has been transformed by the power of the monolith from a human being into the Starchild, the scene nonetheless develops using a succession of ellipses. The transformation of bone to spacecraft involved a significant ellipse requiring a leap of thousands of years. The leaps that Kubrick presents in the "Louis XVI" sequence create a cognitive disturbance through their rapid succession, building on the lingering affects of the journey through the Stargate. Bearing this in mind, the appearance of the Starchild can be interpreted as a kind of visual *koan*—a concluding moment that asks all disparate elements to be called together in meaningful arrangement.

Grodal's cognitive understanding of the style of art films further illuminates the mechanics of Schrader's transcendental style as well as Kubrick's directorial style in *2001*. There are several instances where Grodal's observations align with Schrader's, revealing that directors like Schrader have come to an intuitive understanding of cognitive mechanics even if they are articulated in nonpsychological terminology. On a cognitive level, Grodal's principal observation is that art films disrupt and block PECMA flow and that this works on several levels to create a particular type of film experience. As our brains function in the context of embodied experience, sensory input is processed through systems that have been built for interaction in the world (Grodal 2009: 210). In the cinema, the viewer's perception is guided by what appears on the screen, unlike in everyday life (Grodal 2009: 234). What is shown is more condensed and stimulating than everyday life. Watching a film, the brain is constantly scanning the information that appears, attempting to match what is seen to remembered images and associations, evaluating what is seen in terms of its reality status (Grodal 2009: 185, 149, and 226). One of the common techniques that makers of art films employ is to present the viewer with problems that are left unresolved and associations that do not progress the narrative, maintaining a sense of open-endedness and ambiguity. According to Grodal, filmmakers

> Lure the spectator into endless puzzles, prompting feelings that fuel the hermeneutic process in which the brain automatically searches for some hidden meaning. A filmmaker can activate so many associations that our short-term memory becomes overloaded, giving us the sense of some ungraspable fundamental significance. (2009: 247)

Viewer mikemacisaac makes a similar observation of *2001* saying that it "intentionally offers us more questions then [sic] it can answer, it is made to puzzle and mystify, but leaves the viewer nevertheless with a sense of awe and reverence." The viewer is spurred to consider "large and ominous" questions "concerning the genesis and destiny of the human race, its ultimate place in the cosmic design and the existence or lack of some creative intelligence behind the structure of the universe itself." When the viewer is finished watching, the film's influence goes on with "images that linger in the mind's eye long after the movie itself is over" (mikemacisaac, January 8, 2007, user review of *2001*).

Kubrick uses this technique in *2001*, particularly in the final scene where the image of the Starchild is presented, as the meaning of this scene is not spelled out. Grodal compares the "feeling of deep significance" experienced by viewers who have been overloaded in this way to "religious experiences or out-of-body experiences" (2009: 149). Emotional saturation and hyperactivation can "lead to extreme vividness and also feelings of truth" and "create a sense of permanence and transcendence" that remains with the viewer after the film concludes (Grodal 2009: 149, 221, and 226). Grodal also links this feeling of permanence to the abstract, personalized, and interior experience of art films that is activated through the denial of narrative resolution and straightforward cognition (2009: 218). As Grodal explains, "There is no prescribed way to release the saturated emotions associated with nonnarrative experiences, and these feelings therefore remain permanent," unlike mainstream films (Grodal 2009: 212). This is an important observation that is especially relevant to *2001*. The permanence of the feelings elicited during a viewing experience haunt people for extended periods of time. As will be discussed in greater detail below, films like *2001* can have an affect similar to religious ritual in the way that they become engraved into consciousness and memory.

Grodal's theory that continual open-ended queries can trigger feelings of profundity relates to the central narrative theme of *2001*: human curiosity. It is also in alignment with the mode of spiritual seekership typical of post-1960s Western culture where the individual is empowered to seek out unmediated truth using their intuition as a guide. The sense of seeking an unknown truth through a fog of associations leads to a stronger sense of authenticity—a closer brush with the truth—because it does not feel predictable, formulaic, familiar, or doctrinal. Indeed, Grodal observes that art films are "preoccupied with questions of truth and reality" where "subjective, ambiguous, and transient representations" of reality are more trustworthy than "supposedly objective representations" (2009: 221–2).

The genuine feeling one that does not know and cannot predict the full meaning of what is presented invites the viewer into an encounter with the mysteries of existence. The relocation of agency from the viewer to the film generates a strange sense of presence more likely to be found in religious ritual or practice. If a viewer's expectations are not realized on screen, this is the point where many will become bored or frustrated, while those who have experience with art films are able to "switch into a subjective-lyrical mode," where they begin to "unravel parts of the associative network to which the film gives rise" (Grodal 2009: 234). This method of viewing is described as "a more unfocused mode" where "diffuse semiconscious or unconscious associations and subjective feelings indicate that no actions or focused propositions are possible" (Grodal

2009: 233). A common technique used in art films is the presentation of scenes where the camera lingers for an excessive amount of time without providing any further narrative information (Grodal 2009: 220). Bordwell similarly identifies this feature of art film, interpreting this to be a sign of the auteur's deliberate rejection of film conventions (1979: 59–60). Because this seems so unnatural, the viewer begins to suspect that this points toward some deeper meaning (Grodal 2009: 220–1).

Both Schrader (1972: 64–6) and Grodal (2009: 223) identify distant, emotionally remote characters as being important to the transcendental style or art film, respectively. Grodal identifies the cognitive blocking that takes place when "characters have no stable identities or preferences that might provide them with clear-cut motives and support their actions" (2009: 223). For Schrader, remote characters are important in the enactment of the compositional style that he calls "hieratic frontality" or simply "frontality" (1972: 53). In this mode, the composition is static, flattened, and the viewer is placed in a frontal position in "an I-Thou devotional attitude" (Schrader 1972: 53). Schrader explains this using the example of an actor's face that is non-expressive that takes on a depersonalized and iconic quality. In this context, frontality can "create a respectful, noncommitted attitude within the viewer which can result in a 'stasis' similar to that evoked by a religious icon" (Schrader 1972: 100). Although Kubrick ensures that his actors adopt a non-expressive countenance in *2001*, he does not create a frontal, face-to-face relation between actor and viewer until the final sequence of the film, and this is particularly pronounced when the Starchild turns its gaze upon the audience. The "I-Thou" attitude that is evoked in this powerful closing image also recalls the symmetrical, focalizing compositions used throughout the film as the Starchild glows within a sphere of light.

While many of the features of Grodal's definition of art film and Schrader's description of the techniques of transcendental style are held in common, Schrader places his focus on the culminating moment of stasis. This particular feature is not identified by Grodal, and is not considered to be central to the function of art films. It is useful, however, to take Grodal's insights up until this point, and then to consider how "stasis" might function in relation to PECMA flow. Stasis is brought on when "there is a blast of music, an overt symbol, an open call for emotion" (Schrader 1972: 79). This moment is experienced as "an inexplicable outpouring of human feeling that can have no adequate receptacle" (Schrader 1972: 43). It does not appear, however, to offer narrative resolution that would close the PECMA cycle. Rather, it radically intensifies the flow of unresolvable elements while signaling a "call for emotion" (Schrader 1972: 79).

Most interesting, though, is Schrader's comment that stasis brings about an overwhelming and seemingly sui generis intensity of holy emotion (1972: 43).

This statement, however dramatic it may seem, is verified in the audience responses to *2001*. As Schrader is writing specifically about the *transcendental* style in film, it is fitting to compare his description of stasis with Ralph Waldo Emerson's view that spiritual truth is experienced as "a kind of insanity, a rapture, a ravishment, a blasting excess of light" that he associates with the religious traditions of the East (Versluis 1993: 51). Here again the motif of an unmediated encounter with the divine comes to the fore. For the image of the Starchild to function in this way, it cannot be considered in isolation. Rather, the total experience of *2001* builds to this moment of revelation. Similarly, a religious icon takes on much of its power from the environment in which it is encountered. In both cases, a certain amount of time must be spent in a quiet and focused state where discursive thought is set aside to behold what is seen and to absorb what is heard. It is essential that the perceptive spell remains unbroken to initiate the instinctual rousing of the senses that results in an overflow of ineffable significance resembling the emotion felt in dreams.

Meditative Practice and Focused Awareness

Viewers have drawn attention to the meditative qualities of *2001*, saying that it is "cinema at its most meditative and beautiful" (Steve Pulaski, April 23, 2014, user review of *2001*) and "a meditative piece that is supposed to make viewers think and allow our minds to explore and wander" (Sam Bartos, September 12, 2011, user review of *2001*). The film has been described as "a meditative quest" (moviedude-72, September 25, 2006, user review of *2001*), possessed of "a transcendental/meditative quality" (fearless3003, July 5, 2015, user review of *2001*), requiring patience and interest in "meditative languor" to allow the "vision to unfold" (Antti Keisala, January 10, 2014, user review of *2001*). The film has also been connected with the experience of enlightenment (TheArizonian2014, March 7, 2012, user review of *2001*).

As outlined in Chapter 2, meditative practice has become mainstream in the West and aspects of Buddhism have been woven into the Western worldview where they appear to be compatible with secularism and subjective religiosity. In the context of alternative spirituality, the deconstructive attributes of meditation have had particular appeal where the practitioner is encouraged to let go of all attachments, judgments, and concepts, leaving only the pure experience of the present moment. Such changes in perception appeal to an underlying desire for an unmediated experience where reality can be accessed in its pure and unadulterated state. In *2001*, Kubrick calls upon the spiritual faculties of his viewers, but does not once refer to God or religion. In interviews he explains that the film is a contemplation of the "God concept"—a term that abstracts and de-traditionalizes God—couching the divine in the psychologically objectivized realm of concepts (Gelmis 1969: n.p.). In order to make his audiences feel that they have encountered something sacred in the cinema without referring to religion, *2001* evokes undetermined spiritual feelings. Kubrick achieves this by encouraging meditative viewing practices using the techniques that were outlined above. However, to be successful, this also requires something from the viewer.

Exploring emotional responses to art, Elkins identifies specific techniques that artists like Rothko have used to generate emotive (and often spiritualized) responses as well as viewing techniques that heighten one's emotional receptivity to art. These insights are useful to consider in relation to *2001* as they reveal the role of design and technique in facilitating spiritual impressions. First, Elkins considers Rothko's recommendation that viewers stand eighteen inches from his paintings in order to have an optimal aesthetic experience. Elkins reflects:

> If you step too close to a Rothko, you may find yourself *inside it*. It is not hard to see why people say they are overwhelmed. Everything conspires to overload the senses: the empty incandescent rectangles of color, entirely encompassing your field of vision; the sheer glowing silence; the lack of footing, or anything solid, in the world of the canvas; the weird sense that the color is very far away, yet suffocatingly close. It's not a pleasant feeling: the painting is all around you, and you feel both threatened and comforted, both cushioned and asphyxiated. (2004b: 18)

Through paint and spatial design, Rothko is able to create "weird" sensations that disorient the viewer and "overload the senses." Immersing the viewer in visual "emptiness," they experience an abstract intimacy undergirded by anxiety. Kubrick similarly presents the viewer with a challenging filmic experience, immersing them in the emptiness of space, exposing them to periods of sensory isolation, absence, and affective contrast. The "weird" feelings that ensue are such that they combine holiness with terror, calling on Western tropes of the sacred.

Rothko would declare that he was not a religious man, yet also said that those people who were moved to tears by his paintings were "having the same religious experience I had when I painted them" (Elkins 2004b: 12–13). This apparent contradiction can be accounted for in the modern denial of religion in favor of indefinable and abstracted emotive experiences of the sacred. Like Rothko's enormous black canvases housed in the interfaith Rothko Chapel that inspire meditative contemplation, Kubrick invites the viewer to contemplate the depths of space, and the fundamental questions of existence in *2001*. Rothko's canvases are said to invite deep reflection because they function as a void, confronting the mind with silence, and absence. As a meditative point of focus, their voidness mimics the very act of letting go. Yet they can function equally as a mirror, revealing the action of the mind in a vacuum and providing psychological insight. This type of experience is present in *2001*'s "Pre-Credit" sequence and "Intermission," where Kubrick immerses the viewer in nonrepresentational darkness, and sparse, abstract sound. Kubrick's *2001* has also performed this function through the simplicity of action that is presented and his manner of dwelling in the sparse environments of space and the prehistoric desert. While *2001* does tell a story, and cannot be wholly equated with the experience of standing before a painting, the viewer is given an unusual amount of time to absorb each scene and to achieve a state of contemplative stillness.

Viewers of *2001* who reach a meditative state of immersion are made sensitive to the film's affective power and as Elkins explains, the ability to become receptive to the spiritual and emotional power of art is enhanced in certain conditions. Elkins advises that the viewer should go to see art alone, holding the mind in a state of "concentration and calm" (2004b: 210). Employing an attitude of patience, they should minimize distractions, take their time, relax, and "pay full attention" (Elkins 2004b: 211). Elkins recommends viewing art as if one were in the cinema, experiencing the artwork for a significant duration (at least thirty minutes) and if possible, this should be done in a silent darkened room (2004b: 140–1). Elkins emphasizes, "You need to do nothing but look, care about nothing but looking," "You have to concentrate on understanding what you see. That takes sustained and focused energy. There's a strange state of mind involved, in which you forget yourself just enough to lose track of the boundary between the picture's world and your own world" (2004b: 211). He instructs the viewer, "Let yourself be taken in: allow yourself any thoughts, no matter how bizarre. Let the painting do its work. Fantasize about the picture, if you want. Project your thoughts onto the painting. Let the painting hypnotize you" (Elkins 2004b: 212).

Each aspect of Elkins's advice is replicated in viewer responses to *2001*. Some viewers devote their entire reviews to the preparation of the viewing environment and the type of perceptual comportment that one should adopt, demonstrating the importance of viewer behavior in eliciting a powerful response. Mark Schofield provides an itemized list of possible challenges that viewers may face and advice about how to overcome these and enjoy the film (November 29, 2001, user review of *2001*). Michael O'Keefe stresses the importance of watching the film "uninterrupted, without speaking" and either "alone or with someone who is in as deep focus as you to watch it" (January 1, 2001, user review of *2001*). It is unlikely, however, that viewers literally adopt a set of instructions when viewing the film. In fact, doing so would act as a barrier to the open state of mind that is ideal for a deeply affective experience. Rather, such commentary reveals self-reflexivity following the film event where the viewer attempts to account for their profound experience in relation to negative appraisals of the film. These negative experiences are not limited to the responses of other audience members and often refer to the viewers' previous viewing attempts. Resembling key aspects of meditative practice, the viewer ideally adopts sustained focus (dangerhorse, August 14, 2002, user review of *2001*), a calm and relaxed mood (st-shot, June 8, 2014, user review of *2001*), and openness to visual and aural stimuli as well as spontaneously arising inner impressions without engaging in discursive or rationalized thought. Recalling the challenge faced by the meditative practitioner to achieve a state of nondiscursive focus, viewers highlight the importance of remaining in an immersed and open-minded state (Ken Stephen, February 17, 2011, user review of *2001*; jbirtel, September 11, 2005, user review of *2001*; Juan Mendoza, September 9, 2013, user review of *2001*) where narrative expectation is set to one side (Torgo Approves, August 19, 2006, user review of *2001*; mikemacisaac, January 8, 2007 user review of *2001*; Yates, Immergut, and Graves 2017: 61–2). This viewing style also parallels epistemological features of alternative spirituality, including the rejection of rationality (linked with narrative, dialogue, logic, and discursive thought) as a corollary of institutional systems of control, adopting a form of open monitoring that is passive in the Jamesean sense, and avoiding the cultivation of expectations that might reduce or distort the purity of experience.

The successful pairing of cinematic technique and the perceptual attitude of the viewer results in an unusual state of mind. It is reasonable, given the viewer advice considered thus far, that *2001* involves a distinct shift in perception when the viewer begins to become synchronized with the film. Elkins's mention of hypnotic perception indicates a level of immersion linked with dissociative states where self-awareness and rationalized thought processes become subdued (Butler and Palesh 2004: 65–6). Cereal 11 asks people to "approach [*2001*] not with the mind of a cynical film buff, but with a sort of childlike wonder" (June 17,

2002, user review of *2001*). Childlike wonder here is contrasted with the cynicism and rationalization of intellectual judgment, demonstrating that a nonrational or pre-social state of mind is required to receive the deeper message of the film. The distinct and unusual state of mind that viewers adopt while watching *2001* is in itself difficult to describe. For wawain, "Watching *2001* is similar to holding your breath and trying to observe yourself in relation to your world" (February 6, 2001, user review of *2001*). The notion of holding one's breath could refer to the deliberate pause of internal thought, while the attempt to observe oneself in relation to the world conveys the existential nature of this form of perception. The state of mind that viewers identify as being ideal for *2001* may be difficult for some viewers to achieve but it is a mode of perception that should be familiar to experienced viewers of art films. It is Kubrick's view that *2001* engages the viewer in a manner that closely resembles the appreciation of music or art, highlighting the connection between these modes. However, *2001* appears to ask for an even deeper level of openness and perceptual immersion. As Elkins observes, "Highly emotional and religious responses to art may not be commonplace, but they comprise a significant proportion of viewing experiences" (2004b: 51).

Conclusion

The meditative features of *2001* are instrumental in harnessing the attention of the viewer and pushing them beyond their normal perceptual threshold. Kubrick employs a range of techniques to this end, seeking to stir the audience's spiritual senses. A number of Kubrick's techniques overlap with Schrader's transcendental style, demonstrating that this method is well suited to eliciting the complex and overwhelming feelings associated with mystical experience. However, techniques can only be successful insofar as the audience is prepared to follow to the cues of the film. The specific perceptual mode that viewers adopt comes in response to these filmic cues, and their similarity to religious states of mental preparation can account for the spiritualized responses that result. The next chapter will explore these cinematic experiences of religious feeling, detailing their similarity to James's attributes of mystical experience.

5

2001: A Space Odyssey

Crossing the Perceptual Threshold

The previous chapter analyzed the meditative aspects of *2001*'s design and associated viewing behaviors, highlighting the receptivity to abstract sensations over rationalized narrative appreciation. The adoption of this state of mind supports Hollenback and James's contention that spiritual experiences are preceded by attention focalizing activity. In Hollenback's terms, viewers cultivate their "mind, will and imagination" for a spiritual experience of *2001* (1996: vii–x). The peak moment of a spiritual experience of *2001* is concentrated in the concluding scenes of the film. Resembling Schrader's description of stasis, Kubrick states that *2001* is able to become "a subjective experience that hits the viewer at an inner level of consciousness" (Gelmis 1969: n.p.). Here, the viewer is pushed to a perceptual threshold that when crossed is characterized by feelings of such magnitude that they are thought to be ineffable. Through the lens of James's attributes of mystical experience, this chapter outlines the initiatory qualities and spiritual reception of *2001*.

Ineffability

The first feature of mystical experience that James identifies is that of ineffability (2014: 206). Mystic testimonies from a variety of traditions refer to spiritual encounters and awakenings as being incommunicable to others. These experiences may be spoken of as having a quality that is unlike anything else, that is, sui generis or in Otto's words, "wholly other" (1958: 25–30). It is this type of experience that Schrader associates with the transcendental style, particularly in the moment of stasis. Otto describes a conversation he had with a Buddhist monk where he asked for the definition of Nirvana, and after a long pause came up at last the single answer, low and restrained: "Bliss—unspeakable." And the hushed restraint of that answer, the solemnity of his voice, demeanour, and gesture, made more clear what was meant than the words themselves. (1958: 39)

Here, Otto goes some of the way to understanding what the monk meant by observing his unusually strong emotional response, body language, and tone of great solemnity. The words themselves being ambiguous allowed Otto to make his own connections and to supplement the lack of descriptors with physical cues. This example demonstrates that something of ineffable mystical experience can be communicated to others; however, these experiences are also distinguished by the fact that the experiencer feels unable to cognitively process the fullness of their experience or translate it into words.

As Taves points out, the religious experience has come to be associated with the universal common ground between religions (2005: 7737), so that religious traditions hold no authority and are merely institutionalized interpretations of truth (Hanegraaff 1998: 329). In the Western religious tradition, accounts of mystical experiences attain a sense of legitimacy, in part, through reference to the indescribable nature of a religious encounter. In Buddhism and Hinduism, enlightenment is similarly described as being beyond human understanding. It is clear, however, that the religious encounters and realizations that have occurred throughout the long histories of Western esotericism, Buddhism, and Hinduism, all involve human experiences. As inheritors of this cultural understanding of religious experience, *2001*'s audiences are primed to understand the film on a spiritual level, and Kubrick evokes this category of experience very effectively in the film.

For Kubrick, regardless of a person's socioeconomic background, level of education, or life experience, all are endowed with common perceptual faculties. Designed to stimulate a "subconscious emotional reaction," *2001* affects "an Alabama truck driver" as much as a "young Cambridge intellectual," and Kubrick feels that the film encourages reflection on "man's destiny and role in the universe in the minds of people who in the normal course of their lives would never have considered such matters" (Gelmis 1969: n.p.). Kubrick compares *2001* with modes of abstract communication such as poetry, philosophy, painting, and music that bypass the "rigid" and "limited" socialized mind, engaging with the viewer "directly" at the level of "emotional comprehension." The avoidance of "intellectual verbalization" is considered central in achieving this (Gelmis 1969: n.p.; Schrader 1972: 108). Many of Kubrick's reflections on *2001* that have appeared in published interviews are present in similar observations from

IMDb viewers. For example, Manuel Josh Rivera explains that *2001* "grips you on a subconscious level and speaks to you in the same way any great art does—personally. Once you get the message that Kubrick is trying to give, you can't necessarily verbalize it—you just feel it and are in awe." For those who ask this viewer what the film is about, the viewer simply smiles and says, "It's about everything" (Manuel Josh Rivera, March 23, 2014, user review of *2001*).

It could be argued that Kubrick is successful in triggering spiritual feelings of ineffability through subconscious and emotional means because these forms of communication are more difficult for the viewer to identify. According to the ethos of alternative spirituality (that is present in Kubrick's sentiments above), spontaneously arising sensations are felt to be independent from social systems of manipulation and control. As such, they take on a special truth-value associated with the fundamental nature of reality. Rod Davies comments, "It is the overall feel of the movie, the spine tingling awe that [*2001*] induces that really leaves an indelible mark on your consciousness which itself belies explanation" (April 6, 1999, user review of *2001*). This and similar viewer comments illustrate the connection between the inability to describe the profound nature of their experience and their uncertainty about how they came to feel that way (dead47548, January 8, 2008, user review of *2001*). For Erik G., instead of providing "quasi-religious sermons," *2001* "asks you to feel the answer" on a "visceral, primal level" rather than an "intellectual" one. Its message is not "incomprehensible"; it is simply "difficult to describe in words" (March 2, 2000, user review of *2001*). This mode of spiritual insight empowers the viewer to feel that they are discovering truth first hand. For Gary, *2001* contains higher spiritual knowledge for those who can allow their ignorance to slip away in order to receive its inner wisdom. The viewer uses a quote from Lao Tsu, "One word of explanation, is one too many," to indicate that the meaning of *2001* is ineffable and esoteric. According to this viewer, the message of the film can only be received "in a way that is impersonal and non-intellectual," which involves a connection with "fundamental awareness, or 'ground of being.'" The message of *2001* "precedes thought" and is "purely experiential." Despite the ineffable qualities of this experience, the viewer goes on to explain the insights that he gained, urging other viewers to let go of their fear of truth so that they too may experience realization (Gary, August 20, 2005, user review of *2001*).

As these audience responses show, *2001* is capable of producing feelings of the ineffable that are endowed with spiritual qualities. While these viewers may not be able to describe or fully understand their experience, they still express a sense of awakening where some form of knowledge has been received. As such, the following section continues to explore such responses in their noetic aspect. At this stage, it is important to identify the related concepts that accompany such experiences. The abstract and artful style of *2001* is linked with the pre-social, emotional, visceral, primal, and subconscious faculties. These initial observations show that an ineffable experience of *2001* involves the interplay of film technique, viewing practices, and an underlying worldview associated with alternative spirituality where direct and unmediated experience is privileged.

For Jukangliwayway, the meaning of *2001* is beyond comprehension, yet is nonetheless "unforgettable," lingering in the mind long afterward. Jukangliwayway describes the perceptual responses that preceded this conclusion, providing clues as to how this experience of ineffable meaning develops. Sitting motionless, with "eyes glued" to the screen, "intrigued, hypnotized, [and] enraptured" by the surreal mood of the film, the viewer began to sense that they were "floating in nothingness." Feeling as if time were moving "too slow," and then fast "like a roller coaster," s/he let his/her mind "go blank" in order to experience the feelings that their senses were telling them to feel. The slower scenes and the "Stargate" sequence drew the viewer into "a state of trance" where it was not possible to be bored (jukangliwayway, April 16, 2013, user review of *2001*). Exhibiting a high level of perceptual immersion, this viewer makes a conscious decision to let go of discursive thought in order to engage in a nondeterministic sensual experience. This enhances the power of the film, leading to intense feelings of ineffable significance. In religious practice, the mystic may similarly let go of subjective determinations and inner thought in order to experience the presence of the "other." As the preparatory practices that lead to religious experience involve setting aside discursive thought, the resulting experience exhibits an amplification of these characteristics, making it difficult to describe discursively.

The religious belief that the sacred is beyond human comprehension ties in with the apparent ineffable qualities of *2001*, where the individual is left with the impression that something profound and incomprehensible has occurred. Describing this sense of being overwhelmed by something greater than oneself, eddie olsen compares his experience of *2001* to the moment when he beheld the pyramids of Egypt: "What on earth IS IT? It's both frustrating and pleasing at the same time. A kind of religious feeling" (June 8, 2009, user review of *2001*). This indescribable religious feeling can be considered ineffable, yet it is accompanied by strong emotions such as awe. While this discussion of awe is equally relevant to James's forth category of passivity, it is discussed here in order to explain that the ineffable takes on religious significance where the inability to comprehend or explain is accompanied by amplified emotion—that is, obscurity and ambiguity on their own do not amount to religious experience.

Characterizing religious experience in terms of the numinous, Otto contends that this concept can never be fully defined and one can only be guided toward a manner of thinking where the numinous "begins to stir, to start into life and into consciousness" (1958: 7). This, in itself, embodies the attributes of the ineffable. There are many aspects to numinous experience, the most emotionally vibrant being *mysterium tremendum et fascinans*. This experience of esoteric mystery can involve a "sudden eruption" of ecstasy or can "come sweeping like a gentle tide, pervading the mind with the most tranquil mood of deepest worship" (1958: 12–13). An important aspect of this is a trembling sense of awe (1958: 15). Here Otto refers to Yahweh's wrath as a "hidden force of nature" similar to "stored-up electricity, discharging itself upon anyone who comes too near" (1958: 18). It is further characterized by "awful majesty" or a daunting sense of "over-abounding" awe (Otto 1958: 31 and 85). This feeling is combined with "ineffable joy," "rapture and exaltation verging often on the bizarre and abnormal" that is "uniquely attractive and *fascinating*" (Otto 1958: 31 and 37). This collection of attributes encapsulates various "moments" of numinous experience (1958: 132–3), revealing the interplay between cognitive and emotional aspects. Feelings of the ineffable and the sense that religious knowledge is stirring in one's consciousness are accompanied by moments of extreme emotional vacillation and the near-physical apprehension of an external power.

It is common for viewers to describe their experience of *2001* as one of "awe" (Sahan Fernando, January 11, 2012, user review of *2001*; Rob Snyder, September 13, 1999, user review of *2001*; ackstasis, December 6, 2007, user review of *2001*). Although awe is a typically religious emotion, scootwhoman's comment that *2001* as "an expression of awe at our existence, and faith that we can become more than we are" (May 30, 2006, user review of *2001*) shows that this emotion is not limited to an encounter with the Judeo-Christian God. While Otto does not believe that non-Christian religious traditions are equal to Christianity, he does recognize that subjective, emotionally charged experiences are the primary site of religiosity from which all theological teachings and exegesis emerge. Even morality is derived from this core experiential connection with the numinous (Otto 1958: 107). Feeling a sense of awe in relation to existence and having faith in the progress of humanity are sentiments that sit at the heart of alternative spirituality. Celluloid Junkie's account of being overwhelmed by *2001* is characterized by "tears of wonderment" and a sensation of "endless fascination." Just as Otto highlights the centrality of fascination in experiences of *mysterium tremendum et fascinans*, Celluloid Junkie emphasizes the spiritual nature of their experience by saying that *2001* "has left an indelible impression upon my soul" (August 15, 2002, user review of *2001*). For dbdumonteil, *2001* distorted his/her sense of time and conjured such strong emotions that they felt breathless and close to tears. This viewer felt that the film mesmerized them, turning the audience "into creatures in rapture, in awe," drinking in sensations of the sublime (dbdumonteil, June 22, 2001, user review of *2001*). Ben Harding describes something akin to Otto's "creature feeling" (1958: 10) when he says, "You just feel so small and helpless—but in a somewhat spellbinding way" (May 12, 2009, user review of *2001*). Similarly, when anonymous beheld the face of the Starchild, s/he felt, "This huge thing wash over me"—an awesome, "greater than all of us' feeling" (March 31, 1999, user review of *2001*). As these last comments show, *2001* is capable of stimulating the type of emotional response that Otto describes, that is bound up with the apprehension of a mystery so tremendous that it cannot be adequately conveyed to others.

It is important to consider Otto's own observations about how people can access the numinous and the associated sensations of *mysterium tremendum et fascinans*. Otto recognizes that architecture and the arts express the numinous in the form of the sublime, identifying the use of silence and darkness as crucial in enabling a more direct experience of the numinous via what he generally considers to be the indirect path of aesthetics (1958: 65–8). As Otto traveled the world, visiting North Africa, the Middle East, India, and Japan, he described his encounters with foreign religious traditions. Often, the positive impressions that he formed were inspired by experiences of religious aesthetics. The religious feelings that were roused as he entered temples, stood before great statues, and listened to the sound of chanting, all left a significant impression on him. These experiences were instrumental in the development of Otto's understanding of the numinous (Oldmeadow 2009: 235). Otto describes his visit to the Indian rock temple at Elephanta Island recalling that after climbing the stone steps and entering the temple:

> The eye slowly accustoms itself to the semi-darkness, gradually distinguishes awesome representations—carved into the wall—of the religious epics of India, until it reaches the imposing central recess. Here an image rises up out of the rock which I can only compare with the great representations of Christ in early Byzantine churches. It is a three-headed form, carved only as far as the breast, in threefold human size. . . . Still and powerful the central head looks down, with both the others in profile. Over the image rests perfect peace and majesty. . . . Nowhere else have I found the secret of the transcendent world, the other world

more grandly and perfectly expressed than in these three heads. . . . the spirit of religion which has lived here, one may experience more in a single hour of contemplation than from all the books. (Oldmeadow 2009: 235–6)

As Griffiths has argued, both religious and secular spaces are capable of having a similar effect on the individual (2008: 3). This connection can be attributed to the role that aesthetic experiences play in the development of cultural definitions of religious experience. For example, Griffiths explains that medieval cathedrals were designed to conjure religious feelings and that these experiences of awe, spectacle, and heightened immersion have then come to influence cultural understandings of what religious experience feels like (2008: 18).

Griffiths's case studies, Otto's examples, and eddie olsen's impression of the pyramids of Egypt all convey a connection with "some higher force," and for Griffiths, it is this feeling that makes one shiver and can bring tears to their eyes (2008: 286). In the cinema, scale, volume, and sound quality can play their part in generating sensations of excess, yet *2001* uses multiple devices to this end, ensuring that powerful experiences are possible on the small screen as well. Sensory overload can be identified in each case as the common feature linking aesthetic experiences with the spiritual. Returning briefly to Elkins's work on intense emotive responses to paintings, it is interesting to note that he sees these responses as being "essentially religious, even when religion was the farthest thing from the viewer's mind" (2004b: 149). According to Elkins, whereas the mystics of the past felt the agency of God, in a secular world, people still speak of the "presence" of an artwork referring to this same "fullness, immediacy, pure existence, and urgent mystery that used to be called 'God'" (2004b: 174). This same feeling may also be referred to in terms of enlightenment. Elkins argues that "sudden, unexpected, out-of-control presence is one of the main reasons people cry in front of paintings, and the best meaning I can put to it, the one that explains it most fully, is to say it's a religious feeling" (2004b: 174). Elkins's observations here are crucial to understanding the religious experiences of the film viewers featured in this book more broadly. When viewers approach film as a site of open-minded contemplation where one is sensitive to vision, textures, sounds, and movements, this mode of perception enables the appreciation of abstract feelings and concepts. As has been discussed, abstraction and ineffability are at the heart of the Western understanding of ultimate truth.

In Elkins's work on religion in contemporary art, he argues that one of the functions of art is to "[burn] away what is false in religion" (2004a: 37), leaving the "faint perfume" of true religiosity behind (2004a: 88). The example that he uses here is of one of his students who created a sculpture of the Stations of the Cross that she then abstracted beyond all recognition, seeking a purer representation of her faith (Elkins 2004a: 34–8). Elkins also points to a link between art and mysticism describing mystical art as that which "involves an intimate, personal, or private connection with something transcendental"; it is "an intimate and incommunicable experience of transcendence" (2004a: 106). The apparent authenticity of religion's "faint perfume" can be equated with film experiences of the ineffable (Elkins 2004a: 88). In both cases, there is a shift away from discursive understanding to an ambiguous and embodied perceptual experience.

Noetic Quality

James defines the noetic quality of mystical experiences in the following manner:

> Although so similar to states of feeling, mystical states seem to those who experience them to be also states of knowledge. They are states of insight into depths of truth unplumbed by the discursive intellect. They are illuminations, revelations, full of significance and importance, all inarticulate though they remain; and as a rule they carry with them a curious sense of authority for after-time. (2014: 206)

This professed distinction between "discursive intellect" and states of insight infused with a noetic quality is commonly found in audience responses to *2001*. Viewers contend that the film must be appreciated on an abstract, visual, emotional, or experiential level in order to reach a state of understanding. Monos Z. sees in *2001* the opportunity to "find an answer to our place in the universe," achieved through the application of emotional intensity to bring about a form of understanding that is beyond logic (Monos Z., November 5, 2010, user review of *2001*). Employing psychologized terminology typical of alternative spirituality, tpeterson 1955 classifies the experience as a "'right brain' experience rather than a 'left brained' one" (February 17, 2012, user review of *2001*). The right brain is popularly understood to be the creative, spontaneous, and intuitive part of the mind, while the left brain is the rational and analytic side. Here, the intuitive and rational are juxtaposed in relation to *2001*, placing the film firmly in the former category. Lechuguilla recommends approaching the film from a "transcendental perspective," where "a conventional, egocentric plot" becomes "superfluous." Also employing psychological terminology, Lechuguilla associates narrative and the desire to understand as signs of an underdeveloped consciousness. By contrast, the nonnarrative aspects of the film are understood to be more advanced and less conditioned forms of communication (February 6, 2005, user review of *2001*). This viewer sets apart "perceptive viewers" as those who can overcome the narrative requirements of the ego and experience "an inspirational sense of wonder and awe" (Lechuguilla, February 6, 2005, user review of *2001*).

Viewers have referred to *2001* as a means for overcoming the modern condition—a state associated with existential immaturity. Lost2you2002 realized that the "irritation I felt was not [because] the film was boring," but the result of his/her own "impatience and refusal to stop, take my time, and find the beautiful, majestic pace" of existence. Understanding the need to "break out of my childish mind," the viewer describes their revelation in the following way: "The universe seemed to open up. Kubrick put small layers up slowly until they built into an avalanche and came crashing down" (lost2you2002, September 13, 2002, user review of *2001*). In alternative spirituality, the self is understood to exist in layers of progressive enlightenment. The Higher Self guides the self into situations where spiritual development is achieved through lessons that challenge psychological blocks and unhealthy patterns of thought (Hanegraaff 1998: 211–13). In the quotation above, lost2you2002's comments characterize *2001* as a lesson that is designed to reveal the spiritual immaturity at the heart of their feelings of boredom. Revealing the influence of alternative spirituality, *2001* is identified as an experience of existential wisdom and truth where the synthesis of spiritual and psychological thinking is starkly apparent.

There are numerous examples of viewers who speak of the film's ability to separate those who have a short attention span from those more "advanced" viewers that can bring their focus, intelligence, and openness to the viewing experience. Tvcunningham says, "Depending on the type of person you are, you will either believe that you've just witnessed one of the greatest transcendent pieces of cinema ever, or the most trippy head-scratching bore of your life" (February 25, 2009, user review of *2001*). Secondtake labels *2001* as a "personality sorter," distinguishing between those who are concerned with the mysteries of life and those who require narrative structure. "It is a movie for the intelligent and open-minded" (June 14, 2009, user review of *2001*). Ptsportsguy1 claims that the film encapsulates "what it truly means to be of a higher intelligence" (July 19, 2013, user review of *2001*). Here again, narrative film is equated with the simplicity of the socialized mind, while intuitive, visual, or nondiscursive understanding is considered to pertain to a deeper wisdom.

While the tenor of some viewer comments on this issue is somewhat elitist, referring to the "weak minded, or lazy of Will" (photonutz, October 9, 1999, user review of *2001*) and "juvenile," "conditioned minds" (Jeff [motownmaniax], September 14, 2004, user review of *2001*), they nonetheless present a binary where intelligence, insightfulness, and maturity are aligned with perceptual modes that seek a "truth unplumbed by the discursive intellect" (James 2014: 206). Rationalized interpretations that focus too much on literal meaning and narrative elements are deemed to be inferior and small minded. Viewer comments that make this distinction between "ignorant" rationality and "wise" intuition reveal something of this understanding of truth that is present in James's description of the noetic, in the epistemology of alternative spirituality, and in Kubrick's understanding of experiential wisdom (Gelmis 1969: n.p.). It is also worth noting that scholars like Plate similarly sacralize nonrational and unmediated perception from an academic perspective. For Plate, cinema takes on its religious or mystical qualities when the viewer is moved "not to rational knowledge, but to a corporeal response." This "sensual confrontation with the filmic image" breaks down the ordinary categories of film and the senses and is characterized by its immediacy (2008: 61 and 77). Concerned with finding the "right way" to experience each moment, where nothing is inherently good or bad, alternative spirituality presents the individual with the task of discovering and adopting the perfect form of relation. As st-shot puts it, if one fails to connect with the film "the fault is in ourselves not [*2001*]" (June 8, 2014, user review of *2001*). In this way, the search for noetic understanding, and the suspicion that such knowledge lies hidden in the film, can lead to self-reflexive processes that are integral to the viewer's overall assessment of the insights that they gain.

As James's definition of mystical experience suggests, the ineffable and noetic qualities of spiritual insight are tightly intertwined. The strong sensation of received knowledge is simultaneous with the inability to clearly grasp it or communicate it to others. Viewers that speak in these terms may outline aspects of the film's plot in their reviews but do not spell out the mysterious truth that they have perceived. Graza Shaw comments, "Once you realise the meaning... .You will be dazzled!" "In my personal experience of it, there was a little box that ticked in my head at some point in the movie when I actually realised what this was all about" (September 29, 2011, user review of *2001*). Nowarkfilmstudios says that the film was "designed to inspire an awakening, and it fulfilled it's [*sic*] purpose" (June 1, 2011, user review of *2001*). For john mavety, *2001* is not a movie, it is "a glimpse of the sublime." As the most inspiring cinematic experience he has ever had, he says enigmatically that "it stares right into the abyss of our existence and says YES, it's all worth it" (March 12, 2008, user review of *2001*).

The moment of noetic realization that viewers experience when watching *2001* is characteristically "full of significance and importance" (James 2014: 206) and can be translated into seemingly permanent changes in existential outlook. Vovazhd reports that *2001* changed both his/her approach to film viewing and "the way I viewed life and the universe." This was achieved through the film's ability to make one feel "like a child experiencing something new and special for the first time," leaving the viewer "agape" (vovazhd, October 1, 2007, user review of *2001*). Blakebabe411 similarly felt a correlation between his/her change in relationship to "film" and "life" itself. This viewer stresses that the film had a tangible effect on them, extending beyond an appreciation of the film's themes. *2001* helped him/her to love life with "my consciousness, and how fitting that a movie about the development of consciousness in humanity would be associated for me with the development of my own consciousness" (blakebabe411, May 3, 2006, user review of *2001*). This comment clarifies that a personal experience of revelation is experienced in parallel with the film's themes, but is not produced conventionally in the form of an empathetic connection with the main character. Rather, the subtleties of film design encourage an experience of awakening where most viewers are at a loss to account for the intensity of their experience. For Pulpthatsfiction, *2001* has forced a revaluation of their worldview and has filled their mind with questions. The viewer knows that with repeated viewings they may eventually understand the film's true meaning, but they feel afraid of what they might discover (October 11, 2007, user review of *2001*).

Mikemacisaac classifies *2001* as "a religious film" explaining that this is "not in the conventional sense of adhering to any specific creed, but because of it's invocation of wonder at the vast panorama of existence and it's involvement with the deepest and most vital questions of purpose and truth" (January 8, 2007, user review of *2001*). Reggie Santori goes so far as to say that he has "seen the work of God" in *2001* and that the film has made him religious (December 2, 2001, user review of *2001*), Jacob-28 claims that the film helped him to gain clarity about God's existence (September 5, 1999, user review of *2001*), and erniekelvin associates the film with touching the face of God (December 28, 2006, user review of *2001*). Such comments clearly demonstrate that the intensity and type of experience that *2001* generates are equated with viewers' understanding of religion and God. However, this is unlikely to relate to institutional religion as spiritualized responses to *2001* are invariably of a mystic variety, where subjective experiences of realization are central. Ikorni claims that it is "one of the most mystic journeys" a person can take in their life (June 26, 2000, user review of *2001*). Feelings of realization, awakening, or enlightenment that are evident in viewer comments lend support to the argument that Kubrick is successful in guiding his audiences into a state of stasis.

2001's ability to prompt changes in existential outlook is evident in many audience responses. Some viewers make quite specific comments about the life-changing powers of the film, such as Alexandre Silvolella who says that the film helped him choose his career path (February 12, 2014, user review of *2001*), and Serata who reports that s/he was left in a state of awe with "a new respect for all things natural that humans have destroyed with computers and fossil fuels. Never has a movie made such an impact on my life and the actual way I live. That was how powerful this movie was to me" (December 4, 2003, user review of *2001*). In 1968, one viewer wrote to Kubrick:

> [I]t is within the power of a film such as yours to give people a reason to go on living—to give them the courage to go on living. For *2001* implies much more than just an artistic revelation. On a philosophical level, it implies that if man is capable of this, he is capable of anything—anything rational and heroic and glorious and good.... How can man now be content to consider the trivial and the mundane, when you have shown them a world full of stars, a world beyond the infinite? (Krämer 2010: 87–8)

This impassioned appraisal of the film demonstrates how *2001* can inspire viewers to reorient themselves after coming to a realization of human potential. It can be deduced that the "trivial and mundane" aspects of life are equated with everyday social norms, yet the "rational" is salvaged from this realm to be associated with the "heroic," "glorious," "good," and "a world beyond the infinite." While spiritualized interpretations of *2001* are linked with the religious, they may equally embrace rationality and scientific knowledge in light of the synthesis of various forms of intelligence in alternative spirituality.

Viewer responses show that Kubrick's desire to enable viewers to awaken their senses to "cosmic truth" through *2001* has been, to a large extent, realized (Kloman 1968: n.p.). Kubrick does not ever define "cosmic truth" because it may be something that cannot be explained, so much experienced through the film. Kubrick notes that this state of mind can be reached through other paths such as music, painting, religion, mythology, allegory, and intuition (Kloman 2015: n.p.). The ambiguous end point that all these paths lead toward is that elusive religious feeling that James, Elkins, Griffiths, Schrader, Otto, and others refer to. A sense of awakening brings "meaning" that is experienced intuitively on a "visceral, psychological level" rather than though rational explanation (Kloman 2015: n.p.). This state of mind remains vitally important in Western culture, whether it is understood in psychological, spiritual, aesthetic, or religious terms. Its significance, however, has shifted dramatically with the rise of individualism to the subjective sphere where its vitality is sustained through its uniqueness and inability to be fully explained or institutionalized.

Evidence of the noetic aspects of *2001* can also be found in the characterization of the film as a rite of passage. As R. Barton Palmer explains:

> For the generation that came of age in the late 1960s, seeing the film (often numerous times) became a *rite de passage* thought to be the source of a special knowledge that distinguished them from their parents and "square" adults in general. Many reported undergoing religious conversions, rather than experiencing altered states, during the film's famous twenty-four-minute, dialogue-free final sequence. (2006: 14–15)

As Palmer goes on to say, the youth were drawn to the film because it transformed dominant Christian and scientific discourses into something totally new that seemed to offer both "redemption and renewal" (2006: 15; Krämer 2010: 86–7). While in a traditional sense, rites of passage are designed to initiate the young into the adult community, Palmer's observations demonstrate that *2001* offered initiation into a "special knowledge" that the adult community did not possess. In line with the basic outlook of alternative spirituality, the wisdom of the actual adult community is superseded by a superior spiritual wisdom. Conceived as a free agent, the individual is not determined by Earthly hierarchies, as their true identity issues from, and returns to, the eternal and universal Source. As such, the experience of *2001* provides initiation into the universal spiritual community as part of the process of personal actualization.

Gross Ryder recalls that "as a teenager (around 14 then, the timing was so crucial!) I was hit hard by *2001* when I saw it—both in heart and mind" (May 21, 2012, user review of *2001*). Watercrake remembers the moment as one where

> I was washed over with a sense of awe and absolute wonder. It's as if time slowed and I could see each and every frame of this amazing creation in a distilled and concentrated way. It was more than "movie-magic" happening to me . . . in my 12 year old brain I was finally understanding what it was like to be truly alone and how infinitely small I was in the vastness among the planets. I was overwhelmed. (June 20, 2000, user review of *2001*)

Onumbersix who saw *2001* at the age of fifteen in Cinerama remembered that it felt as if the future was in front of him, "urging the young man I was to proceed into it wholeheartedly" (January 19, 2012, user review of *2001*). Other viewers like serafinogm explain similarly formative experiences of *2001*, especially those who saw the film at the time of its release (October 7, 2015, user review of *2001*).

As a powerful film that has been an important lifetime event for many people, viewers have referred to the film as a rite of passage, highlighting its apparent initiatory function. Audience members like IPreferEvidence (April 4, 2011, user review of *2001*) and Cristian (December 23, 2007, user review of *2001*) believe that *2001* is a film that all people should see because it teaches vital lessons about growing up and facing one's true nature. Dalibor Andric says that one should watch the film in one's youth, middle age, and old age as it is a film that tackles the meaning of existence, life, and the purpose of humanity (October 14, 2013, user review of *2001*). For FilmWiz, *2001* is a film for "a long (in my case LIFE-long) family discussion" (January 8, 2003, user review of *2001*). Similarly, intrepid-s-t-88 remarks: "I will happily spend the rest of my life looking for folks to share this fabulous film with" (August 4, 2013, user review of *2001*). Such comments reveal that while *2001* may be experienced alone or could involve a small group of people, those who share a common experience of the film are drawn to each other in a kind of community of those who "understand."

Conceived as a rite of passage, *2001* has been identified as an important experience for young people to undertake. Tomasasaz refers to the film as a tool for personal empowerment that "digital age children" should be exposed to (January 2, 2011, user review of *2001*). This desire to induct the young into an experience of *2001* is evident in numerous reviews where older viewers have attempted to share the film experience with the young. An experienced *2001* viewer, Kieranmc, took their young friend to see the film and describes his reaction as "silence followed by: Wow!" (April 26, 2000, user review of *2001*). While a positive reaction such as this may be desired, other attempts to initiate the young have not always gone as planned as one young viewer, arcadefreak2000, reports, "(MY teacher made me watch it) and trust me it will make u go insane!" (May 10, 2005, user review of *2001*). Another young viewer, oreo1013, says, "I totally agree with whoever it was that said this was a movie for adults. I'm 14, and this movie totally bored me out of my mind. . . . Sorry if I've disappointed anyone" (September 8, 2001, user review of *2001*). On the other hand, viewers like LMAN JINA (February 2, 2013, user review of *2001*), Panapaok (July 14, 2013, user review of *2001*), and David Johnson (June 30, 2006, user review of *2001*) recommend that young people should not see *2001* because it contains disturbing content that is beyond their years. As a film that is classified as suitable for children (United States [G], United States-TV [PG],

United Kingdom [12], and Australia [G]), *2001* does not include any overtly explicit content, so these comments can be interpreted as an acknowledgment of the film's affective power as a force that should be handled wisely by those who are equipped for the experience.

According to Eliade, modern Western culture is marked by the retreat of initiatory rituals (1965: xi). For Eliade, the function of initiation is to reveal the meaning of existence to the next generation so that they may become responsible participants in culture (1965: xi). A successful initiatory ritual should engender "a basic change in existential condition" (1965: x). Traditionally, Eliade argues, initiatory practice consists of a series of ordeals that bring about religious experience or an "encounter with the sacred" (1965: xii). Dramatic and visceral elements are essential in bringing about such an encounter, as is the ritualistic preparation of sacred ground (1965: 4 and 12–19). While viewer responses correlate with these initiatory features, overall the filmic experience can be considered less intense and formative than physical ritual. In a general sense, the preparation of sacred ground can be compared with comments from the previous chapter insisting upon the arrangement of the viewing space to exclude external distractions, and the adoption of a specific perceptual mode that is conducive to feelings of awe or deep knowing. Similarly, the dramatic techniques employed in film may affect the viewer intensely, but perhaps not to the same extent as physical techniques. There are also differences to consider in terms of the distinction between a living community of elders who are connected with a spiritual hierarchy and the generalized artistic evocations of a de-institutionalized spiritual essence. However, for those viewers who are primed for the experience of existential awakening, it appears that *2001* functions as an initiatory tool by providing an "encounter with the sacred" (1965: xii). The noetic qualities of the film generate feelings of revelation correlated with universal wisdom to the extent that it is considered capable of passing the meaning of existence to the next generation (1965: xi). Like ritual itself, film experiences offer viewers the opportunity to engage in a different mode of perception for a specific period of time where the attainment of wisdom may actually be achieved in subsequent reflection. The temporary nature of religious experience will be discussed in further detail below.

Transiency

James's definition of mystical experience is defined by "transiency" (2014: 207). Acknowledging preparatory aspects, such as focused attention, the experience itself is marked by a perceptual shift into an altered state. Generally, the act of film viewing involves temporary focused engagement in the fictional world of the film for a set period of time, lasting between one and three hours. This is the same amount of time that James ascribes to mystical experience (2014: 207). On this point there is little more to say; however, James also mentions the accumulation of significance and profundity each time the practitioner returns to this state of mind (2014: 207; Schrader 1972: 11). Watching *2001* on a single occasion is only the tip of the iceberg when considering the depth of awe and wisdom that viewers have gained through repeat viewings.

During *2001*'s cinematic release, the *Toronto Telegram* reported many cases of repeat viewing (Agel 1970: 360). *IMDb* viewers refer to their annual (jimmoir, November 7, 2014, user review of *2001*), biannual (loufalce, December 10, 2007, user review of *2001*), or monthly viewing rituals (deodatgyorei, April 2, 2016, user review of *2001*). John Lennon of The Beatles fame claimed that he watched *2001* "every week" (Schwam 2010: front cover). The capacity that *2001* possesses to reveal new knowledge has been compared with the living wisdom of the Bible where new interpretations can always be found while the text itself remains unchanged (Daniel Little, February 17, 2003, user review of *2001*). Here it is *2001*'s capacity to generate multiple interpretations that makes it a suitable subject of continued exegesis.

For deodatgyorei, *2001* "grows with you as you age, it inspires you to gain more knowledge about the world you live in on a scientific and a spiritual level as well" (April 2, 2016, user review of *2001*). For bgiamou, the film "constantly evolves [and] evokes new meaning upon each viewing" (September 29, 2015, user review of *2001*), while rooprect echoes this sentiment saying that *2001* "EVOLVES WITH US" (January 25, 2012, user review of *2001*). These responses demonstrate that *2001* has been conceived as a source of wisdom that reveals itself progressively to the viewer. While the experience itself is transitory, a return to the perceptual state associated with the film increases feelings of "inner richness and importance" (James 2014: 207). Although the ultimate truth that *2001* is thought to possess may never be fully revealed, repeat viewings appear to unveil successive layers of insight. This esoteric or gnostic understanding of layered truth is one of the formative epistemological features of alternative spirituality, and *2001* provides a framework that is adaptable to changing personal interpretations. However, many viewers who now preach fervently about the wisdom of *2001* did not originally appreciate the film. *Newsday* film critic Joseph Gelmis also had this experience where his initial negative appraisal of the film was revised.

While James's definition of religious experience is focused on its overt characteristics, Hollenback's broader view of mysticism includes the preparations that precede it and the response that follows (1996: 1). In the three reviews that Gelmis wrote on *2001*, it is possible to gain insight into areas of preparation and response that are not possible to gain through individual *IMDb* reviews. Gelmis's first review from April 4, 1968, panned the film, presenting *2001* as "pretentious," "patronizingly pedantic in some of its earnest history lessons," a "spectacular, glorious failure" in dramatic terms, and "as a whole, disappointingly confusing, disjointed, and unsatisfying" (Agel 1970: 263–4). Gelmis went on to reprimand the film for its "slow, smug pace" and "awful soundtrack" (Agel 1970: 264). Like many *IMDb* viewers who did not like *2001*, Gelmis seems irritated by the film. In this overwhelmingly negative review, he interpreted the Starchild as "a biblical allusion" where "one must be reborn as a child before being allowed to enter the kingdom of heaven" (Agel 1970: 265). His final comment on the film proceeded: "Instead of suspense, there is surprise and confusion, and, for many, resentment" (Agel 1970: 265).

Just over a fortnight later, on April 20, 1968, Gelmis wrote a second review, where he effectively apologized for rushing his initial commentary and for upholding the "status quo" by judging the film according to existing cinematic conventions (Agel 1970: 265–6). After seeing *2001* again, Gelmis was convinced of its value, referring to it as a "masterwork," saying "this awesome film is light-years ahead of any science fiction you have ever seen and owes more to the mystical visions of Jung and William Blake than to H.G. Wells or Jules Verne" (Agel 1970: 267). This second review abandons all previous critiques but returns to the idea that Kubrick uses "surprise" rather than "suspense," explaining that "the film is full of sequences that seem too long or confusing, until they are seen in context a second time" (Agel 1970: 267). For Gelmis, a second viewing may be necessary in order for *2001* to be effective in touching the audience on a deep level, admitting that during his first viewing, he was not immersed, as he says the film failed for him "because it did not keep me spellbound" (Agel 1970: 267). During his second viewing, Gelmis is more open to the monotonous style and anti-dramatic characterization of *2001* that he now deems essential in making Bowman's transformation "such a joyous reaffirmation of life" (Agel 1970: 267).

It is important to note that Gelmis's shift in appreciation involved several theoretical and perceptual shifts. First, Gelmis put aside the criteria of cinematic convention to appreciate the film on its own terms. Secondly, he allowed himself to become immersed, and in this state, what was once irritating, becomes profound. Thirdly, he changed his religious framework from a Christian perspective to one drawn from the psychologized, mystical, and poetic religiosity of Jung and Blake. While Gelmis does not elaborate on the element of surprise in *2001*, he infers that a contextualized repeat viewing renders this effect more powerful. As previously discussed, Kubrick employs a technique where aural or compositional elements signal a moment of great significance, yet this does not amount to a corresponding narrative revelation. Sensational significance and narrative absence combine to produce the successive apprehension of mystery. This could also be understood, to a certain extent, through Gelmis's explanation of surprise.

Almost exactly one year from his first review, Gelmis wrote a third review of *2001* published April 5, 1969. Gelmis remarks on the eerie similarities that exist between *2001* and two texts written prior to the film's release: Marshall McLuhan's *Understanding Media* (1964) and Alan McGlashan's *The Savage and Beautiful Country* (1966). He refers to McLuhan's view that the artist, as an individual of "integral awareness," can foresee the impact of technological and cultural change prior to its eventuation, so that art is able to provide "exact information of how to rearrange one's psyche in order to anticipate the next blow from our own extended faculties" (Agel 1970: 268). Connecting this concept with *The Savage and Beautiful Country*, he asserts that McGlashan's writing presents "a new direction of perception." He then quotes McGlashan at length, capturing several key aspects of *2001*'s ritual function:

> An almost imperceptible inner change—a willed suspension of conventional judgments, a poised still awareness, a *stillness* in which long-smothered voices that speak the language of the soul can heard again. (Agel 1970: 269)

Gelmis associates McGlashan's view that humanity "is on the verge of a crucial psychic mutation" with the Nietzschean call for humanity to surpass itself, and McLuhan's suggestion that we could perceive what is "beyond space and time" if we were not so distracted by the business of everyday life (Agel 1970: 269).

This interesting review juxtaposes concepts that reflect Gelmis's subjective engagement with the film. Unlike his first and second reviews, this one reveals the pervasive effect that *2001* has had in shaping his personal vision of the world as he discovers serendipitous and seemingly prophetic connections between the film and the writings of McLuhan and McGlashan. Mirroring the religious mode of seekership, Gelmis's review shows how unrelated elements can be brought in to complete each other in what might be considered a "lyrical associative" manner (Grodal 2009: 224). Gelmis's ultimate reluctance to use his own words to capture his final view of *2001*, and to rely almost entirely on quotations, demonstrates that he still cannot find the right expression to capture his experience, suggesting a lingering ineffable quality.

This example of progressive understanding does not necessarily refer to three revelatory film experiences, but rather shows how a return to *2001* yields new and deeper insights. Gelmis's access to the mysteries of *2001* came when he changed his frame of reference from one of conventional cinematic tropes and Christian symbology to a more "open" mode of film viewing where previously irritating techniques start to have a different effect. Returning to the film with a willingness to re-experience it from an alternative perceptual position can be considered a form of preparation, in Hollenback's terminology. Between the reviews, Gelmis clearly spent a significant amount of time reflecting on the film and this, in turn, contributed to the deepening of insight. By the third review, the experience of the film appears to have taken on spiritual meaning. It is at this point that the affect of *2001* extends beyond the film experience itself to be reawakened in other contexts. Reading McLuhan and McGlashan, the words must have leapt from the page, ringing with significance, correlating with the insights of the film. These similarly transient experiences then become a part of *2001*'s successive revelation of wisdom.

Passivity

Continuing with the theme of ritualistic engagement, Whitehouse's work on ritual memory provides useful insight into James's fourth category of passivity. According to Whitehouse, ritual can be divided into two basic modes: the "doctrinal" and the "imagistic." The doctrinal mode employs frequent "low-arousal" rituals that enable religious teaching to be "stored in semantic memory, reproduced stably and spread efficiently as oral tradition," while the imagistic mode is distinguished by infrequent "high arousal" rituals that "etch themselves in episodic memory" by stimulating strong emotions (Atkinson and Whitehouse 2011: 51). However, he qualifies this binary by recognizing that regularized, highly emotive rituals can overcome the "tedium effect" that the doctrinal mode is open to (Whitehouse 2004: 327). James inadvertently stresses the peculiarity of memory function in relation to mystical experience by mentioning it in three of his four categories. For James, the memory of mystical experience may be difficult to grasp, but some recollection "always remains" along with "a profound sense of . . . importance. They modify the inner life of the subject between the times of their recurrence" and "as a rule they carry with them a curious sense of authority for after-time" (2014: 206–7).

Whitehouse uses Christianity as his principal example of the doctrinal mode, stating that Christians often "participate in liturgical rites on autopilot" and are not inclined to reflect on the meaning of their practices (2002: 93–4). By contrast, "high arousal" experiences of the imagistic mode are often traumatic, triggering both "flashbulb memory" and a high level of reflexivity after the event (Whitehouse 2002: 91). An example of this can be found in Melanesian puberty rites that employ fear, physical pain, and various theatrical devices to bring about a genuine sense of trauma. While in Whitehouse's example participants experience pain and trauma first hand, Dimitris Xygalatas et al. found that those who watch such high ordeal rituals are similarly effected through an empathetic response (2013: 1602–4), just as a viewer might be through their imaginative engagement with filmic stimuli. Reflexivity occurs because the event is so disturbing and anomalous that the individual must find ways to come to terms with the experience in their own mind (Whitehouse 1996: 711). By producing "unforgettable, vivid and haunting" episodic memories, these experiences are "'printed' on the mind," giving such memories a "canonical structure" that stays with a person for life (Whitehouse 1996: 710–12). Although James does not specifically mention trauma in his definition, some of the visceral power of mystical experience is captured in the category of "passivity" where "the mystic feels as if his own will were in abeyance, and indeed sometimes as if he were grasped and held by a superior power" (2014: 207). Overall, James's comments regarding memory situate mystical experience in Whitehouse's "imagistic" category.

The cinema provides an environment where the embodied experiences of life are concentrated and intensified to create an engaging experience that affects the viewer, often on a physical level. Action and horror movies use a range of effects to make the viewer's heart race or make them jump in their seat. *2001* does not employ these particular cinematic tropes, yet through its slow and hypnotic style, the film nonetheless generates strong physical responses and feelings of terror and awe. Grrrr97 who experienced "shivers of wonder and awe down the spine" stresses the rarity of this bodily reaction saying (in capitals) "THIS IS NOT A FILM ITS SOMETHING ELSE, SOMETHING WONDERFUL, THAT I DOUBT WILL EVER BE EXPERIENCED AGAIN" (January 24, 2003, user review of *2001*). Such sensations allude to James's attribute of passivity and Otto's description of *mysterium tremendum et fascinans* as the viewer's prelogical systems respond to the film in an uncontrollable manner. Juan Mendoza believes that *2001* operates using "direct mental stimulation" (September 9, 2013, user review of *2001*), while other viewers note that the film affected them viscerally (Metal Angel Ehrler, August 13, 2009, user review of *2001*; Berlioz747, November 9, 2008, user review of *2001*; Jeff Hatfield, May 23, 2005, user review of *2001*). Audience responses show that *2001* brings on strong emotions that cause the hair to stand on end, eliciting tears and chills (The Centurion, January 26, 2009, user review of *2001*; BUNI, February 25, 1999, user review of *2001*; Wunderwaffe, September 30, 2013, user review of *2001*). Each time he watches the film, David H. Schleicher experiences shivers and insists that "no other film in my mind is this innately powerful." The viewer goes on to say that the experience "gives me enough energy to fuel a thousand dreams" (November 21, 2005, user review of *2001*). Here, physical sensation comes as the result of emotional overflow that in turn generates extended creative reflexivity. At times, the physical or psychical experience of *2001* is described in a manner that is suggestive of possession. ElMaruecan82 reports, "A strange feeling inhabits me when I watch this film," where it touches the deepest part of the viewer's soul (October 4, 2010, user review of *2001*).

As Whitehouse suggests, highly emotional, visceral, and traumatic ritual experiences have the capacity to burn themselves into one's memory, taking on a lasting vividness. It may be commonplace to say that a film is memorable, but *2001* viewers go further than this, seemingly to imply that they are *unable* to forget the film (Mr. Hulot, August 21, 2002, user review of *2001*; royale_w_cheez44, February 10, 2006, user review of *2001*; Gorie Catalin, January 31, 2002, user review of *2001*). Further to this, viewers refer to its haunting qualities, saying that the film "stays with you" and that unintentional rumination continues for days, weeks, or years (atomicpunks22, May 6, 2008, user review of *2001*; donald willy, February 19, 2002, user review of *2001*). In imagistic ritual, participants experience a series of ordeals that produce visceral reactions as well as extreme emotional states such as terror. However, Atkinson and Whitehouse note that recent experiments suggest "even low-arousal one-off rituals produce some reflexivity (albeit lower than for high arousal variants)" (2011: 57). The level of reflexivity here is an indicator of how the ritual experience is processed in the brain and stored in memory. While religious ritual and initiation practices are less common in the modern West, film directors still hold many tools at their disposal that can bring about experiences that perform a ritual function. At that point where the viewer begins to feel their sense of personal agency overwhelmed by the ineffable, film can serve this transformative function. The power of such experiences is evidenced in the way that they are retained in memory and the transformative or initiatory role that they play in viewers' lives. According to wwe7961, *2001* "takes your brain, chops it into little tiny pieces, puts it back together perfectly, and puts [it] back in your head at the end of the movie." For this viewer, "By the end of the movie I felt like I was a different person. I was still exactly the same, but something felt different" (August 2, 2010, user review of *2001*). This evocative review suggests a high level of single-pointed focus where the viewer has been able to "feel every moment" of the film, where immersion facilitates the subtle transformation of self that the viewer reports. The "chopping up" and reassembly of the brain is also reminiscent of initiation where the participant experiences ritual death and rebirth through ritual.

The lifelong impact of Sandra's experience of *2001* highlights ways in which film can come to resemble imagistic ritual, albeit in a less intense manner than initiation rites. Sandra recalls that twenty years ago, at the age of seven, she saw *2001* for the first time: "The sky seemed so very different that night. I won't forget that feeling, ever." Over the years, this "impression remained intact." Every time she watches the film, she "eagerly awaits" the "paralyzing" final scenes that offer her something she cannot pinpoint but could be "some kind of hope . . . or simply—life and all that life represents." Referring to the Starchild as "God" and "the ultimate destination," she says, "the image of the fetus is HERE, in my mind, [it] doesn't go away, and never will!" (November 28, 2008, user review of *2001*). According to Ilkka Pyysiäinen, the more intense the sensory and emotive elements are in a ritual, "the stronger feelings of uncontrollability they evoke" and the more they are able to "enhance religious belief" (2011: 158). In the cinema, audiences are immersed in an experience that has been designed to manipulate perception, sensation, and emotion. *2001* has also been specifically designed to help viewers to tap into their "mythological" sense and intuitively discover "cosmic truth" (Gelmis 1969: n.p.; Kloman 2015: n.p.). Those viewers who attribute agency to *2001* approach the film in a similar way to a ritual participant who is affected by spiritual forces. As both Whitehouse and Pyysiäinen argue, intensely emotional and visceral experiences have the capacity to remain burned into the memory of the participant for life, triggering subjective reflection and enhancing religious belief. The "religious belief" here that is being strengthened in viewer's minds is a subjective worldview articulated in terms of alternative spirituality. As Plate argues, "Religions persuade believers using experiences that impress feelings of certitude, where the concepts being conveyed are secondary or incidental" (Plate 2008: 15–16). What Clifford Geertz refers to as the "aura of factuality" is elusive and ever changing, yet directors like Kubrick are able to endow the film experience with this feeling (2017: 97).

On the one hand, sensations of unattributed agency can be disturbing, and can replicate aspects of Whitehouse's imagistic ritual mode. However, this can also be explained through Grodal's claim that the use of open-ended and ambiguous ideas in film overloads the cognitive faculties through the endless search for hidden meaning and associations. As the viewer cannot close these mental queries, a sense of saturated emotion and disorientation builds up which can "create a sense of permanence and transcendence" (2009: 226). Furthermore, the mental work that is performed by the viewer develops a network of personally significant associations that generates a strong feeling of veracity and authenticity (2009: 227). Tribble-841-35156, who describes *2001* as "opaque" and "subliminal," echoes Grodal's description of art films when s/he says, "[We] want to understand it, but what we are told is vague or uncertain, we keep guessing and trying to figure it out, and that uncertainty keeps us going to achieve enlightenment" (September 24, 2010, user review of *2001*). Viewers reports that *2001*'s ambiguity compelled them to think about the film for an extended period, lending support to Grodal's claim (Tony Mathew, November 19, 2013, user review of *2001*; Cameron-lee, July 9, 2013, user review of *2001*; JoH-2, December 27, 2000, user review of *2001*). Grodal's insights provide a means of understanding how *2001* takes on its mysterious power to affect the viewer and to act as a point of access to esoteric wisdom. For RFS23, agency is attributed to the universe that transmits "pure magik" through Kubrick as the creator of *2001*. The viewer repeats, "I really believe that the universe itself is speaking to us in this movie, using Kubrick as it's [*sic*] vessel. . . . The movie really does start to look deep into you . . . try it and see" (October 21, 2001, user review of *2001*).

In religious ritual and practice it is common for participants to feel that spiritual forces or entities are exercising agency and affecting the participant in life-changing ways. Taves explores examples of religious experience that seemed spontaneous to the experiencer, but that actually involved preparations that increased the likelihood of a mystical experience through focus of mind and subconscious expectation (2009: 94–119). The preparatory practices that Taves identifies include prolonged focus on an idea, wanting an experience to happen, and visualization. As these manifest through unconscious processing, they may bring about an experience that appears somewhat predictable to the objective researcher. However, this does not change the subjective feeling that something is happening in the absence of personal intention (Taves 2009: 94–119).

As Taves observes, people attribute causality based on their existing beliefs and assumptions; however, at other times, individuals merely "have feelings, sensations, and perceptions that are suggestive of agency" (2009: 41). In a study on sleep paralysis, individuals reported feeling a "presence" that they described using religious terminology even if they did not consider themselves religious (Taves 2009: 137). According to Taves, "Human beings ascribe counterintuitive agent-related properties to objects because they have a basic tendency to overattribute agency, particularly in situations of ambiguity" (2009: 43). "Hyperactive agency detection" is also found where an individual may feel threatened by an unknown cause (Taves 2009: 138). Viewers of *2001* certainly report a sense of being threatened by the film through feelings of "horror" (T RajahBalaji, February 20, 2002, user review of *2001*; Chance_Boudreaux19, April 7, 2016, user review of *2001*), "terror" (ackstasis, December 6, 2007, user review of *2001*; Spleen, November 7, 1999, user review of *2001*), and "fear" (Andariel Halo, January 20, 2010, user review of *2001*). At the extreme end of the scale, beetleborgs69 recommends that people protect their friends, family, and loved ones from the film and may need "an exorcism" after watching it. S/he reports that *2001* "traumatizes you into submission" in a "terrifying assault on the soul" (March 2, 2015, user review of *2001*). For a film that many describe as being beautiful, optimistic, sublime, and awe-inspiring, it is vital to detect the element of terror that is implicit in experiences of awe.

Highlighting the unusual power attributed to *2001*, Mr. Blockbuster says, "If you let it, [*2001*] will take control of you and change you forever" (January 1, 2001, user review of *2001*). Similarly, Robb 772 (who refers to the film as "visceral") contends that *2001* "demands full submission on the part of the viewer" (May 25, 2006, user review of *2001*), and DeathFish refers to the need for the viewer to "succumb" to the film (January 2, 2007, user review of *2001*). These viewer comments clearly position the viewer in a passive relationship to the film, where it seems as though the film is exerting a spiritual power over them. Each of these comments acknowledge that the viewer must first be willing to allow the experience, but once they have adopted the correct perceptual mode, the film will exert its own agency over the passive or submissive viewer. As previously mentioned, buckdharwin sees the Stargate sequence as an experience of "forcible Enlightenment," further highlighting the independent power of the film that can override the will of the viewer (May 2, 2009, user review of *2001*). As Wood argues, experiences of "possession" are central in the religious culture of neoliberal societies (2007: 22–3). Including practices that involve the perceptual receptivity to external forces such as healing, meditation, and divination, this also refers to activities that seek to bypass the conscious mind in order to gain wisdom from the responses of the subconscious (Wood 2007: 12,

98 and 134–6). Here, the subconscious is thought to communicate in a primal and automatic manner, presenting truth in its unvarnished state. By temporarily deferring to the authority inherent in religious experiences (of a spirit or force), individuals are able to legitimize other aspects of their spiritual worldview (Wood 2007: 163). This may also be the case where a person's worldview is not overtly articulated in spiritual terms. That is, powerful experiences that adhere to James's four attributes of mystical experience provide a sensation of certainty in the context of relativized, pluralistic truth.

Viewers often believe that the film is exerting its will by affecting the subconscious mind, as Maz Murdoch (asda-man) (December 14, 2014, user review of *2001*), Michael (February 6, 2016, user review of *2001*), rcj5365 (December 18, 2008, user review of *2001*), and dbdumonteil (June 22, 2001, user review of *2001*) attest. For raymond chandler, *2001* "forces its way into the subconscious, engaging the viewer on a much more primal level than most movies even attempt" (July 31, 2001, user review of *2001*). Juan Mendoza feels that Kubrick "presents the viewer with a visceral experience that seeps deep into the mind and conveys messages" (September 9, 2013, user review of *2001*). These viewers speak about *2001* as a film that is communicating with, affecting, and changing a part of them that they know exists, but that they may have no tangible sense of. More importantly, the subconscious is beyond perception and control. As Nick Formica puts it, Kubrick creates a space for "discovering something in yourself that you never knew existed" (July 24, 2000, user review of *2001*). In a similar vein, Indy-52's says that *2001* has changed his/her "mentality and perceptions" about "life and our place in the Universe," but that the film "buries itself into your subconscious and doesn't leave you," having unpredictable effects on one's outlook (November 1, 2001, user review of *2001*). These descriptions of *2001* show that the film does not merely operate subliminally; it is also instructive. While alternative spirituality has been discussed in terms of seeking an ultimate experience of truth, it is also evident in this consideration of spiritual passivity that *seekership* relies upon experiences of perceived *guidance*.

Conclusion

This chapter considered the resemblance between *2001*'s reception and James's definition of religious experience. Viewers report intense responses to the film and a confusion of the senses that overwhelms their ability to fit the experience into familiar categories. Also bearing similarities to mystical experiences typified by Otto's concept of *mysterium tremendum et fascinans*, viewer accounts are a reflection on the culminating affects of the film. Viewers slip into a religious frame of reference when they feel themselves to be experientially overpowered. Crossing a perceptual threshold marked by increased feelings of dissociation and ineffable insight, the viewer no longer feels that they are in control of the experience. Where this sensation is most intense, the film's presence continues to affect the viewer in memory recurrence. As an irresolvable event that resists cognitive assimilation, the persistent affect of the film encourages continued reflection, leading to an increasingly personalized interpretation. As correlations arise between the broad existential themes of the film and other instances of insight, the sacredness of multiple pseudo-mystical experiences begin to interrelate and reinforce each other. In this way, Kubrick succeeds in stimulating the religious impulse of his audience, and for receptive viewers, the experience enables the realization of noetic meaning.

6

Enter the Void

The Initiatory Moment

As a director who has experienced the initiatory power of cinema through a powerful childhood encounter with Kubrick's *2001*, Noé's filmmaking explores similarly affective experiences that bypass the viewer's capacity for psychological resistance. *Enter the Void* is a direct tribute to *2001*, working with similar film techniques and generating mystical sensations, as will be discussed in the following chapter. Working nearly a half-century after the spiritual revolution of the late 1960s and the release of *2001*, Noé (and von Trier) are the inheritors of these cultural influences, yet their films also reflect the increasingly graphic, explicit, and invasive nature of modern culture. Outlining the defining features of the current media environment, this chapter accounts for the extreme techniques adopted in contemporary cinema and their role in bringing about spontaneous revelatory experiences through film.

In the late 1960s, seekership flourished in the spirit of revolution and under the looming shadow of nuclear apocalypse. Religious traditions from around the world were largely an untapped resource, holding the promise of hidden insight. The early twenty-first century, by contrast, is defined by an over-availability of information, options, and opinions. The globalization of communication networks has freed the individual from their local culture, offering alternative means of identity construction. Increased social atomization has generated the corresponding urge to reassemble unity through allegiance with tribal groups and the affirmation of self. Religious fundamentalism stems from this desire to form a durable and shared identity in the face of plurality (LeDrew 2018: 143), while "DIY (or do-it-yourself)" approaches to identity construction embrace plurality through ongoing processes of reevaluation and modification, forming contingent affiliations (Gilmore 2011: 37–42). Mistrust of hegemonic social authorities and the need to discover truth for oneself remain constant in both cases and do not preclude the deferral to alternative sources of authority.

Despite improved access to global spiritual resources and communities afforded by the internet, the predominance of text and dialogue-based communication disallows the spontaneous generation of mystical states of mind that may occur more readily in physical congregations and rituals. Social media interactions involve particularly self-conscious forms of engagement, while news media is flooded with emotionally loaded opinion pieces designed to trigger a response through implicit calls to action. Revelations of unmediated truth are therefore to be found in the abstract realm of the experiential that is accessed most readily through cinema, music, and the arts. Through these overwhelming and vital experiences, the individual can become exposed to spiritual truth, making immersive, sensational encounters an important psychological antidote to the constant discursive engagement encouraged by modern media and communications technologies.

The New Extremism in a Media-saturated Age

Widespread public access to the internet and the subsequent integration of media and popular culture into an instantaneously accessible form have transformed the global communications landscape, making the cultural backdrop of *Enter the Void* in 2009 quite distinct from that of *2001* in 1968. Media now permeates global culture and forms the foundation of everyday perception, being fundamental to the "construction of meaning," "identity," and "social consciousness" (Hoover and Emerich 2011: 2). Life is lived via media, so public and private identities are now deeply intertwined. As people invest more of themselves in the digital world, media platforms come to play a more influential role in shaping society (Hoover and Emerich 2011: 4). In the contemporary context, the internet offers unprecedented opportunities to self-publish and express oneself (anonymously or otherwise) in the public domain, and to be exposed to a constant deluge of opinions, images, and random thoughts, alongside computer-generated content, propaganda, and other forms of manipulative media. The ostensibly democratic nature of platforms that enable self-publishing has given voice to an increasing number of underground organizations and subcultures, allowing them to develop their networks and gain unprecedented influence. However, these alternative voices only remain accessible to the public at the behest of internet service providers, search engines, and communication platforms that may just as easily hide, demonetize, or censor this content in accordance with their business interests.

Consumer choices possessed of the greatest capacity to convey social meaning and identity gain influence in the market, thus increasing the enmeshment of social activism and consumer capitalism in complex ways. Institutional authority may have taken a particular guise in the 1960s, yet the locus of institutional power and mainstream thinking is constantly shifting. As Campbell astutely observed, nothing stays alternative for long as new heresies at the fringe are successively absorbed into the mainstream, prompting the rise of new alternative movements (2002: 15–16). Here it is worth noting that many of the countercultural movements of the 1960s have now become integrated into mainstream culture, academia, government legislation, and public activism. As such, these ideological positions no longer hold exclusive claim to the ethos of antiauthoritarianism, and new countercultural voices now condemn the "liberal orthodoxy" and the "liberal tyranny of political correctness" (Hannan 2018: 219). The deconstructive tendency that has accompanied the pursuit of unmediated truth continually takes on new targets, while in other areas rhetorical certitude has calcified, transforming the character of all points on the political spectrum.

While *Enter the Void* was released in 2009 and *Melancholia* in 2011, it is worth briefly considering trends in the media environment that have emerged subsequent to this time as they have a bearing on conceptions of truth and identity that are central to this study. Following Brexit and the election of President Trump in 2016, the traditional divide between left and right came to sit at center stage in public debate. For Jason Hannan, social media and politics now resemble "schoolyard" popularity contests where online bullying is used as a means of reinforcing group affiliation (Hannan 2018: 220–4). Hannan has expressed concerns that social media is altering "the entire affective structure of public discourse" so that "popularity now competes with logic and evidence as an arbiter of truth" (2018: 215 and 220). This means that people are not primarily interested in the truth of the matter; rather, they are engaging in social point-scoring and trading in status recognition. Along similar lines, Nick Rochlin argues that the term "fake news" (popularized by President Trump as a means of discrediting his media critics) has come to refer to any form of reporting "that is seen to attack a person's pre-existing beliefs" (Rochlin 2017: 386). Online debate and commentary on the value of particular news items therefore engages the individual's desire to defend their chosen identity and affiliations against the threat of competing voices. Observations such as these are linked to the claim that we have entered the age of "post-truth," where traditional forms of expertise seem to hold no traction with a public that privileges instinct, emotion, and social currency over all else (Rochlin 2017: 389). While the "post-truth" prognosis may be premature, reflections on the function of "truth" in current media culture point to changes in the role of language in particular contexts, where "factual" forms of information are repurposed as tools of social interaction.

As online environments have become more politicized, passing comments and social connections are now taken as evidence of a person's fundamental beliefs, without further investigation or contextualization. Here, vilifying buzzwords are frequently employed to encourage outraged readers to "click" and "re-share" with little consideration of the impact that this may have on the accused. Inflammatory headlines are the most effective in generating click-based income for content producers, and research has shown that people are willing to re-share articles without having read them (Rochlin 2017: 386–8). Personal choices and their online expression have become subject to an unprecedented degree of public judgment as the social realm has become more politicized. This has increased the need for individuals (and corporations) to present themselves in ways that are likely to be positively received by the public, thereby enhancing the self-conscious performative aspect of public and online interactions. Equally, as corporations, governments, and other large-scale organizations have become more aware of the power of social media, they have developed innovative means of provoking the individual to think, feel, react, purchase, or vote in a particular direction, as they go about their everyday interactions online. Together, these post-2016 trends reflect a mediatized culture that is intent on shaping the individual, where the private has become public, and there are fewer opportunities for the free and anonymous exploration of cyberspace. Spiritual seekership and religious identity construction still take place online, yet with greater self-consciousness, as online activity is tracked and recorded, and can have unpredictable future implications.

Literary studies academic and lecturer Christopher Schaberg reflects that before the election of President Trump in 2016, he "might have celebrated the idea of arriving at an age of 'post-truth'" as "it sounds like a fundamental goal" of his discipline (2018: 3). Schaberg describes this fundamental goal as instilling suspicion of "truth" as a "subjective vector of power" (Schaberg 2018: 3). As Michel E. Sawyer has argued, the echo-chambers that develop in a social media context and that "operate with their own internal truth criteria" add further weight to the idea that all "truths" are ideological constructions (Zackariasson 2018: 14). For Schaberg, the best way to orient oneself in an environment of competing power claims is to "linger in and learn from uncertainty, ambiguity, and paradox" (Schaberg 2018: 3). Seeking solace in "uncertainty, ambiguity, and paradox" is certainly a significant aspect of modern Western epistemology, particularly in the spiritualized film experiences of the art film tradition. However, the world of news and politics has not been the traditional realm of high affect and personal revelation. The uneasiness that has surrounded commentary on "post-truth" expresses the fear that willful ignorance has become widespread, not that truth claims are being questioned (Rochlin 2017: 386; Zackariasson 2018: 5).

Returning to the mid-2000s and early 2010s, the politicization of social and popular media was not as noticeable and had less impact on the individual. However, appeals to emotion, curiosity, and automatic psychological or bodily responses had nonetheless become essential communication tools for all media players, including mainstream and independent news outlets, advertisers, the entertainment industry, and purveyors of illicit content. As such, the communication and entertainment industries share the common challenge of trying to engage the attention of the individual by resorting to more dramatic forms of expression. Whether media players are appealing to the individual's fears, desires, tribal instincts, sense of justice, or physical sensations of disgust or arousal, the goal is to penetrate the oversaturated mind and to engage people by any means necessary. Intense responses are favored, even if they are negative, as research has shown that strong emotion is connected to belief and recollection (Konijn 2013: 10 and 16). However, it has become increasingly difficult to shock or deeply affect audiences, because they have seen it all before. As such, significant innovation is required of filmmakers who seek to cut through the din and challenge their audiences or who attempt to generate a genuine sense of spiritual awe. Filmmakers must overcome the defensive mechanisms of consciousness not only at the level of the senses but also at the level of social scripts. According to Tim Palmer, Noé's films do just this, as they succeed in producing a "raw, unmediated reaction" in the "age of the jaded spectator, the cynical cinephile" (2006: 22).

Subversive depictions of sex and violence have been a mainstay for filmmakers who wish to challenge their audiences, as they can easily arouse strong and visceral audience responses. However, continued exposure to media violence has been shown to produce a desensitizing effect, especially where violence is depicted in such a way that it provides a sense of pleasure, beauty, moral justification, achievement, or closure, and this is often the case in video games and mainstream film (Brockmyer 2013: 6). Desensitization entails reduced "responsiveness to an arousal-eliciting stimulus as a function of repeated exposure" (Krahé et al. 2011: 631) and is a normal psychological response; yet the type of desensitization associated with media exposure has caused concern as it distorts the reality of violence (Brockmyer 2013: 5). Excessive exposure to sexualized media such as pornography also has a desensitizing effect and like violent content can lead to more "permissive" behavior and accepting attitudes in real-life situations (Konijn 2013: 10–11). The impact of desensitization is certainly evident in Western entertainment and arts industries where the public has built up a tolerance (and a taste) for violent, sexualized, and provocative content; however, there is always a point where content goes too far.

In the late 1990s, Noé and a number of other French directors including François Ozon, Catherine Breillat, and Philippe Grandrieux produced films that crossed this line of social acceptability and were grouped together in James Quandt's scathing 2004 review under the banner of "The New French Extremity" (Quandt 2011: 18). This article sparked further investigations into extreme cinema, where connections were made with earlier directors; however, what is termed "the new extremism" by Tanya Horeck and Tina Kendall (2011) is most strongly linked in its "first wave" with the aforementioned French directors of the late 1990s and in its "second wave" with a number of films from directors including Noé, Breillat, Virginie Despentes, and Coralie Trinh Thi released between 2000 and 2002 (Hickin 2011: 123). All of Noé's feature films fit within the category of the new extremism, and now that the term has come to be more broadly applied, it also includes European directors like von Trier, particularly in relation to *The Idiots* (1998), *Dogville* (2003), and *Antichrist* (2009).

For Horeck and Kendall, the new extremism is defined by depictions of sex and violence where "brutal and visceral images appear designed deliberately to shock and provoke" (2011: 1). Such films are commonly met with "fainting, vomiting and mass walkouts" (Horeck and Kendall 2011: 1). Despite differences in style, the films of the new extremism engage the viewer on a "sensory," "affective," and "visceral" level, deconstructing cinematic conventions along with "moral certainties and established value systems," leaving the viewer to find ways to resolve and understand what they have witnessed (Horeck and Kendall 2011: 3, 5, and 8–9). This has led commentators like Nikolaj Lübecker and Michele Aaron to argue that extreme cinema is not simply depraved and attention seeking, as it offers a unique opportunity for personal ethical reflection that is not supplied by films that operate according to a preexisting moral code or that offer closure for the viewer (Horeck and Kendall 2011: 2, 8, and 14).

William Brown shares this view, arguing that the representations of extreme cinema are so overwhelming that they disallow pleasurable or voyeuristic engagement, instead triggering responses of disgust and revulsion (2013: 25–8 and 33). Physical and affective responses of this kind are important in bypassing the viewer's ability to maintain critical distance from what they are experiencing

(Brown 2013: 29). For Brown such experiences are "designed specifically to make us question our enjoyment of viewing horrific acts, particularly in a world where images of cruelty abound" (Brown 2013: 28). This involves confronting the "dark" and "monstrous" part of the self (and humanity), through identification with the horrific acts on screen (Brown 2013: 37–9). This notion of facing the darkness within and arriving at a more authentic ethical standpoint correlates with the initiatory revelation of spiritual truth that has been discussed in previous chapters. In the case of *Enter the Void* (and *Melancholia*), truth is something that is revealed to the individual through a personal encounter with extremity, and is not prescribed by the film through narrative meaning.

The features of the new extremism outlined above share some conceptual similarities with spiritually significant film, yet the latter need not be graphic, violent, or lascivious. It is notable that Kubrick, Noé, and von Trier are directors that have regularly crossed the line of public acceptability and challenged their audiences. The media-saturated environment of the early twenty-first century when *Enter the Void* and *Melancholia* were released seems to demand harsher techniques to penetrate the viewer's desensitized, "jaded," and "cynical" perceptual field to affect them deeply and directly (T. Palmer 2006: 22). Just as the new extremism has been considered by many to be a form of high art, filmmakers' ability to affect their audience in unexpected and invasive ways is often celebrated and deeply valued by viewers. This is particularly the case where the film's overall meaning is undetermined and ambiguous, as a set interpretation prescribed by the director comes to be viewed as an oppressive narrative to be resisted. When a director employs highly affective devices in the service of an ideology, the view is that they are producing propaganda, not art. As the value of self-determinism is so strong in alternative spirituality, it is crucial that art film directors present moments of ambiguity and paradox, as this provides the opportunity for pluralistic responses, even if audience reactions end up looking rather uniform.

Kubrick, Noé, and von Trier have earned their reputations as controversial directors not merely because of the content they present but due to the strong responses that they are able to elicit from audiences. Exploring social taboos and evoking feelings of horror, disgust, and existential unease in their broader oeuvres grants power to their representation of the sacred in *2001*, *Enter the Void*, and *Melancholia*. Interpreted in a religious sense, this is associated with Otto's *mysterium tremendum* and the awful majesty of God, yet more generally, it expresses the modern belief that truth lies in darkness. *Enter the Void* and *Melancholia* (like *2001*) affect the viewer through a strong appeal to abstract and dissociative sensations and do not contain the level of confronting violence and sexual content typical of the new extremism. It is true that *Enter the Void* contains explicit and prolonged sex scenes and instances of graphic violence, yet these aspects of the film are somehow absorbed into the texture of the film, distinguishing it from the harrowing cruelty of *Irreversible* (2002), for example. Denis Lim notes that *Enter the Void* is unusual in Noé's oeuvre, as it conveys "an almost warm and fuzzy New Age sensibility" (2010: n.p.). This passing comment picks up on the influence of alternative spirituality in the film's conception, and viewers have also noted connections with this religious position in its Buddhist, psychedelic, and psychological manifestations. Hinting at the vital importance of experiential communication employed in *Enter the Void*, Noé postulates that the film was controversial "not because of the story but because of the feelings or perceptions that come out of it" (Rose 2010: n.p.). The unique set of techniques Noé employs in *Enter the Void* that merge extremity with the psychedelic and generate strange and challenging feelings in the viewer will be explored in Chapter 7. At this stage, however, it is sufficient to note that this film is not merely characterized by shocking content.

Agency, Authority, and Epistemology

The religious changes outlined in Chapter 2 that form the broad cultural movement of alternative spirituality involve the rejection of institutional authorities and the impulse to seek alternatives to traditional or normative Western religious traditions. Adopting a mode of meaning-making characterized by seekership, the individual is never wholly or permanently satisfied with a single preconceived interpretation of life's Big Questions. As previously discussed, Campbell has identified important parallels between consumerism, romantic love, and spiritual seekership that reinforce each other in their common orientation toward a yet-to-be disclosed state of perfection and enjoyment (Campbell 1989: 69). Other commentators such as Michael York have used the term "spiritual supermarket" to allude to this connection between successive changes in religious orientation and the act of shopping (York 1999). It is also common for this behavior to be described as the assertion of the freely choosing self against the externally imposed dogmatism of a monotheistic religious tradition with exclusive claim to truth. While it is perfectly reasonable to say that from a subjective point of view the rejection of authority and the enactment of personal autonomy are central, Wood has identified an important omission in this argument.

Disputing the notion that the New Age should be characterized as "self-spirituality" where one places the authority once held by religion into their own hands, Wood argues that individuals defer to external religious authorities and spiritual forces when they engage in activities grouped together under the banner of "spirit possession" such as channeling, Reiki, crystal healing, and meditation and that this serves to endow their worldview with spiritual legitimacy (2007: 21). While each source of authority contributes to the person's spirituality, they remain "nonformative authorities" as none are granted exclusive and enduring power (Wood 2007: 14). Wood argues ultimately that "it is not the self that is authenticated and celebrated, but people's practices and involvement with diverse authorities that are affirmed" (2007: 113).

Wood's insights are essential in understanding the epistemological mode of the modern West, as the concept of the freely choosing self does not fully capture the element of Jamsean passivity accompanying moments of realization. The individual may see themselves as fully autonomous, yet it is in those moments when they are overwhelmed by a superior sensation of truth that they are most likely to reach a strong conclusion about ultimate meaning. As previously discussed, in film, overwhelming experiences of unmediated truth can serve the same function as the spiritual experiences that Wood describes, granting temporary agency to unknown forces. While such experiences have the capacity to open the mind to new reflections related to the narrative themes of the film, they might also be an eruption of subconscious ideas, perceived with new and iridescent clarity. The sense of confirmation that these revelations engender allows film experiences to legitimize the individual's (in part, preexisting) worldview.

Studying a network of spiritual groups in Nottinghamshire in the mid-1990s, Wood discovered a complex relationship with spiritual and social authority that cannot be explained simply in terms of the assertion of the self. Engaging in multiple spiritual groups and practices, Wood found that participants sought out experiences where they could be overwhelmed by external spiritual authorities and were happy to operate within hierarchically structured groups where spiritual authority was granted to its leaders (2007: 96). These spiritual leaders, however, did not adopt a dogmatic style and accepted a considerable variety of interpretive responses from the group (Wood 2007: 111), an attitude captured in Sutcliffe's observation of the pluralistic nature of modern spirituality where individuals express "whatever 'spiritual' values are deemed appropriate for the moment," adopting "a radical tolerance—upholding the rights of others to do the same" (2003: 11). While giving themselves over to experiences of spiritual possession, participants nonetheless determined their own subsequent explanations, bearing a range of influences, so that the meanings supplied by spiritual leaders were regularly "supplanted or ignored" (Wood 2007: 89). Wood rightly points out that deferral to authority is present, but there is a sense of personal autonomy maintained in the desire for unmediated (and unaffiliated) experiences of the spiritual, as one of Wood's interviewees noted, the spiritual community was not totally necessary because he had a "direct relationship with God" (2007: 95).

In the assertion of spiritual self-determinism, an overemphasis on individual authority can make it seem as if the ideas, preferences, and meanings ascribed at the subjective level are sui generis and not the product of sociocultural conditioning and biological influences. In Wood's exploration of nonformative authority, he notes that this tendency is not limited to spiritual networks but is characteristic of neoliberal societies in general. The call for continual improvement, self-development, and discovery works hand in hand with the "proliferation of authority and expertise" linked to "market differentiation" (Wood 2007: 81). Individualism does not result in the triumph of "self-authority" but rather the camouflaged propagation of authorities that interact with the individual in complex ways (Wood 2007: 81). However, Wood is not simply arguing that external authorities dominate the self (thus inverting the conception of the New Age that he critiques); rather, he suggests dispensing with this power dichotomy in recognition of the ways in which "social authorities are woven into the very fabric of subjectivity such that the most private, intimate thoughts and actions are inextricably and inseparably bound up with social structures" (2007: 67).

When considering the authority of the self it is also important to remember that in the context of alternative spirituality, the self is understood as a collection of relational parts that are somewhat independent of each other (Wood 2007: 88). This is best exemplified in the concept of the Higher Self but also in the sense that seemingly external spiritual forces can act upon the self, but be subsequently understood as aspects of the self (Wood 2007: 98). The category of external authority, where it is granted temporary agency, is equally contingent, as authorities must be conceived of as alternative rather than hegemonic in order to be considered legitimate. This distinction is linked to the fact that spontaneous or voluntary experiences are accepted as insights, while socially enforced experiences are deemed to be empty of meaning. While individuals value experiences where their sense of personal agency has been temporarily displaced, agency is subjectively reasserted in the subsequent interpretation of meaning or in the act of witnessing true mystery. Here, the contributing influences of society, nature, and culture are not acknowledged, thereby sustaining the illusion of total independence of will and mastery of external influences.

While Campbell's cultic milieu referred to the emergence of new religious movements and the temporary affiliation that that they attract, the deep parallel between this behavior and political affiliation over the last half-century is the centrality of individualism. Self-development is linked to the modern desire to throw off the constraints of social authorities and pursue one's own destiny, becoming a fully realized person of intrinsic uniqueness. Here, subjectively perceived self-determinism and the deferral to nonformative authorities work hand in hand. People are rarely aware of the influences that shape their personal views, yet the implicit mistrust in modern culture ensures that once a manipulative influence is identified, it can be rejected in favor of a new truth. Nothing is sacred in this process as all things can eventually be revealed as falsehoods. In the modern West, those things that speak first to the senses and that remain pure in their abstraction are the only phenomena that can be granted the status of the sacred. These are experiences that distort time and effect memory, displacing inner dialogue and overwhelming personal agency. In a secular culture, they remain recognizably religious in quality, and it is their ineffable nature that frees them from their religious context and the accusations of corruption that can be leveled at any religious tradition.

The Initiation of a Director

Enter the Void tells the story of Oscar and his sister Linda, whose parents died in a car crash when they were young children. The pair promise to stay together "no matter what," but are separated and placed with different foster families. In his twenties, Oscar is living in Tokyo earning money as a small-time drug dealer. He saves enough to fly his sister to Japan and she begins working there as a pole dancer. Oscar is shot dead early in the film and enters a liminal state based upon the travels of the soul in the *Tibetan Book of the Dead*. From a purely thematic point of view, *Enter the Void* includes references to a religious text and the majority of the film takes place from Oscar's perspective in his postmortem state. On their own, however, these religious references do not necessarily provoke a spiritual response from the audience.

The film itself begins in Oscar's room where the audience is positioned within Oscar's viewpoint, and we can hear his thoughts and see him blink. Oscar smokes some dimethyltryptamine (DMT) and the viewer shares Oscar's experience of gradual intoxication as he repeatedly closes his eyes and reopens them to a blurrier vision of the room around him. Finally, Oscar slips into a vision state punctuated by moments of dim self-consciousness as he descends into a realm of pulsating patterns and fuzzy noise that lasts several minutes. Psychedelic patterns radiate in the geometric structures of nature that morph and shudder, taking on the form of flowers, sea anemones, and the inner body. Eventually he is startled into semiconsciousness by the sound of his mobile phone. Oscar's friend Victor asks to meet him at a local club called "The Void" to undertake a drug deal. When Oscar arrives, the police rush in and Victor says that he is "sorry." In his highly disoriented state, Oscar flees to a toilet cubicle and is shot in the heart through the wooden door. The audience experience Oscar's death from his own perspective where he lies in the fetal position on the floor of a filthy squat toilet. The vocalization of thought in Oscar's mind becomes softer and further away until it is completely absorbed by white noise. Eventually, he/the audience begin to float toward the throbbing fluorescent light on the ceiling and into the psychedelic floating world that comprises the remaining hours of the film.

"Oscar," who has become a depersonalized yet vaguely directional perspective point, follows the abstract pulses of the city, being drawn toward his sister, to aspects of the life he left behind and off again. Throughout this journey, we discover through flashback that what Oscar is experiencing resembles the journey of the soul that his friend Alex described to him from the *Tibetan Book of the Dead*. Linda's life is a mess and the details of her daily existence as a stripper are revealed, along with the betrayals that contributed to the botched drug deal that claimed Oscar's life. The childhood scene of Oscar and Linda's parent's fatal car crash is replayed repeatedly throughout the film along with the whispered promise that the siblings would never leave each other. The scenes that Oscar/the audience explore in the film include events from the past and events following Oscar's death. Many of these are deeply disturbing and also very explicit. One of these is a graphic abortion scene where Linda terminates an unwanted pregnancy.

Once the police begin to investigate the drug ring that Oscar was connected to, his friend Alex is forced to go into hiding. Toward the end of the film Alex and Linda come together after a period of conflict and enter one of Tokyo's Love Hotels. Oscar's awareness follows the highly abstract scene where sexual energy and emanations from countless people are depicted as glowing light. Alex and Linda make love in one of the rooms and Oscar/the audience follows the glowing light from the perspective of Alex's sperm to Linda's ovum. This perspective then evolves into that of a newborn baby who experiences the trauma of that first cut to the umbilical cord when he is taken away from his mother's breast. The child is named Oscar and the blurred focus of this scene makes the identity of the mother ambiguous. Many viewers assume the mother to be Linda, with Oscar reincarnated as her son. This sentimental and reassuring ending is in keeping with the comforting scenes where brother and sister had promised to stay together for all time. Noé, however, clarifies that the woman is Oscar's mother and that he is more likely to be re-experiencing his own birth (Lambie 2010: n.p.). In interviews, Noé suggests that Oscar could be caught in a perceptual loop, reliving the trauma of his own birth (Lambie 2010: n.p.). However, Noé encourages viewers to deduce that the mother could be Linda, and audience responses on *IMDb* demonstrate that this is the most common assumption.

Based on this synopsis, it would already be apparent that *Enter the Void* depicts a very different type of story to *2001*. The focus is not on the vast prehistory and future potential of the species but on a family drama that opens the door to postmortem states of being and challenging reflections on human bonds through the processes of reproduction. The two films are also very different in terms of production scale and target audience. *2001* tapped into the zeitgeist of an era, is consistently listed among the greatest films of all time, and is completely devoid of explicit content. By comparison, *Enter the Void* is a confronting film whose appeal is limited to consumers of art film. The primary means through which *Enter the Void* and *2001* are connected is through their use of techniques designed to affect the viewer on a deep level, pushing them to cross into an altered state of perception that is synonymous with religious experience.

Noé compares his role as a director to that of a magician who uses "every trick" to elicit a strong response (Barney 2014: n.p.) and in the case of *Enter the Void*, he specifically aims to "possess" the mind of the viewer (Mottram 2010: n.p.). A large portion of the sixteen-million dollar budget was dedicated to postproduction special effects created by renowned special effects artists at BUF Compagnie with company founder Pierre Buffin working on the film as co-producer (Harris 2010: n.p.; *The Numbers* 2017: n.p.; Failes 2010: n.p.). Noé describes audience responses to *Enter the Void*, where "people come down shaking from the screening room, and say 'what a trip!' and it takes them five minutes or so before they say anything else!" (Lambie 2010: n.p.). With responses like this, Noé is very conscious of the power a director can wield, and has gone so far as to experiment with mass hypnotism via a television broadcast aired to the French public early on New Year's Day in 1995 (Lim 2010: n.p.).

Such techniques draw attention to the impact of early avant-garde filmmakers like Luis Buñuel and Kenneth Anger on Noé's work, and the director explicitly cites Buñuel's *Un Chien Andalou* (1929) and Anger's *Inauguration of the Pleasure Dome* (1954) as foundational influences (Barney 2014: n.p.; Stephenson 2010: n.p.). Buñuel saw cinema as a tool to generate hypnotic states of "fascination" in his audience (1983: 69), while Anger, who was a Thelema practitioner, felt that filmmaking was akin to "casting a spell" (Rowe 2002: 15). These filmmakers, along with others from the American avant-garde, including Maya Deren and Curtis Harrington, undoubtedly pioneered many of the techniques and conceptions of cinema detailed in *Spiritual Sensations*. Their films drew heavily upon religious ritual, esotericism, the unconscious, dream states, and subjective perception, paving the way for both directors and spiritual seekers of the 1960s (Sitney 2002: 4–11, 17, 33–4, 95–6, 101, 109, and 226). While deeply relevant, their work is beyond the scope of this present study, as are a vast number of other filmmakers whose work reveals the hallmarks of religious experience. As *Spiritual Sensations* identifies the centrality of mystical experience in the modern West and the unique role that film can play in generating moments of personal revelation, it is to be expected that this epistemological phenomenon will be found in a variety of films. A point of difference between the American avant-garde and the films discussed here is the comparative fringe status of their experimental work along with the overt religiosity of their filmmaking practice. By contrast, the spiritual manifests as a concealed influence in the work of Kubrick, Noé, and von Trier, and its presence in their films is holy in its abstraction and divorce from overt religious correlations. As such, Noé makes no profound claims about his filmmaking and admits no religious affiliations.

When he was about six years old, Noé saw *2001* at the cinema, and the experience was life changing, producing a feeling he could only describe as "cinematic ecstasy" (Barney 2014: n.p.). Speaking of this moment, he says, "I felt like I was on drugs. I was overwhelmed. I was mind-possessed" (Mottram 2010: section 12). *2001* made him want to "possess" the minds of others through cinema, and was instrumental in his deciding his career path, as a film director (Mottram 2010: section 12). Noé has obsessively collected *2001* paraphernalia over the years, and has referenced Kubrick's film in *Irreversible* and *Love* (2015) in addition to *Enter the Void* (Chodorov and Szaniawski 2018: n.p.). Noé mentions that he has watched *2001* "more than any other [film] in my life," up to "60 times," but does not connect with Kubrick's oeuvre overall (*Sight & Sound* 2012: n.p.; Chodorov and Szaniawski 2018: n.p.). Visually, *Enter the Void* embraces the psychedelic imagery of *2001* through the use of a highly saturated palette where scenes pulse and glow with a synthetic iridescence associated with Japanese cities like Tokyo. The majority of the film takes place at night creating a sense of light emerging from darkness, a mysterious quality epitomizing the "Stargate" sequence from Kubrick's *2001*. *Enter the Void* is Noé's "acid religious movie" (Lambie 2010: n.p.), and viewers discuss the similarities between this film and *2001* in terms of technique, style, cosmic themes, and overall feel (Joseph Sylvers, October 6, 2010, user review of *Enter the Void*; Atavisten, February 6, 2011, user review of *Enter the Void*; gizmomogwai, April 21, 2014, user review of *Enter the Void*).

Noé's experience of *2001* exhibits numerous hallmarks of mystical experience, including ecstasy, ineffability, passivity, and feelings of otherness. Given that Noé intends for *Enter the Void* to have the same effect on his audience, it is reasonable to say that one of the director's primary goals is to engender Jamsean passivity. As Plate has argued, film has the capacity to generate direct experiences where it is the "body that believes" (2008: 16 and 66). As was the case with *2001*, viewers make a point of saying that *Enter the Void* is an "experience" above all else (KineticSeoul, March 4, 2011, user review of *Enter the Void*; Roman James Hoffman, July 27, 2014, user review of *Enter the Void*; ashleym9000, October 1, 2011, user review of *Enter the Void*). This designation sets the film apart as something different to ordinary cinema, requiring alternative modes of viewing.

Despite the director's use of the term "religious" above, Noé is generally hesitant to admit that his films hold religious significance, due to his atheist upbringing (*Trinity-X* 2016: n.p.), and his critical view of religious traditions like Catholicism and Buddhism that sell people a "lie" about life after death and the continuation of the soul (Lambie 2010: n.p.). He makes it clear that he does not want to promote belief in any religion and advises people to live in the moment because there is no such thing as divine intervention (Stephenson 2010: n.p.). However, he does acknowledge that religious belief is a part of the human condition, a "collective dream" that has psychological reality for people and should therefore be represented faithfully in film (Erickson 2010: n.p.; Lambie 2010: n.p.). Noé's approach to religious concepts is pragmatic, focusing on the psychological function and usefulness of belief instead of treating religious concepts as truth propositions (*Trinity-X* 2016: n.p.). Like Kubrick, Noé balances his rejection of institutional religion with alternate forms of existential inquiry. His interest in psychological explanations for religious belief extends to his research into the human brain and his fascination with the idea that the mind is comprised of "three brains"—the reptilian, mammalian, and neocortex—that create a tension between opposing urges (Ebiri 2010: n.p.).

Noé recalls that when he was an adolescent he started smoking marijuana, pondering death and postmortem experience, taking particular interest in reincarnation and Raymond Moody's *Life after Life* (1975) (*Trinity-X* 2016: n.p.). The topic of astral projection was also of interest to him (Lambie 2010: n.p.). Growing up, Noé admired hippie culture and psychologist Timothy Leary's "psychedelic voyages" that were designed to achieve insight into the nature of reality with the assistance of LSD (*Trinity-X* 2016: n.p.). An academically polarizing and antiauthoritarian figure (Moreno 2016: 113), Leary had a profound impact on spiritual seekers of the 1960s and 1970s by offering them a radical and direct path to spiritual revelation. As Versluis explains, Leary's experiments fit into a wider spiritual tradition of what he calls "immediatism" where unmediated experiences of the divine are privileged (2014: 110). For Leary, institutional Christianity acted like a straightjacket, limiting individuals to "one God, one religion, one reality," whereas entheogens like LSD could instantly "open the mind to multiple realities [and] inevitably lead to a polytheistic view of the universe." As Leary goes on to say, "We sensed that the time for a new humanist religion based on intelligent good-natured pluralism and scientific paganism had arrived" (Versluis 2014: 110). The term "entheogens" is defined as "substances that generate god within," "(from *en* [inward] *theos* [god] *gen* [generation])" (Versluis 2014: 110). The notable Buddhist influence on Leary's religious views is evident in *The Psychedelic Experience: A Manual Based on the Tibetan Book of the Dead* (1965), a spiritual manual coauthored with Richard Alpert and Ralph Metzner that guides the individual through the various stages of psychedelic experience to self-realization (Versluis 2014: 115). It is highly likely that Noé modeled his vision of *Enter the Void* on this text, which shares the film's use of the *Tibetan Book of the Dead* as its thematic framework.

Psychedelic explorations into subjective experience embody the ethos of seekership at the heart of alternative spirituality where various tools are employed with the overarching goal of revealing a hidden truth. This distinction clarifies why Noé wishes to avoid being associated with a Buddhist tradition that he does not have any particular connection with, because he is more likely to have discovered the *Tibetan Book of the Dead* in the context of the alternative exploration of consciousness. Like *2001*, *Enter the Void* is more aligned with Buddhist concepts than Christian ones, yet this does not necessarily mean that these are "Buddhist films." *Enter the Void* viewer comments do make reference to Buddhism; however, many of these are simply related to the film's overt themes (HumanoidOfFlesh, January 15, 2011, user review of *Enter the Void*; Chris Blachewicz, March 10, 2011, user review of *Enter the Void*; dallasryan, March

1, 2012, user review of *Enter the Void*). As Stefan Schmidt points out, Eastern religions have a long history of the subjective and experiential exploration of consciousness through practices like meditation (2014: 2). This aspect of Eastern religiosity is attractive to modern Western religious sensibilities and is pertinent to films like *2001* and *Enter the Void* that take the viewer on experiential quests where one is invited to know by feeling.

Noé's interest in altered states of perception extends to his personal experiments with psychoactive drugs that have traditionally been used as tools to access hidden spiritual knowledge. In these experiments, one gives oneself over to the experience, allowing the mind to follow whatever thoughts and sensations arise in an open and nonanalytical manner. The world of *Enter the Void* appears to operate in a similar fashion, as the point-of-view perspective is drawn this way and that. Noé's personal experiences of altered states of perception involve a spiritual state of mind that he seeks to replicate in his audience, yet he is not interested in convincing his audience of religious ideas. As has been discussed in previous chapters, spiritual knowledge as perceived experientially by the individual is anti-institutional and antiauthoritarian in nature. Despite the absence of overt religious references in *2001*, Kubrick's comments about the goal and purpose of the film made it clear that while an institutional form of religion was rejected, a perennial quest for spiritual knowledge was embraced (Kloman 1968: n.p.). Noé's interest in psychedelic dissociative states and those that may follow death (or extend beyond normal embodied experience) have clearly inspired the design of *Enter the Void*. Such liminal states are commonly associated with religious experience or spiritual reality as they begin to slip out of normative modes of being and perceiving.

Conclusion

The power of film to generate perceptions of spiritual significance lies in the capacity to innovate as the features of religious experience—ineffability, noetic quality, transiency, and passivity—can only be experienced where the viewer is taken beyond the familiar structures of conventional film. The evolution of media and communication networks in the early twenty-first century have had a notable impact on the social function of truth, and have amplified processes of identity construction via consumer choice and performances of affiliation. While aspects of religious identity may be formed through these processes, the increasingly self-conscious and argumentative character of online interaction encourages continual dialogic engagement, ensuring that moments of mystical revelation are sought elsewhere.

As the public craves reality and the exposure of all illusions, the entertainment industry has responded with gruesome violence, grotesque representations of human nature, and believable sex scenes. Ever available pornography has followed suit, exposing the curious and the addicted to anything they can imagine, along with things that they could not. Forming a new baseline, entertainment media and pornography influence art film by encouraging directors to seek new extremes. However, it is not simply a matter of presenting the most disturbing content possible; for film to function as art, the putative meaning of extreme content must be transformed, thereby awakening a new sense in the viewer. Wood's investigation of spirit possession in this context demonstrates that temporary (freely chosen or spontaneous) experiences where personal agency is overwhelmed by a superior force are specifically sought out and are used to legitimize thought patterns not yet endowed with the weight of truth. As an epistemological pattern, experiences that initiate the individual into noetic understanding are the defining feature of alternative spirituality, functioning as a sacred space where the individual communes with the essential in a world of relativity. The ineffable nature of this encounter protects both the logic of relativity and the incongruousness of the posture of passivity.

7

Enter the Void

Trauma, Psychedelics, and the Lightning-Bolt Path

Bearing the hallmarks of ineffability, noesis, transiency, and passivity, *IMDb* viewer experiences of *Enter the Void* are generated by a set of techniques reminiscent of Kubrick's directorial approach in *2001* and Schrader's transcendental style, operating at a new level of intensity. Like Kubrick, Noé seeks to affect the viewer's perceptual state, and in this sense, *Enter the Void* shares *2001*'s appeal to the viewer's "subconscious" and "religious" impulses (Gelmis 1969: n.p.). Noé diminishes focus on narrative, maintaining attention through complex visual effects and sound techniques. Reducing the presence of verbal content in *Enter the Void*, Noé seeks to replicate the experience of the dreaming mind, encouraging the viewer to attain a nondiscursive state.

Employing the affective power of extreme cinema with the overarching goal of generating a psychedelic and spiritualized film experience, Noé channels the sexual in such a way that it transmutes arousal into an entirely abstracted form. Reflecting the invasive nature of contemporary media culture, Noé's techniques leave no room for the viewer to escape the intensity of film, and this lack of respite is harnessed as a tool for revelation.

Sex, Stasis, and the Spiritual

Returning to Noé's formative experience with *2001*, he remembers that this was the time when his mother "finally explained what a fetus was and how I came into the world" (*Sight & Sound* 2012: n.p.). Speaking about this moment at the fifty-year anniversary of *2001*'s release, Noé told his interviewers, "In one go, I got to realize what a psychedelic trip could be, where life came from and how it was conceived. The origin of life. I was so fascinated" (Chodorov and Szaniawski 2018: n.p.). This initial association between the Starchild and Noé's initiation into the mysteries of human reproduction (and his own existence as a living being) is quite significant. Noé's depiction of sex, procreation, and infancy in *Enter the Void* appears to involve the search for primal origins. Throughout the film, Noé employs juxtaposition to create correspondences between sexuality and the familial bonds of childhood. In a memory of his childhood, Oscar shares a bath with his mother and baby sister Linda. Oscar is hidden in shadow and the camera is positioned behind his head. Expressing the simple intimacy of this moment, each of their gazes is directed inward, toward each other. In another scene, a younger Oscar reclines on a bed, with his head shown from behind, in shadow, as he watches a childhood version of Linda asleep on the other bed with her teddy bear. The angle of the bed is sloped in a disorienting manner. Mirroring the previous shot, brother and sister are depicted in the same positions as adults, with Linda sleeping topless in a pair of cotton underpants, hugging her teddy bear. The continuity of the child's perspective lingers with the obvious sexual impropriety of the latter scene, conveying a complex vulnerability.

In *Enter the Void*, Noé presents his audience with an unconventional and multifaceted view of sex. The film features scenes from Oscar's point of view that include childhood visions of his parents having sex, the vision of his mother's breast as a newborn baby, seemingly incestuous invasions of privacy as Oscar's point-of-view moves into the perspective of two of Linda's lovers during sex, and sexual transgression in Oscar's secret affair with his friend Victor's mother. While Oscar's relationship with Linda is platonic, his sister is often semi-clothed or stripping in front of him. The "Love Hotel" sequence then depicts countless bodies in varied forms of sexual engagement. Infancy is depicted in a primal yet nurturing sense in the final scenes of the film in stark contrast to Linda's graphic abortion scene earlier on. In short, sex is depicted as being exploitative, meaningless, desirable, curious, loving, familial, universal, and the source of life. Demonstrating the full dramatic potential of sex, Noé's other films have also broken boundaries in this area. *Irreversible* features an arduous nine-minute rape scene while *Love* is an uncensored depiction of sex in the context of a loving yet volatile romantic relationship.

Hollywood cinema rarely presents anything challenging in this area, but rather varies the level of explicitness along a predictable scale. As all sex scenes are viewed through the point of view of Oscar's disembodied spirit, the camera is strangely involved in the scene, revealing Oscar's abstracted responses through special effects such as flickers, color changes, and pulsating light effects. It is important to note, however, that Oscar/the audience observes not with the interested gaze of a person, but with the markedly dissociated perception of the spirit. Like dream or drug-induced perception, Oscar's point-of-view is drawn equally to random objects and lights as to the primary source of action, whether this is in a sex scene or a conversation between characters. For example, Oscar watches Victor's mother crying in distress, regretting the consequences of their affair, but the light of the stove catches his awareness and he becomes absorbed by the all-consuming vibrancy of light. This circular image of the iridescent gas flame shudders and blurs like Oscar's previous psychedelic visions, as he hovers above it, and the camera moves as if about to dive toward the flame.

Despite the pornographic appearance of certain scenes, the camera does not behave in a desiring manner, thus transforming the affect of such imagery. OgierdeBeauseant (February 17, 2011, user review of *Enter the Void*) and Tom Clift (January 13, 2011, user review of *Enter the Void*) refer to the subdued lighting and ghostly quality that Noé employs to generate a sense of detachment to what is happening on screen. Further to this, mwbartko describes the depiction of sex in *Enter the Void* as "surprisingly graphic (yet not at all stimulating) pornography" (December 7, 2010, user review of *Enter the Void*). These comments are in line with Brown's observation that extreme cinematic styles may include "potentially pornographic content" but it is depicted in an "incongruous 'art house' style" that prevents desire or enjoyment (2013: 33). The removal of conventional cinematic eroticism is also captured in Benjamin Bergery's description of the "luminous mating couples" in the "Love Hotel" sequence. This comment conveys an almost scientific distance where people act instinctually and without self-consciousness, like animals in a nature documentary (2010: 10 and 18). Noé's unconventional use of sexual content is one of several techniques that assist in developing a dissociative state of mind. For those who can reach the mystical state that *Enter the Void* is equipped to induce, this extended contemplation of sex can prompt feelings of primal knowledge akin to Noé's personal experience of the Starchild.

In the Love Hotel, Oscar's point of view floats through the rooms where patrons are freely indulging their sexual desires. There is something grotesque in this vision of countless bodies moving in one long meandering take. However, these images have been abstracted in such a way that the bodies are bathed in a pink glow, natural sound has been swallowed by a thick ambient haze, and beautiful golden light blooms and flows from each site of sexual stimulation. This gives the base act of sex a spiritual dimension, where the apparent orgy taking place is recast as a part of some greater process that individuals instinctively take part in, even though they do not understand the significance of their acts. The spiritual tone of this sequence is evident in Joseph Sylvers's comment that in the scene "sex makes everyone glow like angels" (October 6, 2010, user review of

Enter the Void). Despite this observation, the scene is nonetheless arduous and disturbing.

Noé's depiction of sex in *Enter the Void* is reminiscent of tantric practice where the practitioner utilizes transgressive experiences in order to achieve rapid spiritual development via the "lightning-bolt path." Associated with Tibetan Buddhism and other Eastern religious schools, tantra aims to enable enlightenment within the practitioner's lifetime through the direct confrontation of desire. As Hugh B. Urban explains, tantric teachings gained popularity in the 1970s "at the height of the countercultural revolution's search for alternative realities through drugs, Eastern mysticism, and other intense psychic or physical experiences" (2012: 231). In the translation of tantric practices to the West, Urban observes a shift from "Tantra conceived as *dangerous power and secrecy* to Tantra *conceived as healthy pleasure and openness*" (2012: 205). Calling on the esoteric *Tibetan Book of the Dead* as a symbolic guide for the film, Noé restores some of tantra's former meaning. As desire and attachment to dualistic categories—including the distinction between right and wrong—stand as an obstacle to enlightenment (Reed 2004: 263), practitioners deliberately seek out forms of illicit activity including "sex, violence, lying and stealing," "meat eating, and liquor drinking" (Jackson 2004: 871) and in particular schools, this involves ritualized group sex and drug use (Davidson and Orzech 2004: 820). By deliberately violating social taboos and conventions, the practitioner is able to transcend dualistic thinking (Ohnuma 2004: 306). Ultimately, desire is used with the intention of attaining "desirelessness" (Priestley 2004: 685). As the polarizing countercultural guru Rajneesh Osho (1931–90) taught, if sex were approached meditatively it would facilitate spiritual transformation to a higher state of being where sex itself would "become irrelevant, meaningless. You have grown beyond it. It makes no sense to you now" (Shay and Bogdan 2014: 65). In *Enter the Void*, Noé engages the viewer in an extended contemplation of sex to the point where conventional perceptive responses are exhausted and radically transformed. Viewers do not refer to the arousing qualities of the "Love Hotel" sequence, and come away from the film's final scene unable to think or feel in a normal manner. If anything, viewers' immediate reactions to the film tend to be existential, including reflections on consciousness and reality (Hector Asensio, June 25, 2015, user review of *Enter the Void*), philosophy and morality (Roman James Hoffman, July 27, 2014, user review of *Enter the Void*), ontology (awmurshedkar, June 11, 2012, user review of *Enter the Void*), metaphysics, and life and death (Ben Hinman, January 19, 2015, user review of *Enter the Void*).

The special effects used in *Enter the Void* are of a psychedelic intensity, having a notable dissociative effect on viewers. *Enter the Void* adopts a psychedelic palette and disorienting framing techniques, such as those used in images of the neon nightlife of Tokyo, where the camera swoops and rears in tilted visions of light. However, the strange manner in which Oscar's point-of-view/the audience perceive the world also conveys something of the Buddhist concept of dependent co-arising in the representation of reality, identity, and perception (Macy 1979: 38). This concept finds expression in *Enter the Void* through the deconstruction of Oscar's identity. In meditative traditions, practitioners are encouraged to let go of any sense of permanent identity in the realization of dependent co-arising. *Enter the Void* conveys this in two ways. First, Oscar revisits the situations and relationships of his life in a way that is emotionally disconnected from their outcome and secondly, Noé employs techniques of abstraction, sensory intensification, and meandering camerawork to transform reality into a realm of abstract stimuli. To provide an analogy for this transformation, it is similar to a lesson in drawing where one ceases to see the features of a face and instead sees the shapes of light and shade that comprise the form. The sense of dissociation inherent in Oscar's point of view reflects his perception of self. In the world of the film, life is depicted as a flow of sensations, lights, and sounds where the aimless consciousness is drawn blindly toward pulsing light. Noé creates visual associations between instinct, desire, attachment, and procreation through the camera's fascination with luminescence. *Enter the Void* demonstrates the pull of emotional attachment as Oscar's soul is drawn in and out of memories, and to those he knew in life. Together, sensation and desire lead consciousness in endless cycles through samsara. In Buddhism, samsara refers to the aimless cycles of life, death, and rebirth experienced by those who have not attained enlightenment (Harvey 2013: 32–46). As Elsa HOnkemup notes, Noé transforms sex from a meaningful, desiring, or consequential act into a "dull sensation" that the individual engages in just as they would float toward a bright light (May 26, 2011, user review of *Enter the Void*). As events move from one tragic situation to the next, this independent life of light carries on its own secret purpose, remaining unwavering and indifferent to humanity as it guides them on. This strange primal force could be compared with Kubrick's monolith in the sense that it draws humanity in with curiosity but does not ask first before it changes them irreversibly. In von Trier's *Melancholia*, the forces of nature operate with a similar disregard for human intention or welfare. The fact that all three films suggest a natural order beyond human interests is linked to their common evocation of the sacred as an intense inexplicable sensation.

During the "Love Hotel" sequence, Oscar's vision eventually moves from a big-picture perspective to focus on Linda and Alex. Oscar moves into Alex's perspective as he makes love to Linda. To continue the comparison between *2001* and *Enter the Void*, the "Stargate" sequence that has been interpreted by some commentators as a symbolic creation myth (Webster 2010: 53) is replicated in Oscar's point-of-view journey into the pulsing light of their genitals, along the path of Alex's sperm toward Linda's ovum, that appears like a red planet with cosmic storms shifting around it. The conception scene has prompted mixed responses from viewers. Charlene Lydon found herself vacillating between shock and hilarity, saying that it is "difficult sometimes to know whether to laugh or be shocked." This viewer elaborates, "For every roll of the eyes, there is a gasp of astonishment in terms of the intensity of the cinematic experience" (Charlene Lydon, September 14, 2010, user review of *Enter the Void*). Noé says that he did not intend for this scene to be funny and explains this audience response as a "nervous reaction" (Adams 2010: n.p.). Rather, the director wanted to stir the audience's mythological senses, saying "if you saw that in your own dreams, you would not laugh" (Adams 2010: n.p.). The techniques that Noé uses overall in *Enter the Void* are designed to generate a suggestive mental state that resembles the dreaming mind. According to Noé, *2001* achieves this connection with the "inner world" and the "unconscious life" that we live in our sleep (Chodorov and Szaniawski 2018: n.p.). For viewers that can become immersed in this state, the film has the type of mythological power that Noé intended, but some audience members only achieve partial immersion.

Viewers like tieman64 have observed similarities between concluding scenes of *2001* and *Enter the Void* that both involve the motif of birth (February 19, 2011, user review of *Enter the Void*). In the final scenes of *2001*, the planets align, strange sounds begin, and the perspective of Bowman/the audience enters a prolonged psychedelic sequence entering the Stargate. While the forms that emerge from the darkness are entirely abstract, they appear to recall the birth of the universe. Bowman then progressively ages, before the monolith casts its gaze upon him for the last time, and he becomes the Starchild. At this point, the softly glowing fetus looks into the eyes of the audience, causing many viewers to be overcome with emotion (anonymous, March 31, 1999, user review of *2001*). The concluding sequence of *Enter the Void* commences as Oscar/the audience follows Alex and Linda into the Love Hotel. Here, creation is depicted in the physical acts of sex, conception, and birth. However, unlike Kubrick's Starchild who looks toward the audience, the newborn of *Enter the Void* is never physically depicted. Rather, the audience follows the point-of-view through birth and into life, beholding the face of the mother.

During the conception scene, the point-of-view perspective following the path of Alex's sperm is enveloped in the naturalistic tones of the inner body. Rather than being anatomical, this sequence takes on a surreal blur where life-giving elements glow brighter. Visual distortion is so thick that it becomes impossible to determine forms. Sound has dropped away, and now that we have entered the consciousness of the unborn child, the screen goes black for around a minute, offering a soothing reprieve from sensory input. The baby perceives a bright, blurred, and muffled world, and the barely distinguishable face of his mother. He moves toward the breast, and as he begins to nurse, the umbilical cord is cut. The shock of separation is felt in his distressed cries as he is taken to the weighing station. The film ends abruptly with the words "THE VOID" emblazoned across the screen, closing the phrase from the film's beginning: "ENTER." This technique revives feelings of irresolution that may have dissipated during the birth scene. Whether the audience has been comforted by the idea that Oscar was reincarnated or that he is reliving his first moments of life with his mother, the intrusion of these words undercuts feelings of closure and encourages the viewer to seek symbolic correspondences.

While the birth scene conveys emotional rawness, it could be fairly described as "warm and fuzzy" compared to the rest of the film (Lim 2010: n.p.). After the traumatic experience that the viewer has lived through watching *Enter the Void*, this final scene of innocence and protection is like a soothing balm after hours of torture. This is the moment of stasis, which is most certainly a call for emotion. In an initiatory context, this method of emotional contrast creates a sense of cognitive certainty and commitment. Trauma is used to stimulate great anxiety, which is then substituted with comfort and safety, thus prompting the conversion of fear into powerful elation (Whitehouse 1996: 709–12). Here Noé moves into a realm of hazy vision, muted sound, and into absence, evoked through dark silence. This technique conveys the innocence of infancy through the evocation of perceptual simplicity, of a state before thought, image, and sound. Perhaps recalling Noé's initiatory insight into the nature of birth in the aftermath of cinematic "possession" (Mottram 2010: section 12), the noetic quality of this scene comes as an overflow of feeling. Chapter 5 highlighted the role of trauma and sensory overload in the development of highly affective cinematic experiences that haunt the mind long after the event. Noé exploits the power of trauma to a higher degree than Kubrick, to the point that the experience becomes too horrific or sickening for some viewers to maintain a spiritual reading of the film. However, audience responses still adhere to the main categories of mystical experience, involving ineffability, noesis, transiency, passivity, and an appeal to alternate states of consciousness.

The structure of *Enter the Void* follows the shape of Schrader's movement from the everyday, through disparity, and into stasis. However, Noé inverts the quality of the everyday through a fullness of sound, color, and stimulation. Like the sparseness that Schrader describes (1972: 38–9), *Enter the Void* is unrelenting in the uniformity of oversaturation. Where contrast in intensity is featured (in the car crash scene, for example), it only serves to further stimulate the viewer, and does not provide the opportunity for resolution. The apparent sentimentality of the birth scene connects with the repeated "sibling vow" flashbacks, providing some closure through the suggestion that Oscar is reunited with his sister through rebirth. However, this scene remains ambiguous in meaning. In this scene, Noé introduces a radical stylistic change by moving from an extreme cinematic mode to a clichéd ending befitting of Hollywood tearjerkers. While facilitating the emotional overflow and complex euphoria associated with stasis, this is no doubt a deliberate move to maintain the echo of disparity after the film's conclusion that will ensure its haunting affect in memory.

This outpouring of emotion can also be attributed to the cognitive challenge of processing highly stimulating imagery that has been subjected to numerous levels of distortion. At first the audience may be shocked by the presence of pornographic imagery in a film that has been approved for public distribution; however, this explicit vision is in fact obscured on many levels. First, the viewer is kept at an aural distance through the use of abstracted ambient sound. Secondly, Noé draws attention to the "X-rated" aspects of the scene while simultaneously censoring them with golden light. The viewer's ability to imagine what is hidden is prevented through the excessive duplication of bodies and the muddied glow of Noé's oversaturated palette. Barely perceptible color flickers are also used, creating strange subliminal impressions. According to Brandon Harris, in this section of the film, "One frame out of six is all blue, one frame out of six is all red and out of focus" (2010: n.p.). Noé further confuses the viewer's conventional apprehension of this sex scene by introducing the confronting inner-body shot of a penis (a taboo even in contemporary film making), followed soon after by that of a newborn baby searching for his mother's breast. A second example of Noé's unusual depiction of sex is exhibited in the strip club dressing room scene where Linda has sex with her boss. In this scene, Oscar's disembodied consciousness follows the action that is taking place, but the movement of the camera and murmurings of his mind convey a sense of distance through a general attraction to bright lights. Despite the many boundaries that are abused in this scene, Noé is able to depict sex explicitly but evoke feelings of distant curiosity and compassionate sexless kinship. Here, Noé encourages the viewer to view sex from a higher perspective typified by the distancing of desire.

Forming associations between a complex set of sexual and relational themes, Noé makes it difficult for the viewer to focus completely on any one of these themes in isolation. The composition of the "Love Hotel" scene is reminiscent of pornography; sexual exploitation is represented in the fleeting image of Victor's sexual insubordination; romantic love is present in the connection between Alex and Linda; familial love exists in the bond between Oscar and Linda; procreation is depicted literally through inner-body footage; infancy and motherhood are portrayed in the image of a newborn baby in his mother's embrace; and the audience views the scene through the disembodied gaze of the soul. This triggers a range of responses in the viewer, and the challenge of trying to reconcile them presents the opportunity for the type of perceptual overload that can trigger feelings of spiritual awakening. Given the suggestible mental state that Noé has developed through visual and aural distortion at this point in the film, it becomes possible to exploit the transgressive power of crossed boundaries and mixed categories to generate a realization of archetypal oneness, rather than clear-headed revulsion.

Sensory Possession

2001 and *Enter the Void* share the ability to create an experience that encourages unusual viewing behaviors and responses. As will be discussed below, Noé draws the viewer into a trance-like state through the use of rhythmic patterns, meditative devices, and sensory overload, transforming a story about the death of a small-time drug dealer into a psychedelic journey to a liminal state of being. The mode of spiritual seekership prevalent in Western consumer culture, that places great value on the individual's journey through the unknown to a realization of truth, maps onto this film quite effectively. Turning the experience up a notch for desensitized modern audiences, *Enter the Void* stimulates every sense until viewers find themselves mesmerized and unable to fully control their experience of the film. Both *2001* and *Enter the Void* are films that engage the viewer on a level where critical distance can be circumvented if viewer immersion is first achieved. For some, this unusual and challenging experience is referred to as life changing.

From the very outset, Noé assaults the viewer with visual and aural stimuli as the opening credits—all in different fonts, colors, and textures—strobe and flicker in kaleidoscopic succession to LFO's hammering techno track *Freak* (2003). Rick Poynor describes this as an intensely disorientating experience where the viewer is arrested "by an irresistible vortex of brain-scrambling sensation and sucked down into the film's chemically modified consciousness" (2010: 8–9). For Greg Hainge this sequence is an immersive strategy that serves to "pummel the spectator into submission via a massive multisensory overload, her eyes assaulted by a machine-gun-fire succession of strobing psychedelic typefaces" (2012: 321). Hainge was seized by "the kind of full body semi-involuntary rhythmic throbbing normally experienced at raves" that left him with "sea legs" (2012: 321). Jimi99 postulates that the intense opening credit sequence has been designed in order to capture the full attention of the viewer and prepare their mind for the slow movement of the remainder of the film. This viewer also refers to the repeated intrusion of "extremely loud, sudden shocks" that leave them feeling like they have survived an ordeal (January 28, 2011, user review of *Enter the Void*).

These observations can be further explained in relation to the structure and rhythms of *2001*. Both Kubrick and Noé seek to capture the attention of the viewer within the opening minutes of the film in an abstract manner that utilizes imagery and dramatic music, but that does not yet introduce narrative elements. *2001* opens with the darkness of the pre-credit sequence and the eerie sounds of Ligeti, to be punctuated by the heralding tones of *Thus Spoke Zarathustra*, and the rising image of an eclipse. Noé transforms the function of the opening credits of *Enter the Void* into a cacophony of sound and flashing imagery, annihilating any thoughts that may exist in the viewer's mind as they struggle to withstand the onslaught. Using different stylistic approaches, both directors seek to empty the viewer's mind and focalize their attention. Kubrick shocks the mind with absence by using the black screen to accompany the creeping movement of music, while Noé similarly shocks the mind with an excess of visual and aural stimuli. As both films progress, slow and abstract pulses are punctuated by highly stimulating shocks in order to maintain a mesmeric affect. The shock of the monolith's periodic appearance throughout *2001* finds its equivalent in the repeated car crash sequence in *Enter the Void*. The narrative meaning of these moments of high stimulation differs in the two films, but the effect that they have on the viewer is similar in terms of rhythmic structure. As both films are comprised mainly of slow and hypnotic scenes, these periodic shocks refocus the viewer so that they can continue to be both absorbed and stimulated by the film and not drift off to sleep. In meditative practice, the sound of a bell or gong can be used to refocus and enliven concentration. Viewers have recognized the meditative qualities of *Enter the Void* along with its ability to bring about a trance-like state, mirroring the technique of "logic relaxation" in meditative practice (Schmidt 2014: 139; Hardeep Pthak, May 13, 2012, user review of *Enter the Void*). Ashleym9000 comments that when Oscar's internal dialogue ceases in the scene of his death, his "thoughts stop and you find that yours do too." This viewer describes the resulting state of mind as one of "meditative trance" where one perceives image and sound with their "primal sense" (ashleym9000, October 1, 2011, user review of *Enter the Void*). In meditative practice, letting go of conscious thought is of principal importance in allowing meditative perception to arise. Noé's techniques do not so much create a quiet space for contemplation as override the viewer's inner dialogue through the intense and unrelenting stimulation of the senses.

Downtek-889-148371 refers to a line from the *Tibetan Book of the Dead* that s/he believes captures the experience of *Enter the Void*: "At that time, sounds, lights, and rays—all three—are experienced. These awe, frighten, and terrify, and cause much fatigue" (November 5, 2010, user review of *Enter the Void*). Viewers like Fighterdan6, Nanthande, and Indyrod similarly note that *Enter the Void* challenges the capacities of the brain. They observe that the film elicits mixed emotions that are difficult to process (Nanthande, June 30, 2013, user review of *Enter the Void*), and features "frenetic visuals" that challenge the mind's capacity to digest what is being seen (Indyrod, October 18, 2010, user review of *Enter the Void*), leaving the viewer speechless for a significant time as the experience is processed (Fighterdan6, June 28, 2012, user review of *Enter the Void*). The experience is also described as being physically and psychologically arduous (jjanerney, April 2, 2016, user review of *Enter the Void*; radioheadrcm, October 4, 2010, user review of *Enter the Void*; chaos-rampant, February 4, 2011, user review of *Enter the Void*). Interviewer Hunter Stephenson refers to his own viewing experience of *Enter the Void* as "the first time I have witnessed so many grown men squirming in their seats during a movie," "they were twitching," and "overstimulated." Stephenson goes on to say, "There was a point where I'm not sure I could have told you which way was up or down in the room" (2010: n.p.). As these comments demonstrate, Noé makes extensive use of sensory overload in *Enter the Void*, distorting and layering sound and image to disrupt ease of cognitive processing. Cinematographer Benoît Debie approached filming with the aim of creating the illusion of an unbroken shot wherever possible to make Oscar's journey "look like one continuous movement of the mind"

(Bergery 2010: 22), and employed postproduction effects such as color flickers to complicate cognitive processing (Harris 2010: n.p.; Failes 2010: n.p.). Denying audiences' moments of rest or resolution, Noé creates an unyielding viewing experience that contributes to increasingly dissociative sensations. As Grodal has argued, this technique can bring on feelings of profound significance.

Enter the Void, like *2001*, contains a distinct narrative, yet viewers often refer to Noé's film as a nonnarrative or purely visual film (Radu_A, December 13, 2010, user review of *Enter the Void*; macocael-353-951088, June 8, 2012, user review of *Enter the Void*). Colin George's experience of *Enter the Void* was one where "somewhere along the way, the lines of the narrative are obliterated" to be replaced by hypnotic effects that mesmerize the mind (October 10, 2010, user review of *Enter the Void*). *Enter the Void* viewers also discuss the necessity of preparing themselves by getting into the right state of mind (Michael Kenmore, January 23, 2010, user review of *Enter the Void*), opening themselves to the experience of the film (SiilentMiike, January 11, 2012, user review of *Enter the Void*), and letting it wash over them (jaredmobarak, September 19, 2009, user review of *Enter the Void*). It is evident from audience responses that *Enter the Void* requires a special type of focus where the mind held in an open and non-ruminative state of awareness. As w-sky puts it, one must allow the film to affect them by opening their mind and allowing themselves to "flow through the pictures, [and] accept moments of strange nothingness" for several hours (September 2, 2010, user review of *Enter the Void*). The viewer's preexisting nature and aptitudes are also identified as determining their ability to access the deeper meaning of the film (kentuckyfriedpanda42, August 23, 2010, user review of *Enter the Void*; uglyzombie, January 27, 2011, user review of *Enter the Void*). All of these features are similarly evident in *2001* viewer comments, demonstrating that the two films call on a similar perceptual state, albeit using a different set of techniques.

As this state of mind requires the viewer's focus, vacillation between absorption and disengaged boredom can commonly occur. For example, Greg Magne initially found it easy to become absorbed by the film, but he began to check his watch frequently as the film tested the limits of his patience. However, he was repeatedly drawn back into focus through the film's shocking scenes (September 15, 2009, user review of *Enter the Void*). The skills employed by meditative practitioners to reach a relaxed state of undirected focus, and those utilized by audience members to sustain a contemplative and open attitude during viewing, are somewhat similar. However, the sensation of moving in and out of focus is also a deliberate technique used by Noé to create feelings of altered perception. Noé refers to a visual technique that he uses in the film, in which the image is unfocused and then imperceptibly refocused, so that "you feel like you're falling asleep," which is exhausting to the mind (Adams 2010: n.p.). Bradleybean86 observes that *Enter the Void* is "effective at keeping your attention, then causing you to wonder if your mind has lost its train of thought or if you're just 'missing something'" (November 16, 2012, user review of *Enter the Void*).

Noé adopts a slow and meandering pace throughout *Enter the Void*, where visual and aural intensities increase to a fever pitch and subside. Frequencies emerge and disappear in a similar manner to the lines of music in a wall of sound. This device is used both visually and in the sound design of the film. As Oscar's point-of-view follows the swelling white light that exists as a living force in the *Enter the Void* universe, the viewer's attention is subtly shifted from the narrative action of the scene into an abstract and visual mode of viewing. The camera moves toward the light, the synthetic hum increases, and the scene becomes muffled as it dissolves away. Overall, Noé spends an inordinate amount of time lingering in each scene, working against expectations of action-based plot progression. Viewers like RachyLovesRattys refer to the "gratuitous" amount of time that Noé spends as being crucial for the overall affect of the film (September 2, 2013, user review of *Enter the Void*). While slow in pace, these scenes can be confronting, graphic, sexual in nature, or simply excessive in vibrancy. Radioheadrcm notes that this means the viewer is not allowed time to rest, even for a moment (October 4, 2010, user review of *Enter the Void*). This combination of slowness and intensity continues to overwhelm the senses, and as thismango puts it, there is "the sense of escalating spiritual tension, like a static charge building up" (November 10, 2012, user review of *Enter the Void*).

Noé also uses sound in order to affect his audience. According to Noé, *Enter the Void* includes the use of "drums and frequencies" designed to put the viewer in a "hypnotic state" and "feel stoned" (Lambie 2010: n.p.). According to CinemaPat, these sounds have been designed "to alter the brain waves in an effort to change perception" (December 9, 2010, user review of *Enter the Void*), an observation echoed by Jorge Campoverde (March 19, 2011, user review of *Enter the Void*) and ashleym9000 (October 1, 2011, user review of *Enter the Void*). In *Irreversible*, Noé also used "a barely perceptible but aggravating bass rumble" for a total of sixty minutes that was intended to unsettle his audience. According to Tim Palmer, Noé recorded this sound "at 27 hertz, the frequency used by riot police to quell mobs by inducing unease and, after prolonged exposure, physical nausea" (2006: 29). Using techniques like this enables the director to elicit a strong and predictable response that the viewer themselves may not understand.

Robert Barry refers to the music of *Enter the Void* as being a "maelstrom" of musical fragments that are "mixed and blended 'like a river, where all the waters are mixed inside,' blended beyond distinguishability" (Barry 2010: n.p.). Noé's sound design references Kubrick by featuring a prominent and well-known orchestral leitmotif, Johann Sebastian Bach's *Air on the G String* (1731), but the overall "maelstrom" that Barry describes recalls something of the quality of Ligeti's dense web of sound where melodies and phrases are enmeshed to the point of being indistinguishable from each other. While the viewer struggles to decipher a path through this thick and enigmatic mass of shifting sound, the effect is both disorientating and a form of cognitive excess. From the mesh of sound, occasional moments of striking clarity and familiarity shine through, and the audience can move from aural disembodiment to find their feet on the ground in the repeated "sibling vow" scene featuring Bach's *Air on the G String*. However, the repetition of this scene and musical motif create an unsettling feeling of narrative immobility, transforming it into a rhythmic pattern underscoring the narrative, rather than a moment of action progressing the plot.

Noé's near exclusive use of point-of-view camerawork is one of *Enter the Void*'s the most obvious departures from conventional film. Viewers report that this technique transforms the film into an inescapably personal experience, removing critical distance (Siddharth kalkal, June 27, 2013, user review of *Enter the Void*; liebeistderweg, February 26, 2012, user review of *Enter the Void*; oOgiandujaOo, October 17, 2009, user review of *Enter the Void*). Cassandra Kelsey describes the visual effects of the film as leading the viewer "to almost physically sense" what Oscar is experiencing (June 13, 2013, user review of *Enter the Void*). For Gino Monaco, *Enter the Void* felt "more real than life," and at times he forgot that it was a movie (August 9, 2012, user review of *Enter the Void*). Noé's representation of subjectivity that is achieved through point-of-view camerawork along with other subtle effects can be considered innovative on several counts. Physical embodiment (or its memory) is suggested through the sound of Oscar's heartbeat, breath, and the muffled sound of his inner thoughts that vibrate as though they are resounding through the body, as one might hear their own voice (Birks 2015: 139). In flashback sequences, Noé incorporates a silhouetted figure that Jeeshan Gazi argues is faithful to the dynamics of spatial cognition in memory. Here, one remembers by placing themselves in the scene, either in a first- or third-person perspective. This type of memory is distinct from "eidetic memory," which includes all detail in sharp clarity and is not often experienced. Noé also makes use of "associative memory" in sequences that recall multiple versions of similar scenes in consecutive developments so that the point-of-view appears uncertain of what really happened (Gazi 2017: n.p.). Noé included this dimension based on his own experience of memories and dreams where he is aware of seeing himself in silhouette (Bergery 2010: 18). Noé seeks to replicate human perception as closely as possible in order to capture what it is really like to be asleep, in pain, or in an altered state of consciousness (*Trinity-X* 2016: n.p.).

In particular, Noé is interested in replicating dream perception as dreams lead to heightened feelings of profundity (Adams 2010: n.p.) and "stay in your mind" (Barney 2014: n.p.). As liminal experiences, dreams resist recollection, and their logic is clouded by ellipses and gaps. As Grodal explains, a "dreamlike" quality can be generated through the avoidance of narrative resolution and through a variety of techniques that impede or cloud perception. This might include devices as simple as fog or heavy rain that prevent the viewer from full access to the visual information of their environment (Grodal 2009: 243 and 237). Linking dream states with "supernatural" encounters, such experiences are characterized by a "lack of control of vision" and an impenetrability that encourages one to seek access to what is hidden (Grodal 2009: 237, 241, and 245). One of Grodal's principal examples of lyrical-associative toning—Robert Montgomery's *Lady in the Lake* (1947)—is also a major influence on *Enter the Void* (Grodal 2009: 241; Bradshaw 2010: n.p.). Lyrical-associative toning resembles the way in which dreams combine images, thoughts, and feelings that the awoken dreamer attempts to make sense of. In his description of dream perception, Noé demonstrates a sensitivity to experiential subtleties that enables him to create uncanny renditions of these states for his audience. The director acknowledges David Lynch's *Mulholland Drive* (2001) as a particularly good example of dream perception, where Lynch recreates the telepathic communication and unfinished sentences of dreams (Harris 2010: n.p.). Lynch is another director who is renowned for creating deeply immersive films that have a supernatural undertone. In Episode 8 "Gotta Light?" from the third season of *Twin Peaks* (directed by Lynch and Robert Frost), there is an extended scene replicating the cinematic techniques that Kubrick used in the Stargate sequence of *2001*. This deeply disturbing scene depicts the explosion of an atomic bomb and the mutation of elemental forces that gave birth to evil (in the form of the supernatural character of Bob). Like Kubrick, Lynch and Frost make extensive use of repetitious sound, and long static takes of evolving visual patterns, to draw the audience into a state where their mental guard is down for the final horrifying scene. It is worth noting that Lynch is both a cinematic master of mood and a meditation practitioner. Since 2005, the David Lynch Foundation for Consciousness-Based Education and World Peace has raised money to teach Transcendental Meditation, a classic 1960s alternative spiritual practice. It is likely that the regular reflective practice of meditation provides a director like Lynch with a level of expertise in the subtleties of cognition and perception that enables him to manipulate these faculties in his audience. Similarly, Noé's personal experiences of perception-altering drugs, and research into spiritual practices, such as out-of-body experiences, demonstrate that the director has dedicated considerable time to investigating the nonnormative states of mind that his films seek to replicate.

Noé mimics visual perception through nuances such as blinking and subtle blurring to convey the selective focus of subjective attention. Gazi compares Noé's point-of-view work with *Lady in the Lake*, arguing that *Enter the Void* more faithfully mimics natural perception. *Lady in the Lake* does not include blinking, misapproximates the height of actors, and it feels like characters are speaking to the camera, not to the character's point-of-view. Noé, on the other hand, uses a helmet with a camera attached, includes more real-time footage, and makes effective use of blinking effects. Noé's use of subtle blurring techniques to capture the limited focus of human perception is a striking innovation and departure from conventional cinema, where many scenes subtly constrict focus to particular areas (Gazi 2017: n.p.).

During Oscar's conversation with Victor, Noé includes the effect of "gaze avoidance" reflecting the natural movement of the eye as it responds to inner thought processes such as recollection and simultaneously scans the external environment (Gazi 2017: n.p.). In this scene Oscar's point-of-view blinks are consistent with the observation that a person who is conversing will blink more often when they speak and less when they listen; however, Gazi points out that this tendency is reversed during the opening scenes when Oscar is under the influence of DMT (2017: n.p.). Following his death, Oscar's point of view can be felt through the emotional responsiveness of the camera and lighting effects. As Linda responds to her boss's advances in her dressing room, Oscar's point-of-view adopts various attitudes from curiosity to affection, but at one point appears to "violently strobe as if in distress" (Gazi 2017: n.p.). Similarly in *Irreversible* the "sensorially consistent world" that viewers might expect from conventional film is undermined through Noé's use of special effects. Noé employs visible grain and disruptions to camera stability as deliberate aesthetic strategies to convey meaning. The story, which is told in reverse, proceeds from grainy texture and unstable camera work to less textured, sharper imagery, with saturated color (Rios and Davis 2007: 95–105). Debie also used disco lights to illuminate scenes during filming in order to express Oscar's changing emotions through color changes (Bergery 2010: 19). The intricate detail applied to the task of generating subjectivity leads to an almost invasively personalized experience for the viewer (robocopssadside-1, January 28, 2011, user review of *Enter the Void*). The experience is "uncanny" because one feels "subjected to the full force of the events taking place on-screen, yet unable to control them" (Hainge 2012: 318).

Gazi's observations are mirrored in comments that attest to the visceral power of the film. Colin George claims that *Enter the Void* is a film that "hijacks your consciousness" (October 10, 2010, user review of *Enter the Void*) while for others like tom van de Bospoort the film brings on feelings of illness, dryness of the mouth, and spontaneous weeping (September 25, 2010, user review of *Enter the Void*). Physical responses to the film are common, including shivers (jaredmobarak, September 19, 2009, user review of *Enter the Void*; Simon Kraft, November 22, 2009, user review of *Enter the Void*), nausea (Gino Monaco, August 9, 2012, user review of *Enter the Void*; Radu_A, December 13, 2010, user review of *Enter the Void*), tension (John DeSando, November 28, 2010, user review of *Enter the Void*), and feeling drained by the film (jaredmobarak, September 19, 2009, user review of *Enter the Void*). Such responses only serve to intensify the viewer's sensation of truth. As Winfried Menninghaus explains, the twentieth century saw a decisive shift in the conception of truth from that of the beautiful to the abject, where feelings of trauma and disgust were cast as primal and unmediated irruptions of reality (2003: 384–7). Menninghaus provides a useful overview of the transformation of philosophical truth from the beautiful to the disgusting through the work of figures like Nietzsche, Freud, and Julia Kristeva. Menninghaus explains that "truth is henceforth something that posits itself in the miscarriage of 'normal' modes of symbolization, . . . it implies a more far-reaching claim: namely in the dissolution of all constructions of reality, to let 'the "real" itself break through'" (2003: 384–7). While the reorientation of truth that Menninghaus describes is especially relevant to this study, it is felt that the dense terminology of writers like Kristeva and the political application of her work would confuse the existing characterization of truth employed here that traces the concept through alternative spirituality.

The repeated car crash scene has been singled out as particularly traumatic for viewers (Nicholas Lopez, February 16, 2011, user review of *Enter the Void*;

CinemaPat, December 9, 2010, user review of *Enter the Void*; makelajanne75, June 31, 2013, user review of *Enter the Void*). TheCultureSlut goes so far as to refer to *Enter the Void* as "psychologically damaging" (April 15, 2012, user review of *Enter the Void*) while felipedigre categorizes the film as a form of "shock therapy" (September 12, 2015, user review of *Enter the Void*). This scene involves loud noises, screaming, and disturbing imagery that has triggered involuntary movements in some viewers, such as jumping from their seat (Simon Kraft, November 22, 2009, user review of *Enter the Void*). Jaredmobarak recalls that this scene created "the visceral, physical feeling of being rocked back" by the impact of the crash (September 19, 2009, user review of *Enter the Void*). In Noé's personal experience of a taxi collision, he felt the resonant affect of trauma on memory, saying that the event is "still engraved" in his mind (*Trinity-X* 2016: n.p.). The continuing power of this personal event is replicated in viewer responses to *Enter the Void*'s car crash scene. While some are comfortable to go with the experience, others resent the feeling of losing control (Stephenson 2010: n.p.). For Richard Alex Jenkins, the only way to withstand the affect of the film is to shut his eyes and count to ten (January 16, 2014, user review of *Enter the Void*).

Viewer comments testify to the intense and continued impact of *Enter the Void* that remains in the viewer's consciousness beyond ordinary recollection. Radioheadrcm comments, "Watch it once and you'll carry it with you forever" (October 4, 2010, user review of *Enter the Void*). A Different Drummer says that the film mesmerized and hypnotized him so that "EVEN IF I WANTED TO FORGET THIS FILM, I could not" (November 28, 2013, user review of *Enter the Void*). These comments bear a clear similarity to *2001* audience responses that attribute agency to the film. Rumid appears to attribute a willful presence to the film where it "enters your system and stays there for a while, visiting you in dreams and thoughts" (May 26, 2013, user review of *Enter the Void*). As previously mentioned, the mind often attributes agency to that which appears to behave uncontrollably or unpredictably (Taves 2009: 43). While this characteristic was often positively received by *2001* viewers who experienced simultaneous feelings of awe and wonder, *Enter the Void* is a much more difficult journey. The "lightning-bolt path" is not for everyone, and where the moment of stasis fails to offer transcendence (and the ineffable knowledge that comes with it), its lasting affect would be more fittingly compared with demonic possession. In the latter case, it does not herald the circumvention of earthly authorities to experience an unmediated connection with sacred truth; rather it becomes psychic millstone, stifling the propensity toward freedom and potentiality that characterizes alternative spirituality.

Profane Paths to the Sacred: Cinematic Journeys of Realization

Another way of conceiving of the dark side of cinematic possession is that is a "bad trip," determined in large part by the existing psychological propensities of the viewer. Unlike conventional cinema, Noé is not content with imaginative engagement; rather he seeks to guide the viewer into an alternate state of perception using any means possible. *Enter the Void* not only depicts drug-induced states of mind but also appears to generate the experience of taking hallucinogenic drugs in audiences. For Taylor_Gillen *Enter the Void* is "like an actual hallucinatory experience, minutes feel like hours, and hours feel like days" (January 2, 2016, user review of *Enter the Void*). Vikram-ry123 felt that s/he was losing control of his/her senses as if they had taken drugs (February 12, 2011, user review of *Enter the Void*), while otuswerd remarks that the cognitive effects resembling a "heavy trip" were so intense that they could not be sure whether "what was going on was real" (August 13, 2010, user review of *Enter the Void*). The latter aspect of *Enter the Void* sets it apart from other films as it exerts its strong influence on the viewer's perception. While a small number of audience responses provide evidence of drug-assisted viewing, the majority verifies the perception-altering powers of the film itself. Viewer Ben Hinman was smoking marijuana while watching the film but notes that the film made him feel as if he had taken acid. This viewer identifies the technique of using strobe lighting effects as assisting in inducing a "drug like state" of mind and specifically warns others not to take drugs before seeing the film, as the effect can be too strong (Ben Hinman, January 19, 2015, user review of *Enter the Void*).

The relationship that Noé first felt between "cinematic ecstasy" and the feeling of being on drugs highlights the complex relationship between sacred and profane experiences of nonnormative mental states in the modern West. This overwhelming sense of being mesmerized into an alternate state of consciousness is equally associated with profound meaning and quasi-religious significance in Western culture. *Enter the Void*'s depiction of drugs may fit the category of the profane in some respects, but the film does not draw its inspiration from party culture. Rather, shamanic ritual can be said to have influenced the film's vision, where drugs are used as entheogens—tools to access esoteric wisdom. Oscar and other characters in the film may not actively seek wisdom, but they find themselves enveloped by, and confronted with, something greater than themselves. This dynamic is mirrored in the cinematic encounter where viewers suggest that *Enter the Void* works like a drug to bring about consciousness expansion (Joseph Sylvers, October 6, 2010, user review of *Enter the Void*; sabareesh10, August 3, 2013, user review of *Enter the Void*). According to w-sky, *Enter the Void* is "not a pro-drug or antidrug film: It shows drugs as just what they are. Mind-altering substances, that may be used with caution and expert knowledge" (September 2, 2010, user review of *Enter the Void*).

In late 1960s, alternative spirituality and perception-altering drugs such as LSD, mescalin, and marijuana were viewed as tools to be used for the purpose of consciousness expansion and breaking out of the confines of the socially conditioned mind. Jungian psychologist Luigi Zoja points out that there is a distinction between the "drug initiate" of the 1960s who undertakes intentional drug use in order to pursue enlightenment and the "drug addict" who is aimless in their pursuit of a "high" (1989: 7). The reality of drug use in the 1960s may not be so clear-cut, but it is worth noting that particular forms of drug use and experiences associated with them are correlated with spiritual awakening in Western culture. Drugs like LSD and magic mushrooms that were used recreationally, and in pursuit of spiritual revelation in this period, enable vivid hallucinations. Drug-assisted spiritual experiences typical of late-1960s alternative spirituality involve feelings of oneness with the universe, dissolution of identity, recognition of interconnectedness, and the reality of religious universalism. This type of experience may involve visions of bright lights, patterns, and encounters with spiritual beings, animals, and religious figures. Reference to spiritually inflected drug experiences can be found in popular culture of the period, demonstrating their importance in the countercultural movement. "Hippie" revelations from the 1960s about the nature of self are remarkably similar to the earlier experiments of psychical researchers. For instance, James reflected that individuals are like "islands in the sea" that "hang together through the ocean's bottom. Just so there is a continuum of cosmic consciousness, against which our individuality builds but accidental fences, and into which our several minds plunge as into a mother-sea or reservoir" (Nicotra 2008: 206–13). This very concept is used by Clarke in *Childhood's End* (1990 [1953]), the novel that is recognized as being crucial to Clarke's vision of *2001*. In the novel, Clarke makes the following postulation:

> Imagine that every man's mind is an island, surrounded by ocean. Each seems isolated, yet in reality all are linked through the bedrock from which they spring. If the oceans were to vanish, that would be the end of the islands. They would all be part of one continent, but their individuality would have gone. Telepathy, as you have called it, is something like this. (1990 [1953]: 168)

Such reflections demonstrate that the 1960s did not necessarily see the emergence of something new in the activities of consciousness expansion but rather, the continuation and popularization of this trend. Without the traditions and frameworks of religious traditions to facilitate transformative or initiatory religious experiences, individuals are positively disposed toward situations that bring about similar experiences in a seemingly spontaneous manner. Drugs bring about a dramatic loss of agency, and a perceptual shift, that can provide a powerful encounter with spiritual truth if the experiencer is inclined to view drug experience as an authentic epistemological avenue.

Medical doctor Rick Strassman, working in the field of psychedelic research, has undertaken experiments with DMT, recording the experiences of a range of participants. Typically, participants recall experiences where time crumbles, the self no longer exists, attachments are stripped away, and the overall sensation of ineffability is beheld with awe (Strassman 2000). These experiences possess mystical qualities and are defined by intense stimuli such as colors, sounds, and heightened emotional states. As Nayar has argued, Schrader's transcendental style favors a still and spare articulation of the divine, as this type of mystical experience is often granted the highest status in Western culture (2012: 105–17). However, Nayar points out that authentic religious experiences from non-Western cultures such as Hinduism are stimulating to the senses (2012: 95). Hollenback also argues that mystical experiences involving colors, images, sound, and emotion are just as valid as those of stillness and nothingness (1996: 202–3 and 305). Considering the religiosity of cinematic experiences and the mystical qualities that films like *2001* and *Enter the Void* engender, it is enough to note that viewers feel a lingering sense of realization or revelation. Both films engage the senses as they guide audiences into contemplative modes of perception. Kubrick assists the mind in "letting go" through the use of quiet, repetitive sound, and scenes that bring quietness to the mind through their simple, symmetrical composition, or their slow, steady movement. Noé keeps the viewer in a more heightened state of anxiety throughout, but creates his own sense of slowness. The thick, ambient hum of sound, swirling camera movement, and fuzzy, saturated color that permeate the film keep the viewer submerged in a continuous state, deactivating mental processing linked with action-based narratives. Both films also utilize techniques that overwhelm the viewer with a high level of stimulation that mirrors the type of experiences described by Strassman's participants.

Given that Noé cites *2001* as the primary influence on *Enter the Void*, it is worth considering Kubrick's view of the role that drugs played in the making of what has become known as "the Ultimate Trip." In Kubrick's view "drugs are basically of more use to the audience than to the artist.... The artist's transcendence must be within his own work; he should not impose any artificial barriers between himself and the mainspring of his subconscious" (Rowe 2013: 53). In contrast to Noé, who approaches psychedelic drug use in an unstructured manner as an interesting investigation of the unknown, the Jungian framework that underpins Kubrick's thinking is evident in his desire to access his subconscious with clear perception. These directors share a desire to experience and convey altered states of consciousness, and both seem to value these states as sites of some ambiguous ultimate truth.

Noé actively experimented with DMT as he was formulating his vision for *Enter the Void*. As a part of his creative process, Noé took ayahuasca after a period of research into reincarnation and out-of-body experiences (Lambie 2010: n.p.). On ayahuasca, he was able to forget his "human form" and Earthly existence in the face of "visions that are far scarier or far more futuristic" than visions facilitated by other means (Lambie 2010: n.p.). In recreating the experience of DMT, the special effects team drew on the botanical drawings of Edouard Marie Heckel (1843–1916) as these images were at the same time "beautiful" and "troubling," abstract and organic (Failes 2010: n.p.). Other directors like Alejandro Jodorowsky have also used drug-enhanced spiritual practice in a similar way. While preparing to film *The Holy Mountain* (1973), he and his wife underwent a week of sleep deprivation, and the entire cast was required to live in Jodorowsky's house for three months undergoing spiritual training under Zen master Oscar Ichazo (1931–) (Hoberman and Rosenbaum 2008: 291). This training involved an eclectic blend of religious ritual and meditation combined with the controlled use of psychoactive substances. Reportedly, Jodorowsky expected to attain enlightenment during filming, so that the experience of acting in, and creating the film, was akin to the spiritual journey undertaken by the film's characters.

For Jodorowsky, the cinematic journey into the subconscious was an affective experience for himself, his crew, and his audience. Comparisons can also be made with the approach of filmmaker Nathaniel Dorsky (1943–). Dorsky employs techniques influenced by spiritual practice and drug experimentation in an effort to lead his audience into alternate modes of seeing (MacDonald 2006). According to interviewer Scott MacDonald, Dorsky's films provide "a form of visual/conceptual training in apprehending the world" in a more "reverent" way (MacDonald 2006: 78). Dorsky's silent films are intended to be projected at eighteen frames per second in order to draw the viewer into a form of meditative focus. Employing what Grodal would call lyrical-associative toning (referred to by Dorsky as "polyvalence technique") the director seeks to produce "mental linkages" that cannot be organized into narrative meaning. Dorsky's polyvalence technique (interrelationship of scenes) serves to "place viewers into a cinematic present that cannot be reduced to verbal codes and analysis" (McDonald 2006: 79). He achieves this by avoiding narrative and ideological meaning in favor of a purely visual and intuitive experience (MacDonald 2006: 93). Dorsky's spiritualized filmmaking was influenced by his experimentation with marijuana and LSD which taught the director how to see, hear, and experience the world in new ways, insights that he then sought to pass onto his audience (MacDonald 2006: 93).

As has been previously discussed, personal experiences that are difficult to understand or explain are granted a higher truth-value in alternative spirituality. Seeking out such experiences involves a willingness to experiment, enter the unknown, and to observe one's own experience in a reflective manner. James, an earlier proponent of such experiential self-experimentation, provides evidence of the cultural continuity of this mode of epistemology in Western culture. The Western scientific method that dominated James's era may have considered interior experience and testimony to be unreliable, and self-experimentation especially so, but this did not dissuade him from pursuing this method of inquiry in addition to his observation of professed spirit channels, clairvoyants, and cases of telekinesis. James's techniques of self-experimentation involved sleep deprivation and the use of mind-altering substances including nitrous oxide, mescal, ether, chloral, and amyl nitrate in order to understand the nature of consciousness (Nicotra 2008: 200–201). This form of surrender to unknown affects, undertaken with openness of mind, and the absence of expectations, is also practiced by viewers of *2001* and *Enter the Void*.

In one particular self-experiment with nitrous oxide, James attempted to record the experience but was only able to record fragmentary impressions as they streamed through his mind in a torrent of oppositional concepts: "Good and evil reconciled in a laugh!," "*In*coherent, coherent—same," "And it fades! And it's infinite! AND it's infinite!" (Nicotra 2008: 206-7). Colleagues who attempted similar experiments faced the same challenge of adequately capturing the experience and communicating it to others, and as Nicotra points out, "the only thing the reader grasps adequately is that *something* very interesting and powerful happened" (Nicotra 2008: 206-9). These experiences, like mystical accounts and viewer recollections of *2001* and *Enter the Void*, share this same quality of ineffability steeped in profound significance. James also experimented with affective states of intoxication (nitrous oxide), acute physical pain (tooth extraction), and emotional duress, where stimuli took on a truth-value unrelated to reason or subjective desires (Nicotra 2008: 208, 211, and 239–40). Analyzing these experiences in retrospect, James could not unhinge their veracity. "One conclusion was forced upon my mind at that time, and my impression of its truth has ever since remained unshaken" (Nicotra 2008: 211). It is clear that these accounts bear a striking similarity to James's definition of mystical experience, highlighting the blurred boundary between religious practices and those that may be considered profane.

As a form of filmic experience that resists rational understanding by exceeding the brain's ability to process what is being seen, *Enter the Void* has been referred to as a film that has a an ineffable quality. As was the case with *2001*, *Enter the Void* is referred to as an experience that exceeds the capacity of language (Matt_Layden, January 23, 2011, user review of *Enter the Void*; jaredmobarak, September 19, 2009, user review of *Enter the Void*) and that leaves one speechless (DonFishies, January 23, 2011, user review of *Enter the Void*; Fighterdan6, June 28, 2012, user review of *Enter the Void*). Audiences stress the unique nature of their cinematic experience, saying that they have never experienced anything like *Enter the Void*, nor do they expect to again (AMadLane, November 11, 2010, user review of *Enter the Void*; Greg Magne, September 15, 2009, user review of *Enter the Void*). The special or unusual nature of this experience sets it aside as something other than the norm, an attribute that Taves has identified as being important in the attribution of spiritual qualities in mystical experience.

In Chapter 5, the revelatory and transformative power of *2001* came through in a number of reviews. Similarly, viewers like Brian Daly (November 6, 2014, user review of *Enter the Void*), Imaocarrots (November 16, 2011, user review of *Enter the Void*), sabareesh10 (August 3, 2013, user review of *Enter the Void*), and RachyLovesRattys (September 2, 2013, user review of *Enter the Void*) felt that the film affected them and changed their perspective of life and death in ways that are difficult to articulate. Downtek-889-148371 describes the experience of *Enter the Void* more specifically in religious terms. As a film that works on an energetic level, rather than "a narrative or doctrinal one," this viewer feels that the film employs shock to bring about enlightenment in the same way that religious teachings use the realization of death to trigger spiritual awakening. As a deeply confronting experience, downtek-889-148371 sees *Enter the Void* as an experience that challenges the individual to engage in "raw, sincere confession" and overcome the ego in order to be redeemed. In this particular case, the film appears to have succeeded in prompting a spiritual transformation as the viewer goes on to say,

"I feel that I may have received new power to make the right choices in many of the finest details of my life, through the jolting, loathsome ugliness ... misery and force of this film" (November 5, 2010, user review of *Enter the Void*).

Responses such as this suggest that *Enter the Void* can play a very important existential role in viewer's lives. However, this role may or may not be as far reaching as their words suggest. In Strassman's study of DMT experiences, he found that while participants described profound spiritual experiences, over time, these individuals did not typically adopt corresponding changes in their approach to daily life. However, Alissa Hirshfeld-Flores points out that while Strassman may have been disappointed that participants did not adopt spiritual or psychologically reflective practices following their experience, "several reported a stronger sense of self, less fear of death, and a greater appreciation of life" (2002: 1448). As an experience that takes place outside of a structured religious tradition, the ongoing influence of spiritually revelatory cinematic encounters are most likely to involve a personal reflection on the basic premises of one's worldview, including understandings about life, death, self, and consciousness. However, the haunting affect of the film may have a less traceable impact. In the changing cultural conception of the sacred, the harsher and more abstract manifestation of truth that Menninghaus identifies sees the beauty of the sublime recede, becoming perhaps less romantic and more modern. Here, *Enter the Void* makes its unique contribution to the cultural imaginary in the depiction of that which lies at the limit of human perception.

Conclusion

Noé's *Enter the Void* and Kubrick's *2001* are very different films in terms of style and content, yet they share common techniques, fostering the practice of meditative viewing. In this state of focused immersion, viewers are encouraged to let go of conscious thought, allowing the sensations of the film to wash over them. The affective qualities of the film are built up until they culminate in a final outpouring of feeling. As with *2001*, audiences find the overall sensations of the film to be profound and difficult to explain, haunting them long after the film is over.

Noé uses a vast array of techniques that harness the energies of perception, overloading the senses and then dissipating these frequencies rather than resolving them. Working in a layered rhythm, these sources of stimulation push the brain to reach a certain limit, while retaining a constant state of immersion. Noé's techniques include but are not limited to visual techniques that over-stimulate the senses while impeding cognitive processing; sound techniques that encourage mental drifting with moments of sharpness to renew focus; and the compositional manipulation of intensities, where excessive brightness, loudness, violence, sex, and moments of extreme emotion are used to generate dissociative sensations.

As a film made forty-one years after *2001*, the spiritualized viewer experiences can no longer be attributed to the hippie culture of the late 1960s. On the one hand, the ethos of alternative spirituality continues to permeate the Western orientation toward the sacred, and on the other, these films can be identified as sharing common film techniques that manipulate perception in specific ways. Noé consciously cites *2001* as the principal influence on the design of *Enter the Void*, yet it does not mimic Kubrick's film in any recognizable way beyond the use of psychedelic imagery. The common link between these films exists at the level of feeling. Due to the disturbing themes and graphic imagery in *Enter the Void*, it is a more difficult journey than *2001*. However meditative practice also has different paths, some of which are focused on the most disgusting and horrific things imaginable including the contemplation of one's own death and decaying corpse (Gyatso 2000: 81; Thepyanmongkol 2008: 52). By confronting the most difficult subject that is fraught with the deepest attachments and fears, it is thought that the practitioner might be able to achieve sudden enlightenment.

The desire to reveal, confront, and overcome the darkest aspects of the human consciousness is an impetus toward truth that has developed increasingly toward the horrific. This stems from a mistrust of society and a psychologized approach to personal and social development through the revelation of truth. What might have previously been classed as taboo by previous generations takes on a special power as a gateway to something real that has been hidden through a fear of the unknown. Evidence of this tendency can be found throughout Western culture. In each case, individuals are geared to seek out hidden truth and to look past what they think they know. Each successive layer is expected to be more confronting than the last.

To replicate something of the "cinematic ecstasy" that he felt as a child of six when he first saw *2001* (Barney 2014: n.p.), in the present context, Noé is required to transform Kubrick's approach so that it can attain the continually renewing frequency of truth. Because convention and familiarity lead to predictability, it is a challenge to maintain the elusive feeling of undetermined potentiality associated with the sacred. However, like a magician, Noé uses every device at his disposal to take his audience to that special place of primal terror and elation that is beyond words.

8

Melancholia
In Dreadful Beauty and Trembling

Released forty-three years after Kubrick's *2001*, von Trier's *Melancholia* is situated in the same cultural context as Noé's *Enter the Void* and was also produced by a controversial European director. *Melancholia* is the second installment of von Trier's "Depression Trilogy" that includes *Antichrist* (2009) and *Nymphomaniac* (2013). Like Kubrick and Noé, von Trier is renowned as an enfant terrible and has been associated with the new extremism that exploits cinema's potential to affect the viewer on a visceral level (Birks 2015: 131–2). During *Enter the Void*'s premiere, von Trier's *Antichrist* stood as its main rival in terms of shock value and visual excess. Von Trier has been described as a director who makes "us see more than we want to see, for longer than we should endure" (Figlerowicz 2012: 21). However, *Melancholia* does not do this with sex, violence, or similarly transgressive content. Rather, the audience is plunged into a world of physical beauty, aural tragedy, and emotional sickliness, in von Trier's unyielding depiction of depression. As a film that is also about the end of the world, personal and cosmic themes intertwine following the strained relationship of sisters Justine and Claire.

Both *Enter the Void* and *Melancholia* are films that belong to the art film genre; however, *Melancholia* has been able to reach a wider audience than *Enter the Void* for several reasons. Von Trier is a more established director who has cast popular actors and music personalities in his films, for instance, *Dogville* (2003) stars Nicole Kidman, and *Dancer in the Dark* (2000), the Icelandic singer Bjork. *Melancholia* itself features Kirsten Dunst, famous for her roles in Hollywood films like *Interview with the Vampire* (1994) and the *Spiderman* trilogy (2002, 2004, 2007), and Alexander Skarsgård, from the Home Box Office (HBO) vampire television series *True Blood* (2008–14). These personalities, and other renowned actors featured in *Melancholia*'s cast, such as Kiefer Sutherland, Udo Kier, John Hurt, Charlotte Rampling, and Charlotte Gainsbourg, draw viewers to see *Melancholia* who might not normally be attracted to von Trier's work. *Melancholia* is also one of the rare films in von Trier's oeuvre to be classified as suitable for audiences under seventeen (United States [R], United States-TV [14], United Kingdom [15], and Australia [M]). By contrast, Noé works with relatively unknown or inexperienced actors, with famous actors occasionally featured, and his films are consistently rated for audiences over the age of eighteen, where a classification is granted. However, neither *Melancholia* nor *Enter the Void* is able to compare with the mass popular appeal of *2001*, or with its longevity as one of the key films in the history of cinema.

Like *Enter the Void*, *Melancholia* bears the influence of Kubrick's 1968 classic, although von Trier does not stress the influence of *2001* with the fervor of Noé (Cheung 2015: n.p.). While viewers of *Enter the Void* were assaulted with visual and aural stimuli in a seemingly endless Stargate journey, the intensity of *Melancholia* is emotional. As a melodrama, *Melancholia* is quite different to Kubrick's space odyssey. However, the resemblance between *2001* and *Melancholia* can be found in the use of silence, darkness, and an understated verbal style, as well as in the planetary scenes and adoption of evocative classical music that are used in both films. Structurally, the films are also similar as they start with a short but highly evocative introduction and then slowly build to a single extreme and prolonged climactic moment.

Broadly speaking, all three films follow the pattern of Schrader's transcendental style, moving from the everyday through disparity and into stasis. However, each film does this in its own way, creating culminating feelings of different qualities. As each film establishes its own baseline depiction of the everyday, it is from this point that disparity is created. Linking these alternate versions of the everyday is the generation of monotonous continuity where emotional cycles are stimulated without being allowed to resolve or dissipate. Further to this, all three films engage a set of techniques that lead to cinematic responses that can be considered religious in their adherence to James's categories of mystical experience. In terms of the core thematic elements of the three films in this study, *2001* asks archetypal questions about the nature of existence, and *Enter the Void* investigates liminal states of consciousness, blurring the line between identity and experience, and between life and death. *Melancholia* also tackles the cessation of experiential existence, creating a symbolic parallel between the destruction of the embodied self, where consciousness resides, and the annihilation of the planet Earth. Both films present a bleaker and more confrontational existential interrogation than *2001*, which included the potentially hopeful image of the Starchild at its conclusion. The broader significance of the treatment of such existential questions will be explored in the following chapter, in particular their interrelationship with the epistemological inferences that come when directors work with audiences at the level of experience. First, however, *Melancholia*'s formal qualities will be detailed, and in the following section, audience responses will be explored.

Frontality, Vibrations, and Inversions

Melancholia opens with a stunning ten-minute sequence featuring scenes from the film's conclusion along with symbolic visions that represent Justine's premonitory dreams. Without introduction or explanation, the viewer is transported into a world of uncanny aesthetics accompanied by the yearning strains of Richard Wagner's prelude to *Tristan and Isolde* (1865). Staged as if they are romantic paintings and moving in ultra-slow motion, these images are made to appear all the more unreal through a color saturation effect that flattens motion, making each frame appear as a living photograph. *Melancholia* cinematographer Manuel Alberto Claro used a special device called the "Phantom camera" that could capture up to 1,000 frames per second, where standard cameras can only capture around 24 frames per second. This footage was then dramatically slowed to reveal detail that would normally be impossible to capture, a technique also used in *Antichrist* (White 2012: 19).

The film begins in darkness, where a creeping luminescence reveals the image of Justine's face as she slowly opens her eyes. The first isolated notes of Wagner's prelude express a freedom of aural gesture while the image struggles to progress. Immersed in turgid color and expression, Justine's face captures the emotion of the film's title. This extreme close up is confronting, yet distant, like an icon. Justine's hazy blue eyes appear to look straight through the viewer, and her expression is painterly in its affected hues. This opening image embodies frontality, a concept that Schrader links specifically to expressionless facial close-ups (1972: 53 and 100). However, it could also be interpreted as melancholic inversion of Kubrick's Starchild, where *2001*'s final scene becomes *Melancholia*'s first. Both the face of the Starchild and the face of Justine behold the revelation of apocalypse, and perhaps their own transcendence, as they gaze into the viewer's eyes. Lingering here, dead birds begin to fall from the sky.

Like *2001*'s "Dawn of Man" sequence, the images that open *Melancholia* appear as minimally animated "stills." Each image is placed before the viewer for an extended duration where movement possesses a dreamy, underwater quality, as if the environment of the film were a thick substance. The next image that appears is a symmetrical shot of a manicured lawn lined by topiary trees, and a large sundial dominating the foreground. Justine can be seen as a tiny speck on the grass wandering in the extreme distance. This image is compositionally reminiscent of *2001*, containing strong perspectival lines and a circular shape in the foreground, with focus drawn to a small distant point. This image, like many others in the film, guides the eye *into* the image, where the central point of focus encourages stillness of the gaze. At this central point, there is a space, rather than a specific object of focus. The sequence proceeds at an arrested pace with an image of Pieter Bruegel's *Hunters in the Snow* (1565) catching fire and the monolithically sized planet Melancholia eclipsing the distant red glow of the star Antares. In the next image, Clare trudges toward the camera holding her son Leo to her breast in anguish and exhaustion. Her footprints leave a dark trail behind her, depicting strong unidirectional movement. Following this, a black horse is shown sinking backward into a marsh. Although barely noticeable to the viewer, the appearance of Melancholia brings with it an unsettling low rumbling sound. As Wagner's prelude gains momentum and the strings call repeatedly for a rush of emotion, each reappearance of the planet increases the effect of the music through the accompaniment of this subconsciously terrifying vibration.

Perhaps heralding her role in the film as someone who lives in between two worlds (whether the "other" world is interpreted as the psychological state of depression or a supernatural one) Justine is shown centrally positioned in a Christ pose, her head slightly tilted and her face expressionless. Illuminated by a surreal yellowish glow as thousands of moths rise around her, this symmetrical image invites contemplative vision. The next frame is highly surreal, presenting a symmetrical image of a castle with three figures in the foreground. Justine, Claire, and Leo walk toward the camera dressed in their finery and each walks beneath the glow of a celestial body. Justine, to the left in her wedding dress, beneath the shadowy glow of Melancholia, young Leo in his suit, centrally placed below the moon, and Claire to the right in a silvery gown, beneath a sort of nighttime sun.

The scene changes to an image of Melancholia circling the diminutive planet Earth. Justine slowly raises her hands as tendrils of lightning connect with her fingertips. She regards the phenomena with the curious wonder of one who no longer fears the fate of their body. Next, Justine is shown trudging across the screen from right to left in her wedding gown as a black yarn-like substance clings to her, pulling her backward. Her determined stride creates a strong sense of unidirectional movement. Melancholia and Earth appear in the following image, face-to-face in intimate symmetry. A window seat with a symmetrical archway frames the distant scene of a tree catching fire. In her wedding dress and veil, with flowers held in funerary position, Claire floats along a river, moving centrally down the screen. This image references Sir John Everett Millais's painting *Ophelia* (1851–52) that depicts the death of Ophelia from William Shakespeare's *Hamlet* (1599–1602). Such images employ strong unidirectional movement that is quite unnatural in mainstream cinema. The next image continues in this manner as Leo strips a branch of its bark with the movement of his pocketknife gesturing rhythmically forward while Justine also moves forward, more slowly, from the background. The music is now reaching its peak, as the spherical mass of Melancholia approaches Earth from right to left in a horizontal trajectory. The Western textual tradition teaches the eye to proceed onward from left to right, moving successively downward. The inversion of this movement mimics the gesture of textual erasure where the Earth is irrevocably deleted by Melancholia, leaving nothing behind. Melancholia's ghostly atmosphere appears to reach out to the Earth in caress before humanity's terrestrial home plunges into the larger planet, to be swallowed utterly as darkness descends. Here, von Trier creates an inversion of "Earthrise" in the apparition of Earth's demise. As the musical crescendo fades, Melancholia's vibrations can still be heard for around half a minute as the screen sits in darkness and the film title appears.

Following this sequence, *Melancholia* unfolds as a two-part narrative that is filmed using a handheld camera and that features naturalistic sound. The entire film takes place at Claire and John's home, filmed at the magnificent Tjolöholm Castle in Sweden, overlooking a neoclassical garden and an unearthly horizon of sea and sky beyond. Fringed by a dark wood, the castle is protected from any contact with the outside world, and it is as if there is a barrier surrounding the property, as cars and horses struggle to cross its threshold.

The first half of the film, entitled "Justine," features Justine's wedding reception, an arduous and drawn-out event that ends in her husband's permanent departure. Michael and Justine are all giggles and affection as they arrive at the reception, but the nature of their marriage is immediately undercut as Claire asks Justine: "So, you want this?" In this one line, Claire has revealed Justine's marriage to Michael as a performance of happiness that she doubts her sister will have the inclination to uphold. This question is posed in front of Michael, whose feelings are completely disregarded. With a demeanor of puppy-dog innocence, he does not seem to notice the affront. Similar confrontations occur throughout the reception, each challenging Justine to assert her happiness and commitment to Michael. As she fails every test, the true shape of her depression begins to show. Justine's face begins to take on a waxen quality, her shoulders slump, and her eyes glaze over. Her absences from the party become longer and less justifiable. Her newlywed husband tries to cheer her, to no avail. By the early hours of the morning, Michael has already given up on the dream of their marriage and the couple part with little to say to one another.

Part Two, entitled "Claire," sees Justine move into Claire and John's house after sinking into a depressive state in which she is no longer able to care for herself. Claire takes on the role of a patient mother as she tries to rouse her sister from her debilitated state of mind. Using all her strength to lift Justine's limp naked body into a warm bath, she is unable to convince Justine to raise her foot to get in. Justine will not eat and sleeps constantly. It is revealed that the planet Melancholia is due to pass close to the Earth in the coming days, and Claire worries that it might collide after reading about this theory on the internet. John is the champion of scientific rationality, insisting that the planet will not hit, rather it will be an astronomical wonder to behold. As Justine becomes more animated and conversational, she adopts a dry and nihilistic demeanor, undermining Claire's attempts to construct comforting illusions or rituals of normality that might distract from the cold fact of impending apocalypse. Throughout this half of the film there are a number of brief moments where Justine regards the planet Melancholia or notices changes in the natural environment that herald its approach. These moments take on an eerie quality through Justine's slight air of exhilaration. Sometimes, a muted phrase from Wagner's prelude comes in, reminding the viewer of the melodramatic and archetypal visions from the film's introductory sequence. Claire regards her sister in these instances with suspicion and fear. Like a witch sneaking into the woods at night to join her coven, Justine wanders down to a river where her sister sees her lying naked beneath the light of Melancholia. The luminescent celestial body returns Justine's desiring gaze in a shot-reverse-shot exchange. This scene and Justine's own assertion that she "knows things" give her a seer-like quality. Being hyperaware of her sister's moods, Claire is liable to fall under the spell of her sister's authoritative statements about life and death. In such conversations, Justine is transformed from a helpless and infantilized woman into the role of therapist, and Claire's role reverses in turn.

All the while, John attempts to convince Claire of the surety of science. John and his son Leo fashion an optical device that can measure the distance of Melancholia from Earth. It is mentioned in the film that the device is made from "steel" wire and Leo calls Justine "Aunt Steelbreaker." She is the only one who does not use the device, presumably because she knows what is coming. The analogy here could relate to humanity's feeble attempts to understand, predict, and control nature. The notion of "breaking" the device could relate to Justine's passive acceptance of death and her privileging of intuition over scientific calculation. When John finally realizes that he was wrong and that the planet will collide, he goes to the barn without a word to his family and commits suicide. Claire's anxieties about immanent death have now been confirmed and she is stricken with terror about the fate of her little boy Leo. Claire tries to keep a brave face for her son, making him breakfast and carrying on as normal. During these scenes, and for the final thirty-five minutes of the film, von Trier introduces layers of anxiety-inducing naturalistic sound. Claire's panicked breathing, the rumbling approach of Melancholia, and the distressed sounds of the horses continue in increasing persistence, interspersed with short Wagnerian phrases that signal the coming of the end. Justine shows her sister no sympathy and is cold in her reprimands about the futility of having a glass of wine together as the world ends. Justine displays a brief moment of empathy as she embraces Leo who is afraid that there will be nowhere to hide when Melancholia comes. She tells him a comforting story, saying that he must have forgotten about the "magic cave." Fashioning a tee-pee of sticks, Justine leads Leo and Claire into the "cave." Justine is centrally placed with her back to Melancholia. She holds Leo's hand to her right, asking him to close his eyes, then holds Claire's hand to her left. As the planet hits, Justine and Leo remain in a calm meditative pose. But Claire looks toward Melancholia, withdrawing her hand in terror to cover her face as they are engulfed in flame. The explosion rolls out in a thunderous white expanse, and the sound of the collision continues after the screen has turned black.

The spiritual significance of *Melancholia* is linked with the powerful and inexplicable feelings that it elicits. Like Kubrick and Noé, von Trier uses visual and aural techniques to stimulate an audience response that exceeds narrative requirements. Bearing the influence of *2001*, *Melancholia* features orchestral music contrasted with extended periods of naturalistic sound, the persistent use of breathing and low rumbling sounds, along with camera movement and compositions that encourages stillness of gaze. Their affect generates an almost hypnotic state of focus where the viewer becomes less analytical and more sensitive to the power of excess. In order for these film experiences to take on mystical attributes, it is necessary to reach a peak moment of stasis. It is this experience of emotional and cognitive overflow that produces the effect of passivity and ineffable noesis. Taking the path of melodrama, von Trier takes the viewer on an emotional journey from the everyday, through disparity, and into stasis. Structurally, *Melancholia* is bookended by sequences that are visually, aurally, and emotionally evocative. The main body of the film, however, is characterized by controlled emotional cycles that are not allowed to fully resolve. Using a variety of devices, von Trier steadily increases emotional saturation that is only released in the film's closing scene.

The everyday style that von Trier adopts in *Melancholia* is not exactly naturalistic, yet it is reminiscent of the Dogme 95 approach to film that stresses the importance of stripping back illusory devices. In the "Dogme 95 Manifesto," von Trier outlines the importance of shooting in color and on location, using a handheld camera, and retaining naturalistic sound. *Melancholia*, however, departs from this manifesto in its use of evocative music and special effects (Koutsourakis 2013: 211–12). Filming on location at Tjolöholm Castle, von Trier asked his cinematographer to adopt an instinctive approach using a handheld camera, and insisted that the furniture stay in a fixed position once filming commenced, limiting the movement of the camera (White 2012: 18–19). The use of naturalistic sound, pace, and camera movement encourages the viewer to follow the film's organic movements rather than anticipate unfolding action through narrative-based jump-cuts and artificial sound cues. As such, von Trier creates a feeling that is unnatural in conventional cinema and that subtly undermines viewer expectations. Viewer Emma Diaz-Nicholson mentions *Melancholia*'s "unpredictable shifts in tempo and tone" that give the film a poetic feel, highlighting von Trier's unusual approach to filmic rhythm (April 14, 2013, user review of *Melancholia*).

The emotional intensity of *Melancholia*, however, sets it apart from Schrader's description of the everyday. Von Trier does not achieve intensity through dramatic tearful outbursts and other familiar melodramatic tropes. Rather, he creates an uncomfortable tension using highly realistic emotionality that is restrained and internalized, often to the point of illness. Realism is heightened through intimate facial close-ups and the expressive subtlety of the breath that is heard where the character will not say what they are feeling. On the night of her wedding, Justine confides in her mother that she is scared of something she cannot define. Instead of reassuring her daughter, she tells Justine that she should be scared, but that she should just "forget it" and run away. This motherly advice is both cruel and bizarre. Justine's response is internalized as she says nothing and disappears downstairs. Many similar exchanges occur between Claire and Justine where it becomes increasingly difficult to understand Justine's motives and character. This pattern of repression and avoidance generates an emotional fog that permeates the film, creating increasingly abstract sensations of anxiety. This element of abstraction is essential in developing feelings of disparity as the viewer must dwell in this realm of unresolved emotional drives. As this feeling builds and is conflated with the mortal threat of planetary collision, its origins become more obscure and as the sense of clear-headed control recedes, feelings of passivity begin to emerge.

Throughout the film, Justine's morose composure and deadpan speech serve a dual purpose. Von Trier's evocation of depression is confronting and realistic, generating many viewer comments that express the similarities between the film and their own personal experience of mental illness (jebophos, August 4, 2012, user review of *Melancholia*; misty 77, February 13, 2012, user review of *Melancholia*; olga255, October 4, 2011, user review of *Melancholia*). Here, the development of cinematically induced spiritual affect and the dissociative features it exhibits becomes interrelated with the dissociative aspect of depressive episodes. However, viewers such as Michael Niebuhr were able to find resonance in the film despite a feeling of disconnection with the character of Justine. For this viewer, it was possible to redirect the emotional power of the film toward a contemplation of "the state of the world. And the future of ... human kind" (May 20, 2011, user review of *Melancholia*). As such, the parallel paths of destruction that *Melancholia* depicts (of the microcosm of subjective consciousness and the macrocosm of planetary survival) can be seen as equally effective paths to revelation.

The synopsis above details numerous scenes where von Trier employs frontality. He uses this technique using facial close-ups, and in symmetrically framed compositions. The transcendental style is present in the frontal or iconic depiction of Justine at key points in the film, where her face engenders a "respectful, noncommitted attitude within the viewer" (Schrader 1972: 100). There are also moments where the placement of her body transforms her from a person into a symbol, such as those featured in the film's opening sequence. While these symbolic apparitions do not necessarily fulfill Schrader's definition of frontality, they depict Justine with an air of distant sacrality that the viewer must attempt to reconcile with her more human traits. This in itself generates disparity as Justine does not appear to offer an enlightening message. While Justine's depressive states are palpable and realistic, other elements of her character create confusion about her ultimate nature. Justine is visually aligned with Christ through the image of her arms outstretched in *Melancholia*'s opening sequence, and is similarly compared with a goddess of antiquity lying naked by a stream later in the film. These references combine with her claimed prophetic abilities to suggest that she serves a religious function. However, Justine's heartless treatment of her sister and other selfish or childish acts diminish her potentially salvific qualities. While she may have special insights that sound grand and authoritative, she is nonetheless crushed by the weight of her mental illness, and in the final scenes of the film, despite her comparative calm, there are signs that she too feels fear and sadness. As all of these aspects coalesce in the viewer's mind, the irreconcilable features of her personality force the viewer to remain in an unresolved state of lyrical-associative reflection (Grodal 2009: 224).

Like *2001*, *Melancholia* features still compositions that evoke the frontal qualities of an altar. In their perfect symmetry, these images guide focus to the center where the viewer's eye becomes still in contemplation of an abstract inner space. Von Trier employs this technique in the introductory sequence of the film. *2001* and *Enter the Void* also employ strong focalizing strategies in their introductory sequences in order to prepare the viewer's mind for an immersive cinematic experience that calls upon nondiscursive perception. Kubrick primed his audience with the apprehension of a black void that stirred with abstract, shifting sounds. Noé pummeled conscious thought from the viewer's mind with an onslaught of hammering techno and strobing typefaces. In *Melancholia*, von Trier similarly immerses the mind in an abstract state before commencing the narrative. *Melancholia*'s introductory sequence that is described above presents the viewer with oblique, visually sensuous images that move in ways that do not conform to the laws of space and time. The uncanny quality of movement combined with the unexplained symbolism of these images makes them impenetrably surreal, yet music is offered as a guide, providing an emotional roadmap for the viewer to follow. As Grodal observes, these scenes combine stimulating and emotive music with "frozen" imagery, so that it is as if von Trier is "touching the accelerator and the brake at the same time" (2012: 47). When Part One commences, the stylistic contrast is dramatic; giving the feeling that one had just stepped out from behind a dark veil into the light of day. This technique clears the mind through the shock of contrast and sets the subconscious to work on the unexplained symbolic content that has just been removed from sight.

Von Trier's approach to characterization, his use of frontality, and naturalistic camerawork has been considered above. However, one of the most powerful means through which von Trier affects his audience is through sound. It is interesting to consider the correlations that Stefano Carta has identified between *Melancholia* and the work of Renaissance philosopher Marsilio Ficino (2015: 741–51), as Ficino viewed music to be the most effective means through which the spirit could attune to planetary influence. Music, he believed, affected the individual through a sympathetic connection of macro- and microcosm: *spiritus humanus* and *spiritus mundanus* (Ammann 1998: 575–9). Melancholy, as it was understood by Ficino, was a negative state of being brought about through the influence of Saturn, yet the Saturnian influence could also be viewed positively, where it was linked with the concept of genius (Ammann 1998: 573). As a sufferer of melancholy, Ficino conducted musical rituals where his "astrological songs are addressed to the compensating benign planets, the Sun, Jupiter and Venus" in an attempt to "temper" Saturn's influence (Ammann 1998: 571). In von Trier's film, Wagner's prelude emits as a call and response between the advancing planet and Justine as Earth's "seer." In line with Ficino's philosophy, a micro/macrocosmic parallel is established between Justine's personal experience of melancholy (or depression) and Earthly apocalypse (Carta 2015: 742).

Wagner's prelude accompanies the introductory sequence of the film, yet after this point, naturalistic sound is employed. At times, a sense of emotional closeness is generated though the detailed sound of the breath. However, it is in the final thirty-five minutes that sound is used to its full potential. At this point, Melancholia rises on the horizon. The vibrations of the planet can be felt in a low rumbling sound and soon the planet is close enough to take some of Earth's atmosphere. Claire begins to hyperventilate but John helps her to become calm again. In the background, the horses can be heard whinnying in distress. These three sounds—planetary vibration, panicked or labored breath, and the sound of distressed horses—remain in the aural landscape for the remainder of the film. While sparse naturalistic sound is still featured during this period, these unnerving sounds communicate biologically familiar signs of terror and foreboding.

Comparing the use of persistent breathing in *2001* and *Melancholia*, the former adopts the tone of calm monotony while the latter conveys monotonous distress. The common link between them exists in the hypnotic quality of repetition, despite differences in tone. In a Hollywood film, such rumbling, whinnying, and breathless sounds would be concentrated at a key narrative point and might last for a couple of minutes, if that. Their presence for an extended period is deeply unnerving, and there is very little action occurring through which to channel this disembodied anxiety. The sense of impeded action and inevitability is perfectly staged when Claire attempts to rescue her son from death in a futile attempt to drive away from the property (Grodal 2004: 133). None of her cars start, so she grabs her son and drives off on a golf cart that soon runs out of power and stops. As she struggles to carry her son in her adrenaline-charged state, Justine stands there completely calm and resigned, making Claire seem all the more hysterical by comparison. When Claire returns to the point she started from, she is utterly exhausted and has achieved nothing, except the expenditure of energy.

The aural texture that von Trier creates using this rumbling noise is reminiscent of Peter Weir's sound design in *Picnic at Hanging Rock* (1975) where the director used distorted recordings of earthquake noise to imbue the Australian landscape (and Hanging Rock in particular) with a supernatural quality. Weir explained that he chose to use natural sounds such as earthquake noise that would be subliminally registered by the audience as an impending threat, and from a cognitive perspective it is no surprise that sounds associated with natural disaster are translated by the brain as signs of danger. Annabel Carr refers to the "vibration of sacrality" that Weir generates, cultivating a metaphysical sensation of "primordial doom" (2005: 123–6). As sound subtly manipulates the viewer's sense of expectation, it periodically stimulates low-level anxiety through aural reference to physical danger. While Kubrick uses a vocal composition to signal the presence of *2001*'s monolith, this strange enmeshment of voices takes on the quality of an unstable electrical charge, similarly generating a sense of the uncanny.

As von Trier develops a heightened sense of expectation through sound, the call of Wagner's prelude is heard on four occasions in the latter half of the film, before it is brought in for the explosive finale. The first of these moments occur when Claire and Justine are out riding. Justine's horse will not cross the bridge and she begins whipping him relentlessly. When she finally stops, they gaze up at the planet. The second instance occurs as Justine lays naked beneath the glow of Melancholia. The third comes after Justine tells Claire that "life on earth is evil" and that all will be destroyed, coinciding with the revelation that she predicted the exact amount of beans in the bean lottery (proving that she "knows things"). The fourth moment occurs when Claire attempts to rescue Leo, and finally falls to the ground in exhaustion as hail begins to fall.

These moments signal the viewer to recall the introductory sequence and the image of Earth's destruction. It is a sound technique that is also utilized in *2001* (signaling the monolith), *Picnic at Hanging Rock* (recalling the spirit of Miranda), and *Enter the Void* (returning to the sibling vow). *2001* and *Enter the Void* connect the musical phrase with a corresponding visual reference; however, *Picnic at Hanging Rock* and *Melancholia* only do so in some instances. Aural presence and visual absence contribute a haunting quality that contributes to disparity. In *Melancholia*, each time this non-diegetic sound intrudes, it draws the inevitable conclusion a little closer. In this way, *Melancholia* creates a strange form of suspense where the viewer is dragged toward a known endpoint. However, films often introduce a plot twist or transformative message where a particular outcome seems immanent. In fact, conventional cinema leads the audience to expect this type of outcome. *Melancholia*, by contrast, passes each of these signposted moments without changing course. As Justine, Leo and Claire enter the "magic cave" the rumbling increases and Wagner's prelude is allowed to play out once again. Aural suspense and emotive anticipation heighten to an unbearable degree as von Trier focuses on each of their faces, before drawing back to behold their demise in a composition of perfect symmetry. The tiniest opportunity remains for von Trier to bring about emotive resolution for his audience, but he does not take it. Claire and Justine do not fully reconcile, and Claire does not even get to hold her son as they are consumed in flames. All the tensions that existed in life (including philosophical tensions between the worldviews presented by Claire, John, and Justine) are left unresolved.

It is in this state of disparity that *Melancholia* builds to a crescendo of light and sound that engulfs the image entirely, leaving nothing behind. This bright light forces the pupil to contract and then to immediately dilate in the cut-to-black. The black screen remains formless for a full twenty seconds while the sound of the explosion rolls out. Peter Szendy describes this scene as a pure and emblematic instance of cinematic apocalypse where "the end of the movie is the end of the world." In his personal experience of *Melancholia*, he tries to remind himself of the fictional nature of cinema, yet cannot be reassured, being haunted by a subliminal trembling (2015: 1–4). The audience is left to sit in this chamber of echoing sound, with the ghostly afterglow of bright light resounding in the eye, before the credits appear. This final high-contrast technique combined with the sudden loss of narrative constitutes a breaking point, where the building dissociative sensations of the film compound. Viewer comments in the following section demonstrate that this moment can be reasonably described as "an inexplicable outpouring of human feeling that can have no adequate receptacle" and a moment of filmic stasis (Schrader 1972: 43).

Mystical Experience

In *Picnic at Hanging Rock*, Weir sought to prompt a "visceral reaction" among viewers, "to induce them into a kind of dream state" where it would become possible to "access the audience's unconscious" (Bliss 2000: 190). Weir's statement sounds strikingly similar to Kubrick's, and while von Trier may not explicitly state the same, the similarities between these films draw Weir's comments into an interesting parallel with *Melancholia*. The approach that Weir describes generates a spiritualized response through an appeal to forms of stimulation that can bypass conscious reflection. As the audience begins to feel themselves responding to these subconscious cues, their sense of control is undermined. In this vein, Grodal alludes to von Trier's evocation of "ungraspable and difficult to verify dangers" in *Melancholia* (2012: 51). As the viewer reaches an emotional peak that they cannot account for, feelings of ineffability and passivity come into play. Where the peak experience is strong enough to fit Schrader's description of stasis, its power involves a shock to consciousness that is likely to possess corresponding noetic qualities.

Viewers describe *Melancholia* using terms reminiscent of James's attributes of mystical experience, and Otto's *mysterium tremendum et fascinans*. The film is "haunting" and "beautiful" ([victor7754@hotmail.com], April 20, 2012, user review of *Melancholia*), "overwhelming" and "traumatic" (Emma Diaz-Nicholson, April 14, 2013, user review of *Melancholia*), "existential," "ecstatic, stunning, dazzling, sensuous," (Roger Burke, June 16, 2012, user review of *Melancholia*), "mystical" (Vincentiu, October 4, 2011, user review of *Melancholia*), "sublime" (jon_orourke45, February 14, 2012, user review of *Melancholia*), "beyond emotions" (blackvenom-1, September 10, 2011, user review of *Melancholia*), and capable of bringing about states of "awe" (aurora7, December 2, 2011, user review of *Melancholia*). Like *2001* and *Enter the Void*, it is described as an experience where perceptual immersion is central in order to attain a focused state of mind (zephyryoun, October 28, 2012, user review of *Melancholia*; Harley Green, December 28, 2012, user review of *Melancholia*; earlytalkie, January 15, 2013, user review of *Melancholia*). Viewer advice in this area closely resembles commentary on *2001* and *Enter the Void*. Samkan says that one should experience the emotions of the film without arranging their feelings into a narrative structure (November 24, 2011, user review of *Melancholia*), while zephyryoun recommends using "empathy and imagination" while positioning themselves as a subjective "witness" to the events taking place (October 28, 2012, user review of *Melancholia*). For Khemaluck Deeprawat one should approach the film as if it was a painting, absorbing the experience, and in this state, *Melancholia* is able to communicate with "some deep part inside the mind" (January 22, 2015, user review of *Melancholia*). Encouraged by the style and techniques of the film, viewers quiet the discursive mind that would follow narrative progression, in order to allow the film to affect them in unexpected ways. Adopting a lyrical-associative style, von Trier calls upon the viewer to make connections between visual and aural cues, as well as parallels between micro- and macrocosmic narratives. This type of cognitive involvement makes films like *2001*, *Enter the Void*, and *Melancholia* well suited to amplifying and reflecting the psyche of the viewer.

One of the characteristic features of *2001*'s affective power is the inability to forget the experience and the ongoing sensation of being haunted by the film. Viewer comments testify to *Melancholia*'s similar effect on audiences. According to Anna19864, "The images will be seared into your brain, continuing to haunt for many years to come" (July 3, 2012, user review of *Melancholia*). Ribeiroworld remarked, "I had no idea that nearly a month after I watched this movie, I would still be haunted by it" (November 19, 2011, user review of *Melancholia*), and Golligow was left feeling as if s/he were "still in that magically imagined world" of the film (May 22, 2012, user review of *Melancholia*). Others found themselves dreaming about the film (sarahmillyhannah, January 16, 2012, user review of *Melancholia*; Xaaralia, November 10, 2011, user review of *Melancholia*). The haunting effect of the film is related to its perceived ineffable qualities and continued reflection on the film can be viewed as an integral part of its ritual function. Malull2 describes the progressive affect of *Melancholia*, where initially the experience resists understanding; the following day one begins to appreciate it, and after two days, it has the same effect as "a strong memory" that "lasts with you until you go old and start to forget things" (November 6, 2011, user review of *Melancholia*).

Viewers such as junkielee and Jess-K confirm that reflexivity has an impact on their existential outlook. For junkielee "after two days of rumination (a spontaneous reaction and I have no reason to explain why)" the slow affect of the film strikes the viewer and s/he feels a personal connection, which reveals an understanding of self that s/he was previously unaware of (December 4, 2011, user review of *Melancholia*). Jess-K reported that the film remained with her for days, "raised a lot of questions of the meaning of life," and "its impact to me was quite profound" (June 29, 2012, user review of *Melancholia*). The affective power of *Melancholia* and its ability to bring about feelings of ineffable significance and prolonged awe is evident in many reviews. Rather than engaging in discursive thought processes about the film after its conclusion, audience members report that they felt they needed to remain in a state of silent, wordless contemplation for an extended period (Summer Black, September 12, 2011, user review of *Melancholia*). M. J. Arocena was left "without appetite or willingness to talk" (November 28, 2011, user review of *Melancholia*), while dr luj felt "numb" and was "silent for quite some time" (November 19, 2011, user review of *Melancholia*). ZombieLittlePony was affected by *Melancholia* in an unprecedentedly physical way where s/he recalls, "My muscles went like water so I could not even stand from my seat. You have to experience it to understand" (October 16, 2011, user review of *Melancholia*). Viewers like by_all (October 11, 2011, user review of

Melancholia), CubeRic9000 (December 5, 2011, user review of *Melancholia*), and Echooche (August 24, 2011, user review of *Melancholia*) similarly describe the paralyzing power of *Melancholia* that renders audiences unable to move after the film's conclusion. However, the opening sequence has also exerted great power over viewers like masoroso whose hands turned "cold like ice" in response to this scene (September 26, 2011, user review of *Melancholia*). The invasive power of the film is noted by sarnela who says that the film "feels like it happens directly to you. You sense it with the hair of your skin" (November 9, 2012, user review of *Melancholia*). Hazefjord, who was deeply moved by *Melancholia*, said, "I felt it in my heart, my guts and in the form of chilly shivers along my spine." Comparing the film to the sight of a "poignant zeppelin," this viewer captures the sense of terror and awe embodying the passivity of mystical experience (June 14, 2012, user review of *Melancholia*).

Marked by an unexpected intimacy, experiences of *Melancholia* can cross the threshold of critical distance, penetrating the viewer's "soul." ZombieLittlePony compares the experience of watching the film to that of understanding someone simply by looking into their eyes. "The feeling is emotionally overwhelming but also very disturbing," as if someone "just opened the core of my very soul" (October 16, 2011, user review of *Melancholia*). References to the soul indicate that *Melancholia* engages the viewer on a level that is associated with their deeper self, as did references to the subconscious in *2001* and *Enter the Void*. According to jmillerdp, "What you experience is something that transcends film and goes to your very soul" (November 22, 2011, user review of *Melancholia*). Mention of the soul can also indicate the exertion of spiritual (or unattributed) agency over the viewer. For instance, bluestemz felt compelled to watch the film twice in a row and reported that it "dug it's [sic] claws into my heart and wrung raw emotion from my soul" (September 26, 2011, user review of *Melancholia*). Responses from audience members like manupravda and Joe Mason add weight to this postulation. According to manupravda, "It is hard to remain insensitive to this film. Like it or not, LVT films leave their print on you" (August 4, 2011, user review of *Melancholia*). Joe Mason remarks, "Say what you want about this guy, he has his finger on YOUR pulse. His film's know us. You can't hide" (September 26, 2011, user review of *Melancholia*). Interestingly, *Melancholia* viewers employ the term "soul" with relative frequency, whereas "subconscious" is less commonly used. This could be attributed to the romantic aesthetic of the film where one perceives the terrifying beauty of nature with their "soul." As a melodrama, *Melancholia* engages the emotions, and is therefore less likely to be discussed in terms of consciousness.

However, viewers still attest to sensations of overwhelming perceptual change. According to gradyharp, *Melancholia* is able to "jar the audience into a different level of perception" to contemplate the end of existence (May 16, 2012, user review of *Melancholia*). Further to this, Sarah Cupit says that the film kept her in "suspended wonderment" and that by the end of the film she felt the disintegration of space and time (December 27, 2011, user review of *Melancholia*). This moment of filmic stasis, that is similarly present in many of the reviews considered above, calls upon recognizably mystical sensations. As *Melancholia* builds emotive and anticipatory tension to reach a peak of intensity, the possibility of meaning is stripped away in the simultaneous annihilation of narrative and image. The viewer then fills this void with an overflow of unresolved emotion, leaving the sensation of heightened yet undetermined significance. Having a physical effect on viewers and a lasting impact on memory, the film's unresolved cycles persist in cognitive processes long after the film experience has ended. Rather than being a process that eventually reveals the meaning of the film, these subsequent meditations may be more intimately related to one's experience of similar perceptual and emotional states from a variety of contexts. As such, these mystical experiences build on each other to add a sense of certainty and profundity to one's developing worldview.

Conclusion

In *Melancholia*, von Trier invokes a moment of stasis through techniques designed to slow and focus the mind while maintaining a strong mood that feeds emotive expectation. Like religious spaces and rituals that use sensory cues in order to create an atmosphere conducive to religious experience (Maslow 1994: 31), the techniques evident in *Melancholia* may or may not bring about a spiritual experience. The question, however, is why von Trier seeks to generate this response in the first place. If the cinematic audience is not explicitly religious, why do they crave and highly value experiences that are so close to mystic awe? In the contemporary context of Western consumer society, Zygmunt Bauman has argued that individuals seek experiences through their engagement with the imaginative process of consumerism, so that the acquisition of material things is a by-product of this process (2000: 16). Bauman posits that the contemporary individual is propelled by "the excitement of a new and unprecedented sensation" (2000: 16). This line of argument resembles Campbell's observations about the romantic ethic that underpins consumer culture where he argues that individuals seek "the fundamental pleasure which 'exists' in life itself" (1989: 69).

As previously discussed, conventionally pleasant sensations can be enhanced and made stronger through the addition of harsher elements. The traumatic aspects of this contribute to an unshakable sense of truth that is reliant upon the willingness of the experiencer to accept moments of ineffable sensation as revelatory and to value them as significant. This involves the interplay of cognitive aspects of the experience with cultural predilections that encourage an association with ultimate truth. As this context is predominantly secular, purely religious connotations relating to the presence of God may influence and bolster the signification of truth as an ideal, yet this feeling of truth need not overtly reference such religious concepts. Like Western consumerism that is driven by novelty, and individualism that prizes uniqueness above all else, unprecedented sensations are most desired as they contain potentiality. They embody the promise that there is something more than what has already been experienced in life. Experiencing continued potentiality is vital in secular culture as sacredness can be felt without reference to the promises of religion that are subject to rational scrutiny and doubt. This can account for the appeal of Westernized Buddhist ideas that appear to allow the individual to avoid religious commitment by simply focusing on the present moment, facilitating the celebration of immediate sensations, and reducing the existential burden of future and past.

Where *2001* invites a reassessment of the origin, evolution, and destiny of humankind, *Melancholia* brings about an indirect revaluation of human life by confronting the viewer with a vision of its final end. For Justafilmwatcher, *Melancholia* pushes the viewer to an emotional extreme in the same way that *2001* "forces one to grasp a greater intellectual construct" (November 21, 2011, user review of *Melancholia*). As a contemporary development of Western epistemology, truth has become associated with those affective experiences that resist classification and which overwhelm subjective reflexivity. Recognizing the plurality of the cinematic audience, affect becomes a primary, nonaffiliated representation of religiosity in its pure, emotive state. In the cinema, films like *Melancholia* make it possible for viewers to attain the sensation of unmediated knowing and the ability to feel without affiliation. Being of sacred significance in contemporary consumer societies, the yet-to-be-known can be experienced in these profound states of affect. As audiences possess the ability to learn filmic formulas, predict their trajectory, and diffuse their potential sensational power, filmmakers must continually strive to employ unusual techniques in order to create the desired sense of incomprehensible otherness. The fact that this state of affect is so highly valued in contemporary society reveals much about the ultimate concerns of the West. In a cultural context of relative truth and overwhelming plurality, intense sensations of an abstract and incommunicable nature represent primal, universal, and transcendent ways of knowing. It is clear that contemporary artists and filmmakers recognize this and deliberately choose to work with the auto-reactions of the brain and body. As a film of religious significance, *Melancholia* may tell the story of complete annihilation, yet it leaves behind the vibrations of certainty. Certainty of what, it is hard to say, yet the strength of this certainty is something that transcends the self-reflexive attitude that is so often applied in matters of religious belief. As Brian Massumi so astutely observed, "Belief has waned for many, but not affect" (1995: 88).

Beyond the shared techniques of *2001*, *Enter the Void*, and *Melancholia*, there are strong conceptual links between these films. In their own way, each film confronts the viewer with an apocalyptic revelation of the impersonal forces of the universe, moving away from personhood and the human narrative into pure sensation. The worldview that underpins these films is linked with the individualist spirituality of the modern West that is validated by experience. The film does not try to convince the viewer of a particular argument; it overwhelms them with profound noesis. Those who interpret their experience as spiritual often draw comparisons (or at least terminology and concepts) from Eastern religion, philosophy, romanticism, and psychology. All three films involve the stripping away of identity and society to access the essential power of an awe-inspiring and indifferent universe in the form of pure experience and unmediated knowledge. The source of this knowledge is conceived as a terrifying, impersonal, creative, generative, and destructive force that is spiritual in its strangeness, but constitutes the originative forces of nature. Human life and personhood are in some sense irrelevant, yet as *Enter the Void* demonstrated, the spiritualized forces of nature permeate human beings in such a way that they may not fully understand their own function or purpose. In these films, personhood is consistently denied its usual relevance and the anonymous observing gaze of human awareness is left in its place.

9

Melancholia
Presence in Absence/The Long Withdrawing Roar

As a film ostensibly about the end of the world, *Melancholia*'s release in the lead up to the heralded "Mayan apocalypse" of 2012 placed von Trier's film in the midst of speculation about the destruction of the Earth (Allen, Moore, and Parfitt 2012: n.p.). The conclusion of the Mayan 5,125 calendar in 2012 was variously interpreted in the media as a sign of a new beginning associated with the New Age or of impending apocalypse in line with Christian mythology (Little 2012: n.p.). A global Reuters poll claimed that "one in 10 of us is said to be anxious that 21 December marks the end of the world" (Little 2012: n.p.). While the short-lived, media fueled hype about the end of the world did not necessarily penetrate deeply into the Western psyche, this sense of anxiety that Reuters observed in 10 percent of respondents perhaps revealed more generalized feelings of trepidation about the state of the world and the fate of Western culture.

Viewers often discuss *Melancholia*'s apocalyptic themes in connection with the fall of the West, presenting a strangely accepting attitude about their culture's ultimate demise. The rejection of Western values associated with scientific rationalism, traditional Christianity, sentimentality, and social convention are familiar themes that have been discussed in previous chapters, particularly in relation to *2001*. Through the lens of modernity and drawing on Eastern philosophy and romanticism, *Melancholia* presents the deconstruction of the social, personal, and spiritual values of the West, and challenges the viewer to confront reality. As demonstrated in the previous chapter, this confrontation comes as a moment of enlightenment where attachments are burned away and all that remains is a sense of voidness, where the self no longer exists. *Melancholia* does not tear down one social construct to replace it with a superior one; rather, von Trier captures the orientation toward ultimate reality that's prerequisite is the ruthless deconstruction of all things. To understand the apprehension of this sublime fact, it is necessary to acknowledge the continuation of the dual movements of romantic and modernist thought articulated in Campbell's *Romantic Ethic* and *Easternization of the West*. The romantic influence thus continues to guide the individual to know by feeling, while the modernist influence insists that truth can only be found in the darkest shadows of the human heart. The psychological orientation of this quest is captured in the Jungian archetype of the "shadow" and in the general psychological desire to face and reveal the repressed (Jung 1959: 14; Jung 1966: 103). Taking responsibility for evil is also an important aspect of the "psychologizing of religion" and the "sacralization of psychology" (James 1956a: 47; Hanegraaff 1998: 197), where the individual stands alone in a world without divine "parents," with only the present moment, and the present life, to live. In facing that darkness in an irreligious leap of faith, self and culture fall away, and an ahistorical universal presence is known, providing a momentary glimpse of reality.

Longing for Reality

Unlike Hollywood apocalypse films that apply a moral lens to the topic of human extinction, *Melancholia* presents the end of the world as a cold fact that occurs without reason. The end comes with no one to blame, and no salvation is offered, either in the form of a band of survivors or in postmortem transcendence. *Melancholia* does not extend the plight of apocalypse beyond the perimeter of the stunning castle grounds where the main characters live, so it is as if the rest of the human population never existed anyway. The end of the film is shown in its first minutes, so the audience knows that the cataclysmic collision is inevitable. Von Trier focuses instead on the way in which the main characters face the reality of what is happening. Justine, Claire, John, and Leo are isolated from the rest of the world in their experience of the planet's approach.

Cowboyandvampire interprets John's death as symbolic of society's "misplaced faith in science" that is bound up with the failure of Western civilization (October 20, 2012, user review of *Melancholia*). In this example, John's favored scientific theory is just another convenient narrative used as a balm to provide reassurance in the face of unfathomable danger. Claire's anxiety rises by degrees as she is confronted with the reality that her son Leo (and everyone else on Earth) will die. She tries to save her son, clutching him to her chest in a futile attempt to run away. As these emotional events unfold, Justine, in her depressive state, is accepting of what is about to happen. Her acceptance, however, does not allow for any form of transcendence, as she says, "Life is only on Earth, and not for long."

Justine is not a savior figure; rather, her position embodies the abandonment of hope and the futility of harboring attachment to life, the Earth, or human existence (either physically or spiritually conceived). A conversation between the sisters reveals their contrasting perspectives:

> Justine: The Earth is evil. We don't need to grieve for it.
>
> Claire: What?
>
> Justine: Nobody will miss it.
>
> Claire: But where would Leo grow?
>
> Justine: All I know is, life on Earth is evil.
>
> Claire: Then maybe life somewhere else?
>
> Justine: But there isn't.
>
> Claire: How do you know?
>
> Justine: Because I know things.
>
> Claire: Oh yes, you always imagined you did.
>
> Justine: I know we are alone.
>
> Claire: I don't think you know all that.
>
> (*Melancholia* 2011)

Justine's perspective may seem overly cynical from one point of view, but this conversation can also be interpreted as an implicit challenge to each of Claire's attachments. Claire struggles to confront the truth of impending apocalypse because of her attachment to the Earth, her son, and the possibility of life "somewhere else." In Buddhist thought, attachment keeps one in a state of suffering (Gyatso and Chodron 2017: 46–8). As viewer Khemaluck Deeprawat sees it, *Melancholia* is a call to "embrace the truth that the world is transient and temporary" by letting go of one's attachment to material things, social expectation, and fear of death (January 22, 2015, user review of *Melancholia*).

While Justine is not exactly a model for enlightened thinking, her manner of being has a deconstructive effect in the world of the film, prompting the viewer to disinvest themselves from conventional emotional attachments to the situations presented on screen. Justine herself has been described as "ruthlessly deconstructive" (Cohen 2012: 240). Von Trier draws the viewer into a familiar scenario, and then pulls it apart, leaving nothing behind. This is felt as a narrative ellipse, where the final stage of an emotional process is erased, preventing the viewer from processing it or making sense of its significance. Justine's wedding is the clearest example of this where the newly weds part after surviving less than twenty-four hours of marriage, without a word of explanation. Michael leaves with little complaint, and there appears to be no emotional fallout for Justine. Although the film depicts a subsequent depressive episode, Michael's existence is completely forgotten as he exits stage left. The people who crowd the film during the wedding reception also disappear completely as the event comes to a close. The coming of the end of the world does not even prompt a phone call to mothers, fathers, or friends. Similarly, when John realizes that Melancholia will not be a "fly by," he silently disappears to commit suicide. Claire is initially distressed when she discovers his body, but she does not grieve and does not admit to Leo or Justine that he is gone.

Viewers like Chris_Docker have picked up on the Buddhist theme of attachment in *Melancholia* that he interprets as a critique of "the trappings of happiness" and "transitory and superficial sense-gratification." This viewer refers to *Melancholia* as a film about the concept of "non-attachment" that is "almost Zen-like in its conviction" (Chris_Docker, October 19, 2011, user review of *Melancholia*). Viewers like ZombieLittlePony (October 16, 2011, user review of *Melancholia*) and secondtake (September 23, 2012, user review of *Melancholia*) agree that the rejection of empty ritual is one of the core messages of the film, and von Trier confirms this reading (Thorsen 2014: n.p.). Claro, *Melancholia*'s cinematographer, refers to the yellow lighting used in Part One as "somehow too happy—happy to the point that it becomes disturbing. The yellowness of the lighting is too much; it starts to seem nauseating." This effect is implicitly linked with Catholic opulence as the lighting of the second part is referred to as "Protestant" in its cool neutrality and naturalism (White 2012: 18). Both Chris_Docker and Claro's interpretations embody a sense of alternative spirituality as they align authenticity with the rejection of tradition and a turn toward the cool harshness of reality that is also represented by nature. The act of letting go of ossified social ritual and belief is symbolically linked with Protestant and Buddhist worldviews.

According to von Trier, Justine, as a melancholiac, demands truth, and is willing to surrender to destruction in the search for authenticity (Thorsen 2014: n.p.). Viewers like Rudd Thijs (January 5, 2012, user review of *Melancholia*) and Vlad Coroama (November 14, 2011, user review of *Melancholia*) adopt a similar sentiment in their approach to the film. For von Trier, "Longing is true. It may be that there's no truth at all to long for, but the longing itself is true. Just like pain is true. We feel it inside. It's part of reality" (Thorsen 2014: n.p.). In line with alternative spirituality, this perspective adopts an epistemology of feeling where the path to reality is intuited, but truth itself remains undetermined. Authenticity exists in the openness of intention and the willingness to face truth's ugliness. One's realizations cannot be transferred to another simply by learning, because all things are in a constant state of change and dynamism. Ritual, in this sense, stagnates and distorts the initial encounter with truth by converting it into a repeatable pattern.

For von Trier, Justine's rejection of social expectation is a part of her, "Longing for reality. . . . She is longing for something of true value. And true values entail suffering" (Thorsen 2014: n.p.). The director notes that happy and hopeful art is instinctively mistrusted, in favor of that which contains harsher elements that are considered more truthful. Von Trier recalls that he has always felt compelled to explore the darker aspects of humanity, and to do so without restraint (Heath 2011: n.p.). This comment recalls Menninghaus's observations about the nature of truth in the twentieth century where fear, disgust, and other immediate sensations are granted the highest truth-value (2003: 384–7). For Karen, the revelation presented by the film is "beautiful, it's real, it's disgusting, it's terrifying" (July 14, 2011, user review of *Melancholia*). David senses a "fundamental deeper meaning behind this film" that he cannot define, but it is linked to "the stark truth we all secretly know," involving the acceptance of the reality that "the world is evil, capitalism is evil, and we are all shallow, soulless, empty and materialistic people" (April 8, 2013, user review of *Melancholia*). According to Grumpy, *Melancholia* challenges the viewer to either "meekly submit to death" or to "throw oneself into the fury of pure instinct and native cruelty" (October 19, 2015, user review of *Melancholia*).

Like Kubrick and Clarke in *2001*, von Trier contemplates the question of whether we are alone in the universe in *Melancholia*. In an interview with Nils Thorsen, the director reflected, "When you see pictures from outer space, you shiver and feel that we're awfully alone" (2014: n.p.). Numerous viewers sacralize this sense of human fragility in the face of an indifferent universe that can be understood in terms of the traumatic path to revelation discussed above. Saternbaby felt the "confirmation of wonder and happiness" in the face of "a perceived abyss" (May 9, 2012, user review of *Melancholia*), while oOgiandujaOo had a "calming and beautiful" experience of the "sublime" that offered "the comfort of not caring if the world ends" (October 4, 2011, user review of *Melancholia*). A further example can be found in Jennyhor2004's comment that when faced with "the certainty of annihilation" one can adopt "the serene and passive calmness born of depression and lack of hope" which she sees as a more "reasonable" response than "trusting in a non-existent God or belief systems that so far haven't delivered on their promises of benefitting humans across the Earth." Here we see religion and the psychological act of trusting in God being evaluated for their efficacy against the feeling of "serene and passive calmness" that the viewer attained during the film (December 24, 2011, user review of *Melancholia*). According to AMichaelL, von Trier's nihilistic message is directed toward viewers who already live in a "system of disbelief," and this viewer finds something sublime in the idea that this life may be all we have (January 13, 2012, user review of *Melancholia*). Tieman64 also makes note of the atheist dimensions of *Melancholia* saying that the film is a sincere expression of a crisis of faith that is "atheistic, even when dealing with religious longings" (February 19, 2011, user review of *Melancholia*). From the romantic period onward the scientific revelation of nature's vastness and complexity prompted the development of what Charles Taylor calls "the new cosmic imaginary," where human fragility and the fearsome power of nature spark feelings of awe for the religious believer and atheist alike (2007: 367). The connection between atheism and the reverent apprehension of nature is well established in popular science where human extinction and the destruction of Earth are viewed as sublime facts. For example, physicist Professor Brian Cox explains how life on Earth will eventually come to an end in the BBC documentary series *Wonders of the Universe* (2011). This event (that could be apprehended with fear) is spoken of with reverence as a tragic, beautiful, and poetic destiny that awaits us all. As Tim Matts and Aidan Tynan argue, *Melancholia* reveals nature as "a sheer autonomous objectivity, a self-contained but endangered natural order" that sets humanity in the face of "non-human nature in perfect balance with itself" (2012: n.p.). Tvspace describes feeling sick with fear and anticipation at the "immense scope and power" of "a force that is literally not on a human scale and thus cannot be comprehended by humans, except in the most primitive of ways" (November 14, 2011, user review of *Melancholia*). Similarly, for Bones Eijnar, *Melancholia* forces the viewer to "come face-to-face with the ephemeral nature of our existence," and this is a visceral experience that no words can describe. This primary cinematic experience leads the viewer to the conclusion that the film is about the denial of human fragility in "the face of massive, impersonal forces of nature and a universe of crushing vastness" (June 27, 2011, user review of *Melancholia*). A part of this primitive comprehension of the immense power of nature appears to involve the realization of the utter irrelevance of humanity. The desire to expose the lie and reveal what is hidden by religious institutions manifests in the pleasure of truthful realization. This involves the inversion of traditional

Christian beliefs about God's plan for humanity, and can be partially explained through the psychologizing of religion, as has been previously discussed. Freud's view of Christian faith as infantile is particularly relevant here, as is his overall focus on revealing the hidden desires of the subconscious.

Searching the Darkness

Von Trier's Depression Trilogy, of which *Melancholia* is the second installment, explores extreme states of psychological suffering and evokes the terrifying (and at times abject) beauty of nature and animal instinct. As a set of films that are named after a psychological state (depression) and also reference the religious, emotive, and psychological in the films' respective titles—*Antichrist*, *Melancholia*, and *Nymphomaniac*—it is perhaps unsurprising that these three elements are interwoven into the fabric of the trilogy. Reportedly, von Trier wrote the first of the three films, *Antichrist*, while "in a psychiatric hospital" and was recovering from a major depressive episode during filming (Haubrich 2018: n.p.). Of the three films, *Antichrist* contains the clearest examples of religious symbolism in the archetypically named characters of He and She, and references to Eden, Satan, and the Gospel of Matthew (Haubrich 2018: n.p.). The film depicts the death of the couple's infant son as he falls from a window while they are having sex. Consumed by grief, She is taken by her psychiatrist husband to a place she fears called "Eden," an isolated cabin in the woods, where he imagines that he will remedy her damaged psyche through exposure therapy. She's interior state is increasingly reflected in the environment around them, forming symbolic correspondences of archetypical, religious, and mythological significance.

Unlike *Melancholia*, which depicts the classic features of depression paralleled with impending planetary apocalypse (LeBeau 2011: n.p.), *Antichrist* explores grief, fear, and sexuality through brutal maternal and spousal violence. Connections between evil, sexuality, and the feminine are reflected in an abhorrent vision of nature that is devoid of nurturing qualities, and where decay is everywhere (Plate 2009: n.p.). Von Trier attributes the gruesome image of the self-devouring talking fox that appears in the film to a vision experienced during a "shamanic journey" he undertook ten years prior (O'Hagan 2009: n.p.). He achieved this state using "a Brazilian technique where you enter a trance through this very powerful drumbeat" and von Trier goes on to say that he finds it quite easy to enter this "parallel world" (O'Hagan 2009: n.p.). While the trance-like qualities of *Melancholia* have already been discussed, *Antichrist* draws on some similar techniques, using sensuous imagery and prolonged and repetitive sound to generate mood, such as the relentless thud of falling acorns. While *Nymphomaniac* commences with the sound of drizzling rain against black screen, immersing the viewer in darkness for nearly two minutes, the main part of the film is dominated by dialogue and naturalistic sound, making it stylistically distinct from *Antichrist* and *Melancholia*.

Nymphomaniac revisits the site of emotional pain in the context of female sexuality as Joe retells the stories of her sexual life to a stranger called Seligman, who looks after her after finding her beaten and unconscious in a dark alleyway. While sexually graphic and tragic in its conclusion, the film also offers moments of humor and intellectual reflections on sexuality, as Seligman adopts the nonjudgmental and dispassionate tone of a therapist. Seligman and Joe both declare themselves to be nonreligious, yet Seligman repeatedly connects Joe's stories with religious exemplars and esoteric signs of Satan, while Joe interprets her own behavior as "sinful." In *Melancholia*, the position of rationality is typified by John, and this is also present in *Antichrist*'s He and in *Nymphomaniac*'s Seligman. Larry Gross refers to this characterization as not simply a rational one, but rather that of "self-deluding liberal humanism" (2009: n.p.). By contrast, the suffering female protagonists are enmeshed in embodied states of being and are attuned to both hidden forms of spiritual enchantment and the primal forces of nature. This gendered dichotomy of male rationality versus the chaotic feminine should not be taken at face value as von Trier often represents himself through his female characters (Butler and Denny 2017: 3), and his films do not isolate the ideal in the guise of a single character whose vision triumphs over others. Von Trier's films move through different perspectives, much like the psychological dialogue between different parts of the self, and no film in the Trilogy leaves the viewer with the certainty of closure. *Antichrist* concludes with the possession of He and She by the archetypes of masculinity and femininity in their most horrific guises, *Melancholia* ends with utter annihilation, and *Nymphomaniac* allows openness to develop through the healing processes of dialogue before undoing it all in a final abuse of trust.

As this brief outline demonstrates, the films of the Depression Trilogy share a set of common themes, using the patient-therapist framework as a means of exploring the darkest of psychological states, questioning the origin of our basic human drives, and posing implicit questions about reality. However, the powerful feelings that von Trier generates through the experiential dimension of film both overwhelm and inform how the narrative and symbolic elements are received. To better understand the function of heightened and ambiguous sensations in von Trier's work, and in *Melancholia* in particular, it is worth considering the function of religion, belief, and psychological experience in the director's life more broadly.

Von Trier's personal experiences of psychotherapy have had a significant impact on his filmmaking, leading him to favor artistic instances of psychological confrontation and revelation. As Linda Badley explains, von Trier's extensive experiences with psychotherapy have led him to employ "therapeutic language" in both his films and his public persona(s). Further to this, Badley notes that "therapeutic trauma" is central to von Trier's filmmaking (2011: 6–7). Having grown up in a nudist family, the director explains the graphic depiction of sex that is typical of his films as a "matter of being real." While the sex scene in *Melancholia* is one of the least confronting in his oeuvre, the director's motivation of "being real" is the point of significance (Cheung 2015: n.p.). It has also been said that von Trier's mother raised him "based on a demand for complete openness. Everything was up for discussion" (Badley 2011: 8). This desire for "complete openness" is related to "being real" and both of these are hallmarks of the psychologized alternative spirituality that has been cited as a permeating influence on Kubrick, Noé, and von Trier. According to Caroline Bainbridge, trauma constitutes the "affect and primary aim" of von Trier's films that is a part of his overall tendency to articulate in psychological terminology (Badley 2011: 6). Viewer William O. Tyler lends support to this postulation saying that *Melancholia* is an expression of trauma in its "most beautiful and purist state" (January 28, 2016, user review of *Melancholia*) while sebbastiann compares the experience of watching *Melancholia* with psychological therapy where the film takes "the viewer to the extremes just like a shrink would probably make you face your worst fears before you can feel liberated" (January 8, 2012, user review of *Melancholia*).

This desire to confront reality is echoed in several of von Trier's manifestos. For example, the director wants film to embody the unadulterated, "miraculous," and "physical experience" that "works its way through the body," to a state of trembling ecstasy (Koutsourakis 2013: 209). Bodily engagement is considered more real than the narrative elements of film that von Trier labels as "hackneyed" (Koutsourakis 2013: xx). This point of view is reinforced by von Trier's comments on the religious capacities of cinema:

> We need divine light, a change through the light. For me, that light is cinema or it could be cinema. I watch a lot of films and often I almost want to cry because what I see is that divine light. When Jesus went up the mountain he saw the light, and perhaps there isn't much hope in this light, but there is life. Some of my

favourite films give me this light. I love the concepts of suffering, pain, guilt, but there is another side to life, the luminous side that films can portray. (Lemercier 2011: n.p.)

Comparing the experience of filmic revelation to the moment when Jesus "saw the light," von Trier locates the power of the divine in the common experience that is shared by Jesus and cinematic audiences alike. That the aesthetic path to "divine light" experienced in the cinema is comparable to what Jesus encountered embodies the democratization of religious experience that is typical of the modern period. His comment that "there isn't much hope in this light, but there is life" demonstrates that an encounter with truth may be sublime but it does not necessarily confirm the promises of the church.

This spiritual worldview combines Christian allegory with an undercurrent of existential doubt that is compatible with atheism, revivifying the religious through the aesthetic path of feeling. As a child, von Treir was raised on "hippy" liberalism and communist ideals on the one hand, but was also taught to be firm in his atheism (Nicodemus 2005: n.p.). Ever the iconoclast, von Trier explored the power of identity taboos in his early creative works, demonstrating his willingness to experiment with different aspects of his persona (Heath 2011: n.p.). In his youth, von Trier connected strongly with his paternal Jewish heritage, only to discover at the age of thirty-three that his real father was of Danish/German extraction and that he had been lied to his entire life (Heath 2011: n.p.; Lumholdt 2003: xxii; Kürten 2011: n.p.). His mother, who had raised him to keep nothing hidden and to be "real" and open about everything, suddenly revealed, on her deathbed, that she intentionally chose von Trier's biological father for his creative genes (Badley 2011: 8; Heath 2011: n.p.). This moment of betrayal instilled a seed of doubt regarding the vision of reality that his parents had presented him with, clothed as it was in the pretense of honesty, rationality, and full disclosure. This vision of reality has been described as one lacking in boundaries, but as being built upon "a very clear idea of good and evil, of kitsch and good art" (Nicodemus 2005: n.p.). The insistence on harsh truths extended as far as denying comfort to their child when he was terrified of dying in his sleep, merely offering him the rational response that his sudden death "while unlikely . . . was certainly possible" (Heath 2011: n.p.). Reacting to his parents' beliefs, von Trier asserts, "In my work, I try to throw all this into question. I don't just provoke others, I declare war on myself, on the way I was brought up, on my values the entire time. And I attack the good-people philosophy which prevailed in my family." By doing this, he focuses on "the discrepancy between philosophy and reality, between conviction and its implementation" (Nicodemus 2005: n.p.).

During the chaotic period of his mother's death, von Trier converted to Catholicism, perhaps seeking an alternative way to frame his destabilized sense of self. This newfound religiosity simultaneously flew in the face of his atheist upbringing and the dominant Protestant culture of his country, framing his adoption of Catholicism as an act of rebellion (Ungureanu 2014: 128; Nicodemus 2005: n.p.). In more recent years, von Trier has been dismissive of his Catholic conversion and has expressed difficulty in maintaining religious belief (Muss 2006: n.p.; Nicodemus 2005: n.p.). He has also noted that eventually most people come to adopt similar views to their parents, showing the continued salience of the atheist worldview in his thinking (Fury 2011: n.p.). However, these protestations fit the epistemological mode of alternative spirituality where mistrust of authority is central and where uncertainty about the ultimate veracity of particular teachings is part of drive to seek unmediated truth. Modernity is characterized by the desire to unmask God and to reveal what has been hidden behind comforting illusions and von Trier's personality and upbringing have set him up to pursue this more so than most. As a person with a strong antiauthoritarian streak it is unlikely that von Trier would adopt a straightforward religious identity based on a predetermined set of beliefs and practices. This clarifies why he cannot attain the level of wholehearted belief that he associates with religion and must make up his own mind through self-reflexivity and personal experience.

The presence of religious qualities and symbolism in von Trier's films reveals the depth of his spiritual contemplations despite his dismissive manner of self-representation in interviews. In line with the ethos of alternative spirituality, von Trier exhibits a fundamental appreciation of religious experience and revelatory states of consciousness, demonstrating the continuation of spiritual drive in the absence of set beliefs. According to Freja Dam, von Trier "wrote all of his films on a bottle of vodka a day combined with an unspecified drug," enabling him to enter a state "where ideas arose, creativity flourished and doubts vanished" (2014: n.p.). He refers to this state of intoxication and his experience of trance achieved through a Brazilian drumming technique as examples of entering into a "parallel world" (O'Hagan 2009: n.p.; Dam 2014: n.p.). Further to this, von Trier practices meditation and daily prayer, activities that focalize the mind and cultivate religious forms of perception (Cheung 2015: n.p.; Muss 2006: n.p.). Meditation facilitates the withdrawal from discursive thinking and increases the propensity to experience spontaneous insights. Prayer involves a form of purposeful inner thought directed to an unknowable "other" and the corresponding openness to receive answers or guidance from this unknown source. This range of practices serves, in various ways, to silence the socialized conscious mind and to encourage altered states of consciousness and insight, revealing a somewhat hidden path through which von Trier seeks revelatory experience. Experiencing altered states of consciousness as von Trier (and Noé) seek to do contributes to the effectiveness of their films in manipulating viewer perception.

In "Manifesto One," von Trier asserts that he is seeking "more—of the real thing, fascination, experience—childish and pure, like all real art.... We want to see religion on the screen" (Koutsourakis 2013: 207). The "real," then, is associated with a kind of religious epiphany characterized by "fascination" perhaps akin to Otto's *mysterium tremendum et fascinans*. Importantly, "religion" is understood in relation to the childlike and pure, revealing the desire to attain an unmediated experience of something original and uncorrupted by the institutions of society. According to Camil Ungureanu, von Trier's films express "a deep interest in religious experience and a discontent with secular rationalism of Enlightenment extraction" (2014: 128). Labeling von Trier's approach as "religion against religion," she clarifies that this is a religiosity that is represented through film as "palpable presence" or "riveting silence" in the ultimate denial of "God or Transcendence" (Ungureanu 2014: 127). These observations show that while von Trier may struggle with religious belief and return to the atheist perspective in his considerations of reality, that forms of religiosity that manifest through experience remain vital.

Psychological illness has been a constant presence in von Trier's life, and at times, these invasive experiences have taken hold of him completely (Heath 2011: n.p.). Understanding the feelings and perceptions that arise during periods of marked psychological distress and imbalance has undoubtedly contributed to von Trier's ability to deeply affect his audience and to recreate unusual perceptual states through film. The sensation that personal agency has been displaced is particularly relevant in a consideration of *Melancholia*, along with moments of dark revelation where harsh realities permeate one's entire being. In such times, the individual outsources their capacity to regulate emotion to the therapist, as Justine and Claire do in the film. Von Trier has openly discussed his long-term use of psychotherapy and periods of hospitalization in interviews. Exposure to commonplace psychotherapeutic techniques can be assumed to have encouraged reflexivity and self-observation, creating an inner distance between the self, and the thoughts, beliefs, and emotions that may be experienced. In alternative spirituality, when such distancing is applied to the external world, truth is relativized, making belief in God a situational contingency. In this context, the experience of something akin to faith occurs when one is able to dwell in "uncertainty, ambiguity, and paradox" (Schaberg 2018: 3), accepting both the awesome power of the unknown and the possibility of a Godless universe. The pursuit of this state has been at the heart of modern art, literature, and film where its indefinable quality saves it from the ruthless urge to deconstruct and dethrone all else that is redolent of power.

For Uncle Newgod, the "joy" of *Melancholia* is found in "the vitality and force given to the incommensurable fact that we are all hopelessly alone" and the insistence that there is no form of salvation that will be able to overcome this (December 25, 2011, user review of *Melancholia*). Here, the individual must confront the abyss, doing away with comforting illusions like heavenly salvation. As Jon Pahl's theological reading of *Melancholia* suggests, the film encourages a leap of faith as opposed to the adoption of belief:

> Only those deluded by a superficial rationality, or by cultural convention [which may be the same thing], would wish to escape the end that is the fate of all the living. Better to face the Kierkegaardian dread with equanimity, and to take a leap of faith into the light. *Melancholia*'s affirmation of resurrection is therefore more durable than most. . . . All one has is the film itself, its distinctive and fragile grace, and the faith of the viewer. (Pahl 2012: 3)

Søren Kierkegaard's (1813–55) representation of faith in *Fear and Trembling* is pertinent to von Trier's vision of *Melancholia*. For Kierkegaard, "Infinite resignation is the last stage before faith" as one perceives "the paradox of existence" inherent in the biblical story of Abraham, where he is called to sacrifice his beloved son to God (2005: 14–24 and 52–3). In *Melancholia*'s final moments, the call to let go of attachment is heard by all except Claire who dies screaming in grief and terror as her son, her love, and life itself are sacrificed in the apocalyptic collision. Her repose betrays a failure to heed the call of faith present in the story of Abraham. Justine and Leo, however, embody what Pahl describes above as "equanimity"—a state of emotional evenness perhaps more befitting this moment of faith—and a term often used to describe the ideal emotional state attained in Buddhist meditation practice.

For stan Collin, *Melancholia* systematically deconstructs and destroys the values of the West to be subsumed by the acceptance and transcendence of death (January 13, 2013, user review of *Melancholia*). Bearing in mind the range of viewer responses considered so far, this acceptance and transcendence of death could also be read as the acceptance and transcendence of the death of God. According to Elkins, "The very idea of absence has to be religious. Just as the final model for presence is God, so the final model for absence is God's absence" (2004b: 193). Similarly Michel de Certeau describes the modern individual emerging from "an unaccepted mourning" felt in "pangs of absence" that "afflicts us in a region we cannot identify," and is "akin to the ailment of melancholia" (1995: 1 and 6–8). Elkins goes on to quote the poetry of Matthew Arnold to describe this shift from romantic era thinking to the modern:

> The Sea of Faith, Was once, too, at the full.... But now I only hear, Its melancholy, long, withdrawing roar, Retreating, to the breath, Of the night-wind, down the vast edges drear, And naked shingles of the world. (2004b: 199)

In *Melancholia's* final cut-to-black, von Trier exposes his audience to an abrupt sensation of loss, yet as the vibrations of the collision continue in the darkness, presence is simultaneously felt in the form of a "melancholy, long, withdrawing roar." This continues as an experience of emotional presence and narrative loss, lingering with the viewer and remaining inexplicable. This "fundamental," "inexorable and almost tangible, haunting presence" is present in the premonitory vibrations of Melancholia, moving ever closer to the viewer (tabuno, April 1, 2012, user review of *Melancholia*).

The conflicting sensations of *Melancholia's* finale have also been interpreted in Buddhist terms. According to chaos-rampant, *Melancholia* works in the tradition of the "Eastern mystics" in contemplation of "nothingness," representing this concept in a manner typical of the "Western, post-enlightenment worldview that has pushed god to the side and seated the mind in his place." This comment touches on numerous aspects of alternative spirituality from the psychologizing of religion to the adoption of Eastern concepts into the Western religious lexicon and the important role of mystical epistemology. The viewer compares *Melancholia* with Terrence Malick's *Tree of Life*, released in the same year. Both films are pensive in tone and feature cosmic themes; however, where Malick's film is able to "restore meaning" through its greater focus on human relationships, *Melancholia* simply leaves the viewer to sit with the emptiness that it has revealed (chaos-rampant, September 20, 2011, user review of *Melancholia*). The religiosity of *Melancholia* arises out of the intensity of paradoxical and irresolvable feelings that it leaves behind. For chaos-rampant *Melancholia* draws the viewer into a state of ecstasy where they "feel particles being dislocated inside of [them]." In this "there is the sense of emptying out" that reveals "the impermanence of all things" (chaos-rampant, September 20, 2011, user review of *Melancholia*). Here, the Buddhist concept of impermanence combines with the mistrust of permanent meaning and the tendency toward deconstruction that is present in alternative spirituality. Hedgehog5 experienced the film as "the consummation in fire of all we have ever known" (October 1, 2011, user review of *Melancholia*), and aurora7 saw the film as a lesson in the Buddhist "doctrine of emptiness" (December 2, 2011, user review of *Melancholia*). Mario Nicolaou says that *Melancholia* assaulted him with "painfully delightful emotions" until he reached a "mental state where all my thoughts and emotions were finally out of my head," mirroring the quieting of the mind achieved through meditative practice (May 16, 2012, user review of *Melancholia*). As D. C. Priestley explains, Buddhist meditation practice aims to produce a spontaneous state of "no-mind." When this state has been attained, "Something about the presumed psychological makeup of the meditator is lost, erased, or shown to be an error or an illusion. Hence the theme of 'extinction' or 'cessation' that is so common to many theories of meditation." This "serene and clear awareness" is sometimes experienced as "a literal absence of thought" (2004: 686). Steve_plumber_man felt that the film could lead one to "absolute acceptance of the present moment" (July 20, 2014, user review of *Melancholia*). Mirroring the sensation of filmic stasis or enlightenment, these comments demonstrate *Melancholia*'s ability to bring about a powerful experience of nothingness and emancipation from thought.

Conclusion

Melancholia is at once a spiritualized experience and a therapeutic journey into the harsh light of truth. The ethos of alternative spirituality that crystalized in the late 1960s is evident in von Trier's filmmaking and in audience responses where the inherent corruption of Western culture is taken as a starting point. Privileging experiences of ambiguity and emotional excess over knowledge and meaning, *Melancholia* seeks revelation via darkness and nihilism, exhibiting an implicit mistrust in social authorities and associated constructs. Truth is made manifest to those who take the leap of faith required in the realization that there may be "no truth at all to long for." Truth is something that one feels to be real, "like pain is true" and one must bear "suffering" to reach this point of revelation (Thorsen 2014: n.p.). Here, the looming terror of environmental apocalypse plays an important role, drawing on climate change fears and the possible erasure of a future path for humanity. Casting a chilling shadow over Western culture, the micro-level psychological cataclysm mirrors the macrocosmic, prompting an assessment of individual failures along with the cultural.

As a director who generally works in the realm of extreme cinema and who has frequently experienced states of possession by strong emotion, the element of passivity becomes central in his filmmaking, and is the key factor in generating spiritualized interpretations. *Melancholia* synthesizes atheism with the holy, maintaining the individualized mode of seekership and the primacy of intuitive noesis. While overall, von Trier chooses the lightning-bolt path of "immediatism" in the Depression Trilogy (Versluis 2014: 110), conjuring moments of cinematic revelation through perversity, pain, and the stripping away of comfort, one must not overlook the sublime glow of the "luminous" that permeates *Melancholia*, especially in its final moments (Lemercier 2011: n.p.). As von Trier reflects, this experience comes with no promises of salvation and no assurances against the awesome fact that we may be alone in the universe (Lemercier 2011: n.p.).

Conclusion

Spiritual Sensations

Religion, Film, and the Transcendental Style

The subdiscipline of religion and film remains an eclectic space where there are many opportunities to establish new approaches. As objects of analysis, the religions and films that can be brought into dialogue are numerous and constantly changing in form. Equally, the methodologies of religion and film can be conceived with different purposes in mind, drawing influences from disciplines beyond religious studies (and theology). The methodological approach employed here takes the religio-cultural insights of the religious studies discipline as a starting point, placing the film, its creators, and audience in their cultural context. This allows the researcher to get to the heart of what religion is (by their definition) before drawing correspondences with the cultural product being studied. Films are incredibly complex cultural products, attaining their final form as the result of thousands of design choices over several years, with the intention of conveying particular meanings and experiences to audiences. Any aspect of film can become a focal area for study, and it is vital for religion and film scholars to broaden their frame of reference beyond narrative and symbolism to notice the full suite of design elements—including editing, composition, camerawork, and postproduction aesthetics—that each contribute to the essence of the film and its subtle affects.

This study has picked up the thread of Schrader's *Transcendental Style*, highlighting the insightfulness of this classic (yet little used) text. Looking past Schrader's insinuations about the existence of a transcendent reality, his observations regarding film technique religious experience are turned to a new application—that is, to investigate the relationship between film form and perception in the generation of spiritualized cinematic experiences. Here, viewer comments have been called upon to paint a gestural picture of the experience itself. Finding correlation with all four of James's attributes of mystical experience (2014: 206–7), these audience responses also exhibit hallmarks of religious experience in their effect on memory, their initiatory qualities, and their tendency to trigger existential reflection (Whitehouse 1996: 710).

As Schrader's *Transcendental Style* demonstrates, the shift into a religious frame of perception is brought about using specific cinematic techniques (1972: 3–5). Elkins similarly identifies a set of aesthetic conditions that can facilitate the "religious feeling" of "sudden, unexpected, out-of-control presence" (2004b: 174 and 210–12). In line with Plate's general observation that filmmakers apply "millennia-old aesthetic tactics from religions" (2008: 3), Griffiths discusses the common features of immersive environments (both religious and nonreligious) that are able to bring about a bodily sense of awe (2008: 18 and 32–6.). These observations establish a framework for understanding the connection that exists between religion and the arts, at the level of experience. As this study has demonstrated, filmmakers invoke a religious experiential model when subconscious forms of stimulation overwhelm the viewer, taking the experience out of the realm of rational comprehension and control. Generating a sense of "presence" and "agency" (Taves 2009: 41, 94–119, and 137), films like Kubrick's *2001*, Noé's *Enter the Void*, and von Trier's *Melancholia* provoke a cognitive shift characterized by a noetic feeling of higher unity (James 2014: 206; Schrader 1972: 51) and "the sense of some ungraspable fundamental significance" (Grodal 2009: 247).

The Many Paths

Spiritual Sensations has explored the film experiences offered by *2001*, *Enter the Void*, and *Melancholia*, seeking to account for the spiritually toned responses found in *IMDb* reviews. The religiosity of these films has involved the discussion of various categories of experience, including the meditative, the mystical, the initiatory, the dissociative, the psychedelic, the aesthetic, and the drug-assisted. While it is reasonable to say that these films are capable of bringing about an experience that has notable mystical qualities, the aforementioned categories are so deeply intertwined that it may not be possible to completely separate them. Frames of reference also overlap, where religion, psychology, popular culture, and the methodologies of religious studies find points of correlation. Adopting James's definition of mystical experience (2014: 206–7) and incorporating features from Otto (1958: 12–40) and Hollenback (1996: vii–xi and 94–5), one must acknowledge that their respective insights are drawn from mixed categories of experience. This can be seen in James's drug revelations (Nicotra

2008: 199–213), Otto's aesthetic apprehension of awe (Oldmeadow 2009: 235–6), and the seemingly meditative terminology that Hollenback applies (1996: 94–5), along with the cross-cultural comparisons that inform their respective definitions of religious experience. Similarly, Schrader calls upon the common features of religion, art, and meditative practice in his vision of the transcendent (1972: 108). As a process of analogical comparison, distillation, and mixture, a universally applicable definition of religious experience is bestowed with a religious significance all of its own. That is, at the level of cultural influence, adaptable and nondenominational definitions of religious experience come to act as a model for the subjective experience of spiritual reality.

This conflation of terms, categories, and experiences may seem problematic at first, yet correlations points to a deeper truth. The films, audience responses, and scholarly material presented here are the product of a culture of unprecedented plurality. Alternative spirituality (and its antecedents) share an orientation toward truth that accepts relativity on one level, but on another, a radical experience of truth's oneness is sought. These seemingly opposed positions coexist in the privileging of transient experiences of the latter variety, while subsequent reflective thought involves the return of critical distance and pragmatic evaluation. The direct and unmediated apprehension of truth that is captured by James's definition of mystical experience refers to a state of mind that can occur in both religious and nonreligious contexts.

2001, *Enter the Void*, and *Melancholia* facilitate this experience through the evocation of ineffability, noesis, and passivity. Alluding to broad existential themes, these films foster perceptual immersion, where the viewer responds by allowing the film to affect them without seeking to engage in discursive thought. Through abstraction and ellipses, these directors encourage a lyrical-associative search for meaning (Grodal 2009: 149 and 224). During the film experience, this search for meaning may occur somewhat unconsciously. Techniques of excess are employed to sustain focus and increase disparity while denying narrative resolution. Pushing the viewer to a cognitive and emotional end point, the culminating moment of stasis is experienced as a shock to consciousness that exceeds explanation. The enduring power of this experience lingers in unresolved feelings and reflexive ruminations that are often related back to the film's existential theme. In this way, the film's theme sets a contextual boundary around the experience that influences the subconscious processing of abstract sensations. Due to this extended process of open-ended reflection, the associated meanings that arise take on special personal significance. While these films incorporate religious aesthetics and focalizing techniques, the ability to adopt a religious frame of reference in the cinema stems from the belief that the boundary between sacred and profane can be crossed spontaneously in daily life.

Sacred Sensations and the Beholding of Truth

The meanings, associations, and behaviors that relate to religious experience change over time, and these inflections of meaning reveal the complex structure of an associated worldview. Within viewer comments that may at first seem to be fairly clichéd reflections on film experience, one finds hints of an underlying worldview that privileges transient sensations of overwhelming yet inexplicable noesis. Audience responses demonstrate little self-reflexive insight on this point, so the task of this study has been to determine how films like *2001*, *Enter the Void*, and *Melancholia* have been able to elicit such reactions. Analysis has then turned to the question of why these experiences are significant within the context of the changing religious landscape of the post-1960s West.

As Campbell has argued, the fundamental tenets of the "East" have come to characterize the West (2008: 11, 15, and 141–2). The associated form of spirituality that has emerged in this process of seeking alternatives to Christianity and Enlightenment rationalism inverts and transforms traditional values. It is telling that the Eastern concepts that have gained ground in the West involve the deconstruction of permanent forms of meaning and identity, focusing on the immediacy of experience. These concepts serve to erode previous systems of power, relocating it in the realm of personal control: the present moment and the individual lifetime. New systems of power and manipulation may continue to operate beyond the individual's awareness, but it is the *feeling* of personal autonomy and potentiality that must be maintained. In a pluralist culture, where freedom is valued and individuality and difference are celebrated, permanent religious affiliation and static beliefs are difficult to maintain.

As James has argued, cultural memory can provide a subconscious platform for the adoption of religious belief for those who have stepped into nonbelief and those who experience spiritual doubt (1956a: 14). As a religious position defined by seeking, alternative spirituality starts in a place of spiritual dissatisfaction (Sutcliffe 2003: 99). While alternative in its ethos, new forms of spirituality build on a cultural foundation as much as they seek the untrodden path. Rejecting the dogmatism of Christianity and rationalism, other aspects of these systems of thought can be revived where their truth is relativized. However, alternative spirituality maintains a longing for a truth that transcends relativity, that represents the unblemished source of religion, and that is beyond human comprehension. This is expressed in Elkins's view that when one has "[burnt] away what is false in religion" the sacred can still be discerned in the "faint perfume" of religious truth that is left behind (2004a: 37 and 88). Nayar similarly refers to the process of "stripping away artifice in order to reveal something more essential underneath" (2012: 118-19). The search for the sacred resembles the search for the self where "mainstream values amount to a form of indoctrination that alienates the individual from their true Self" (Houtman and Aupers 2007: 307). In each case, the rejection of external hegemony involves the simultaneous desire to rediscover something essential and precious that was lost along the way, via personal experience.

In order to be free from Earthly influence, religious truth must be defined as something "other." In the abstract languages of the arts, religious mystery can be renewed without reference to contested religious meanings. Here, religious truth is not recognized in its content but through the "aura of factuality" with which it is endowed (Geertz 2017: 97). This certitude can manifest in cinematic experiences where a perceptual, sensational, or emotive threshold is crossed, impacting cognitive processing and memory and leading to a feeling of unmediated encounter. Such overwhelming experiences of otherness resonate with a truth beyond truth as they cannot be fully accounted for or explained.

The discovery of deepening abstraction produces cognitive effects that are a testament to spiritual power and the fact that they remain undefined imbues them with potentiality. Recognizable forms of manipulation or representation can easily break the spell, and directors like Kubrick, Noé, and von Trier have exploited the resonance of trauma in order to elicit the shock of revelation. Aligning with Menninghaus's observations about the changing nature of truth (2003: 384-7), the suspicion of artifice is continually present, and truth itself is expected to be confronting to behold. As such, the tendency toward deconstruction embodies the thrill of holy terror as all things come to be transformed into an "ever-changing continuum of impermanent and impersonal elements" (Collins 1992: 216). *2001* depicts this in the deconstruction of Bowman's personhood as he becomes the Starchild, *Enter the Void* presents a world of sensation that can be conceived as a flow of impersonal elements, and *Melancholia* enacts the total annihilation of things permanent and personal. The "faint perfume" and "aura of factuality" that these films leave behind then comes to signify a truth of absolute otherness that is more essential than what has been sacrificed in the process (Elkins 2004a: 88; Geertz 2017: 97).

Such experiences of cinematic mysticism are important, yet transitory. Their special value arises from their extraordinary features and their difference from everyday experience. Temporarily inverting the individual's sense of freedom and autonomy, these rare psychic intrusions provide a moment of spiritual legitimation that sparks subsequent reflexivity (Wood 2007: 154–75). In the religious culture of alternative spirituality, unmediated experience is valued, yet the worldview itself is characterized by plurality, relativity, psychological distance, and pragmatism. As such, alternative spirituality constitutes a dynamic between two positions—the autonomous seeker who is free to forge their own path of discovery and behind the veil, the primitive force of the sacred that reveals itself in moments of spiritual guidance.

References

2001: A Space Odyssey (1968), [Film] Dir. Stanley Kubrick, USA/UK: Metro Goldwyn Mayer.

Adams, Sam (2010), "Gaspar Noé," *A. V. Club*, September 24. Available online: http://www.avclub.com/article/gaspar-noe-45554 (accessed February 20, 2014).

Agel, Jérôme (1970), *The Making of Kubrick's 2001*, New York: New American Library.

Allen, Nick, Malcolm Moore, and Tom Parfitt (2012), "Mayan Apocalypse: Panic Spreads as December 21 Nears," *The Telegraph*, December 7. Available online: http://www.telegraph.co.uk/news/worldnews/northamerica/usa/9730618/Mayan-apocalypse-panic-spreads-as-December-21-nears.html (accessed June 15, 2015).

Ammann, Peter (1998), "Music and Melancholy: Marsilio Ficino's Archetypal Music Therapy," *Journal of Analytical Psychology*, 43: 571–88.

Antichrist (2009), [Film] Dir. Lars von Trier, Denmark/France/Germany/Italy/Poland/Sweden: Zentropa Entertainments.

Atkinson, Quentin D. and Harvey Whitehouse (2011), "The Cultural Morphospace of Ritual Form Examining Modes of Religiosity Cross-Culturally," *Evolution and Human Behavior*, 32: 50–62.

Austin, James H. (2014), "The Meditative Approach to Awaken Selfless Insight-Wisdom," in Stefan Schmidt and Harald Walach (eds.), *Meditation-Neuroscientific Approaches and Philosophical Implications*, Studies in Neuroscience, Consciousness and Spirituality 2, 23–55, Basel: Springer International Publishing.

Axelson, Tomas (2008), "Movies and Meaning: Studying Audience, Fiction Film and Existential Matters," *Particip@tions*, 5(1) May: n.p.

Axelson, Tomas (2010), "Narration, Visualization and Mind: Movies in Everyday Life as a Resource for Utopian Self-Reflection," Conference Presentation: CMRC, The 7th International Conference on Media, Religion and Culture, Toronto, Canada, August 9–13. Available online: https://www.diva-portal.org/smash/get/diva2:522166/FULLTEXT01.pdf. (accessed June 15, 2015).

Axelson, Tomas (2017), "Movies and the Enchanted Mind: Emotional Comprehension and Spiritual Meaning Making Among Young Adults in Contemporary Sweden," *YOUNG*, 25(1) February: 8–25.

Badley, Linda (2011), *Lars von Trier*, Urbana, IL: University of Illinois Press.

Barney, Matthew (2014), "Matthew Barney and Gaspar Noé," *Bomb Magazine*, April 1. Available online: https://bombmagazine.org/articles/matthew-barney-and-gaspar-noé-1/ (accessed January 19, 2016).

Barry, Robert (2010), "Suddenly the Maelstrom: Gaspar Noé on the Music of *Enter The Void*," *The Quietus*, October 13. Available online: http://thequietus.com/articles/0509

7-gaspar-no-interview-enter-the-void-soundtrack-daft-punk (accessed May 19, 2014).

Bauman, Zygmunt (2000), "Tourists and Vagabonds: Or, Living in Postmodern Times," in Joseph E. Davies (ed.), *Identity and Social Change*, 13–26, Piscataway, NJ: Transaction Publishers.

Benjamin Bergery (2010), "Contemplating a Colorful Afterlife," *American Cinematographer*, 91(10) October: 18–22.

Bergesen, Albert J. and Andrew M. Greeley (2003), *God in the Movies*, Piscataway: Transaction Publishers.

Beugnet, Martine (2007), *Cinema and Sensation: French Film and the Art of Transgression*, Carbondale: Southern Illinois University Press.

Birks, Chelsea (2015), "Body Problems: New Extremism, Descartes and Jean-Luc Nancy," *New Review of Film and Television Studies*, 13(2) April: 131–48.

Bjørnvig, Thore (2012), "Transcendence of Gravity: Arthur C. Clarke and the Apocalypse of Weightlessness," in Alexander Geppert (ed.), *Imagining Outer Space: European Astroculture in the Twentieth Century*, 127–46, New York: Springer.

Bliss, Michael (2000), *Dreams Within a Dream*, Carbondale, IL: Southern Illinois Press.

Blizek, William L. (2009), "Using Religion to Interpret Movies," in William L. Blizek (ed.), *The Continuum Companion to Religion and Film*, 29–38, New York: Continuum.

Blizek, William L., Michele Marie Desmarais, and Ronald R. Burke (2011), "Religion and Film Studies through the Journal of Religion and Film," *Religion*, 41(3): 471–85.

Bordwell, David (1979), "The Art Cinema as a Mode of Film Practice," *Film Criticism*, 4(1): 56–64.

Bradshaw, Peter (2010), "How Enter the Void Sees Itself in Lady in the Lake," *The Guardian*, September 22. Available online: https://www.theguardian.com/film/filmblog/2010/sep/22/enter-the-void-lady-lake (accessed August 14, 2014).

Brahmasamhara, Yogi (2008), *Awakening: Authentic Meditation for the Beginner and Experienced Meditator*, Sydney: Rockpool Publishing.

Brick, Howard (2000), *Age of Contradiction: American Thought and Culture in the 1960s*, New York: Cornell University Press.

Brockmyer, Jeanne Funk (2013), "Media Violence, Desensitization, and Psychological Engagement," in Karen E. Dill (ed.), *The Oxford Handbook of Media Psychology*, 1–19, Oxford: Oxford University Press/Oxford Handbooks Online.

Brown, William (2013), "Violence in Extreme Cinema and the Ethics of Spectatorship," *Projections*, 7(1) Summer: 25–42

Buñuel, Luis (1983), *My Last Sigh*, Abigail Israel (trans.), New York: Knopf.

Burns, Dylan M. (2014), *Apocalypse of the Alien God—Platonism and the Exile of Sethian Gnosticism*, Philadelphia: University of Pennsylvania Press.

Butler, Lisa D. and Oxana Palesh (2004), "Spellbound: Dissociation in the Movies," *Journal of Trauma and Dissociation*, 5(2): 61–87.

Butler, Rex and David Denny (2017), "Introduction: The Feminine Act and the Question of Woman in Lars von Trier's Films," in Rex Butler and David Denny (eds.), *Lars von Trier's Women*, 1–14, New York: Bloomsbury Academic.

Campbell, Colin (1989), *The Romantic Ethic and the Spirit of Modern Consumerism*, New Brunswick, NJ: Blackwell.

Campbell, Colin (2002), "The Cult, the Cultic Milieu and Secularization," in Jeffrey Kaplan and Heléne Lööw (eds.), *The Cultic Milieu: Oppositional Subcultures in an Age of Globalization*, 12–25, Lanham: Altamira Press.

Campbell, Colin (2008), *The Easternization of the West: A Thematic Account of Cultural Change in the Modern Era*, Boulder: Paradigm.

Carr, Annabel (2005), "Beauty, Myth and Monolith: Picnic at Hanging Rock and the Vibration of Sacrality," *The Buddha of Suburbia: Proceedings of the Eighth Australian and International Religion, Literature and the Arts Conference 2004*: 123–31.

Carta, Stefano (2015), "Melancholia," *Journal of Analytical Psychology*, 60(5): 741–51.

Chandler, Siobhan (2010), "Private Religion in the Public Sphere: Life Spirituality in Civil Society," in Stef Aupers and Dick Houtman (eds.), *Religions of Modernity: Relocating the Sacred to the Self and the Digital*, 69–88, Leiden: Brill.

Cheung, Lucy (2015), "Lars von Trier: 'I've Started Drinking Again, so I Can Work,'" *The Guardian*, April 21. Available online: https://www.theguardian.com/film/2015/apr/20/lars-von-trier-interview (accessed June 14, 2015).

Cho, Francisca (1999), "Imagining Nothing and Imaging Otherness in Buddhist Film," in David Jaspers and S. Brent Plate (eds.), *Imag(in)ing the Other: Filmic Visions of Community*, 169–95, Atlanta: Scholar's Press.

Chodorov, Pip and Jeremi Szaniawski (2018), "'The Absolute and Ultimate Manifestation of the Power of the Mind over Technology': Gaspar Noé Talks 2001: A Space Odyssey," *Senses of Cinema*, (87) June. Available online: http://sensesofcinema.com/2018/feature-articles/the-absolute-and-ultimate-manifestation-of-the-power-of-the-mind-over-technology-gaspar-noe-talks-2001-a-space-odyssey/ (accessed July 15, 2019).

Chopra, Deepak (2017), "What's the Significance of Sensations During Meditation?" *The Chopra Centre*. Available online: http://www.chopra.com/articles/what's-the-significance-of-sensations-during-meditation - sm.0000bv13pz687f8ypub190f6t7b8a (accessed December 21, 2017).

Clarke, Arthur C. (1990 [1953]), *Childhood's End*, New York: Ballantine Books.

Clarke, Arthur C. (2000 [1968]), *2001: A Space Odyssey*, London: Hutchinson.

Cohen, Tom (2012), "Polemos: 'I Am at War with Myself' or, Deconstruction™ in the Anthropocene?" *Oxford Literary Review*, 34(2) December: 239–57.

Collins, Steven (1992), "Nirvana, Time, and Narrative," *History of Religions*, 31: 215–46.

Cowan, Douglas E. (2009), "Seeing the Saviour in the Stars: Religion, Conformity, and the Day the Earth Stood Still," *The Journal of Religion and Popular Culture*, 21(1) March: n.p.

Cowan, Douglas E. (2010), *Sacred Space: The Quest for Transcendence in Science Fiction Film and Television*, Waco: Baylor University Press.

Cusack, Carole M. (2011), "The Western Reception of Buddhism: Celebrity and Popular Cultural Media as Agents of Familiarisation," *Australian Religion Studies Review*, 24(3) December: 297–316.

Dam, Freja (2014), "Lars von Trier Speaks! 9 Takeaways from His First Interview in Three Years," *Indie Wire*, December 1. Available online: http://www.indiewire.com/article/lars-von-trier-speaks-9-takeaways-from-his-first-interview-in-three-years-20141201 (accessed May 5, 2015).

David Lyon (2000), *Jesus in Disneyland: Religion in Postmodern Times*, Malden: Wiley-Blackwell.

Davidson, Ronald M. and D. Orzech (2004), "Tantra," in Robert E. Buswell Jr. (ed.), *Encyclopaedia of Buddhism*, vols. 1 and 2, 820–26, New York: Macmillan Reference Library/Thompson Gale.

Davis, Judson (2016), "The Primordial Mandalas of East and West: Jungian and Tibetan Buddhist Approaches to Healing and Transformation," *NeuroQuantology; Bornova Izmir*, 14(2): 242–54.

Deacy, Christopher (2005), *Faith in Film: Religious Themes in Contemporary Cinema*, Farnham: Ashgate.

de Certeau, Michel (1995), *The Mystic Fable: Volume One: The Sixteenth and Seventeenth Centuries*, Michael B. Smith (trans.), Chicago: University of Chicago Press.

Demerath III, N. J. (2000), "The Varieties of Sacred Experience: Finding the Sacred in a Secular Grove," *Journal for the Scientific Study of Religion*, 39(1) March: 1–11.

Ebiri, Bilge (2010), "Gaspar Noé on Why Enter the Void Is Avatar for the Art Crowd: Both Are 'Like Taking Drugs,'" *Vulture*, September, 27. Available online: http://www.vulture.com/2010/09/gaspar_noe_on_why_enter_the_vo.html# (accessed August 21, 2014).

Eliade, Mircea (1965), *Rites and Symbols of Initiation: The Mysteries of Birth and Rebirth*, New York: Harper and Row.

Elkins, James (2004a), *On the Strange Place of Religion in Contemporary Art*, London: Routledge.

Elkins, James (2004b), *Pictures and Tears: A History of People Who Have Cried in Front of Paintings*, Milton Park: Taylor and Francis Group.

Enter the Void (2009), [Film] Dir. Gaspar Noé, France/Germany/Italy: Wild Bunch Distribution.

Erickson, Steve (2010), "'Enter the Void' Director Gaspar Noé Talks Sex, Drugs and Narrative Cinema," *The Wall Street Journal*, September 21. Available online: http://blogs.wsj.com/speakeasy/2010/09/21/enter-the-void-director-gaspar-noe-talks-sex-drugs-and-narrative-cinema/ (accessed August 15, 2014).

Fabien Lemercier (2011), "Von Trier's Train Wreck," *Cineuropa Film Focus*, April 28. Available online: http://cineuropa.org/ff.aspx?t=ffocusinterview&l=en&tid=2239&did=203318 (accessed January 7, 2014).

Failes, Ian (2010), "Enter the Void Made by fx," December 28. Available online: https://www.fxguide.com/featured/enter_the_void_made_by_fx/ (accessed May 13, 2014).

Faivre, Antoine (1994), *Access to Western Esotericism*, New York: State University of New York Press.

Farber, David (2002), "The Intoxicated State/Illegal Nation: Drugs in the Sixties Counterculture," in Peter Braunstein and Michael William Doyle (eds.), *Imagine Nation: The American Counterculture of the 1960s and 1970s*, 17–40, Abingdon: Routledge.

Figlerowicz, Marta (2012), "Comedy of Abandon: Lars von Trier's Melancholia," *Film Quarterly*, 65(4): 21–6.

Ford, James L. (2000), "Buddhism, Christianity, and the Matrix: The Dialectic of Myth-Making in Contemporary Cinema," *The Journal of Religion and Film*, 4(2): n.p.

Fraser, Peter (1998), *Images of the Passion: The Sacramental Mode in Film*, Westport: Praeger.

Freud, Sigmund (1989), *The Future of an Illusion*, New York: W. W. Norton and Company.

Freud, Sigmund (2002), *The Psychopathology of Everyday Life*, London: Penguin.

Fury, Moe (2011), "Lars Von Trier on Atheism," [YouTube video], February 22. Available online: https://www.youtube.com/watch?v=-HLvTBvSf2M (accessed July 16, 2019).

Gazi, Jeeshan (2017), "Blinking and Thinking: The Embodied Perceptions of Presence and Remembrance in Gaspar Noé's Enter the Void," *Film Criticism*, 41(1) February: n.p.

Geertz, Clifford (2017), *The Interpretation of Cultures*, New York: Basic Books.

Gelmis, Joseph (1969), "An Interview with Stanley Kubrick (1969) by Joseph Gelmis," excerpt from Joseph Gelmis, *The Film Director as Superstar*, New York: Doubleday and Company, 1970. Available online: http://www.visual-memory.co.uk/amk/doc/0069.html (accessed January 28, 2015).

Gilmore, Lee (2011), "DIY Spiritual Community: From Individualism to Participatory Culture," in Stewart M. Hoover and Monica Emerich (eds.), *Media, Spiritualities and Social Change*, 37–46, London: Continuum/Bloomsbury Collections.

Gonzalez, Pedro Blas (2009), "Stanley Kubrick's 2001: An Existential Odyssey," *Senses of Cinema*, 52: n.p.

Griffiths, Alison (2008), *Shivers Down Your Spine: Cinema, Museums, and the Immersive View*, New York: Columbia University Press.

Grodal, Torben Kragh (2004), "Frozen Flows in von Trier's Oeuvre," in Bente Larsen, Iben Thorving Laursen, and Torben Kragh Grodal (eds.), *Visual Authorship: Creativity and Intentionality in Media*, 129–67, Copenhagen: Museum Tusculanum Press.

Grodal, Torben Kragh (2009), *Embodied Visions: Evolution, Emotion, Culture, and Film*, Oxford: Oxford University Press.

Grodal, Torben Kragh (2012), "Frozen Style and Strong Emotions of Panic and Separation: Trier's Prologues to Antichrist and Melancholia," *Journal of Scandinavian Cinema*, 2(1): 47–53.

Gross, Larry (2009). "The Six Commandments of the Church of Lars von Trier's Antichrist," *Film Comment*, September/October. Available online: https://www.film comment.com/article/the-six-commandments-of-the-church-of-lars-von-triers-antichrist/ (accessed July 17, 2019).

Gyatso, Bhiksu Tenzin [The Fourteenth Dalai Lama] and Bhiksuni Thubten Chodron (2017), *Approaching the Buddhist Path*, Somerville: Wisdom Publications.

Gyatso, Geshe Kelsang (2000), *Essence of Vajrayana: The Highest Yoga Tantra Practice of Heruka Body Mandala*, Delhi: Motilal Banarsidass.

Hainge, Greg (2012), "To Have Done with the Perspective of the (Biological) Body: Gaspar Noé's Enter the Void, Somatic Film Theory and the Biocinematic Imaginary," *Somatechnics*, 2(2) September: 305–24.

Hanegraaff, Wouter (1998), *New Age Religion and Western Culture: Esotericism in the Mirror of Secular Thought*, New York: State University of New York Press.

Hanh, Thich Nhat (2016), *The Miracle of Mindfulness*, Boston: Beacon Press.

Hannan, Jason (2018), "Trolling Ourselves to Death? Social Media and Post-truth Politics," *European Journal of Communication*, 33(2): 214–26.

Harris, Brandon (2010), "The Trip," *Features*, July 20. Available online: http://filmmake rmagazine.com/11207-the-trip-2/ - .WiZtc4V5ns0 (accessed May 13, 2014).

Harvey, Peter (2013), *An Introduction to Buddhism: Teachings, History and Practices*, New York: Cambridge University Press.

Haubrich, Wess (2018), "Nihilism, Clinical Depression, and 'Satan's Church' in Lars von Trier's Antichrist," *The 405*, May 4. Available online: https://www.thefourohfive.com/film/article/nihilism-clinical-depression-and-satan-s-church-in-lars-von-trier-s-antichrist-152 (accessed July 16, 2019).

Haunton, Christian (2009), "Imagining God in the Movies," in William L. Blizek (ed.), *The Continuum Companion to Religion and Film*, 260–9, New York: Continuum.

Heath, Chris (2011) "Lars Attacks!" *GQ*, September 19. Available online: https://www.gq.com/story/lars-von-trier-gq-interview-october-2011 (accessed July 16, 2019).

Hickin, Daniel (2011), "Censorship, Reception and the Films of Gaspar Noé: The Emergence of the New Extremism in Britain," in Tanya C. Horeck and Tina Kendall (eds.), *The New Extremism in Cinema: From France to Europe*, 117–29, Edinburgh: Edinburgh University Press.

Hirshfeld-Flores, Alissa (2002), "DMT: The Spirit Molecule: A Doctor's Revolutionary Research into the Biology of Near-Death and Mystical Experiences," *American Journal of Psychiatry*, 159(8) August: 1448–9.

Hoberman, J. and Jonathan Rosenbaum (2008), "El Topo: Though the Wasteland of the Counterculture," in Ernest Mathijs and Xavier Mendik (eds.), *The Cult Film Reader*, 284–93, New York: Open University Press.

Hoch, David G. (1971), "Mythic Patterns in 2001: A Space Odyssey," *The Journal of Popular Culture*, 4(4) March: 961–5.

Hollenback, Jess Byron (1996), *Mysticism: Experience, Response and Empowerment*, Philadelphia: Pennsylvania University Press.

Hoover, Stewart M. and Monica M. Emerich (2011), "Introduction: Media, Spiritualities and Social Change," *Media, Spiritualities and Social Change*, 1–12, London: Continuum/Bloomsbury Collections.
Horeck, Tanya C. and Tina Kendall (2011), "Introduction," in Tanya C. Horeck and Tina Kendall (eds.), *The New Extremism in Cinema: From France to Europe*, 1–17, Edinburgh: Edinburgh University Press.
Houtman, Dick and Stef Aupers (2007), "The Spiritual Turn and the Decline of Tradition: The Spread of Post-Christian Spirituality in 14 Western Countries, 1981–2000," *Journal for the Scientific Study of Religion*, 46(3) September: 305–20.
Jackson, Roger R. (2004), "Usury," in Robert E. Buswell Jr. (ed.), *Encyclopaedia of Buddhism*, vols. 1 and 2, 872–3, New York: Macmillan Reference Library/Thompson Gale.
James, William (1956a), *"Is Life Worth Living?" The Will to Believe: And Other Essays in Popular Philosophy, and Human Immortality*, New York: Courier Dover Publications.
James, William (1956b), *The Will to Believe and Other Essays in Popular Philosophy/ Human Immorality: Both Books Bound as One*, New York: Dover Publications.
James, William (2014), *The Varieties of Religious Experience*, Lexington: Seven Treasures Publications.
Journal of Religion and Film (2014), "Journal of Religion and Film: University of Nebraska Omaha: Homepage." Available online: http://digitalcommons.unomaha.edu/jrf/ (accessed December 20, 2014).
Jung, Carl Gustav (1951), *Introduction to a Science of Mythology: The Myth of the Divine Child and the Mysteries of Eleusis*, Karl Kerényi (ed.), Abingdon: Routledge and Kegan Paul.
Jung, Carl Gustav (1959), *Aion*, R. F. C. Hull (trans.), Princeton: Princeton University Press.
Jung, Carl Gustav (1960), *Collected Works of C. G. Jung: Structure and Dynamics of the Psyche*, Gerhard Adler and R. F. C. Hull (trans.), Princeton: Princeton University Press.
Jung, Carl Gustav (1966), *The Spirit in Man, Art, and Literature*, R. F. C. Hull (trans.), Princeton: Princeton University Press.
Jung, Carl Gustav (1981), *The Archetypes and the Collective Unconscious*, Princeton: Princeton University Press.
Kay, David N. (2007), *Tibetan and Zen Buddhism in Britain: Transplantation, Development and Adaptation*, Abingdon: Routledge.
Kickasola, Joseph, John Lyden, S. Brent Plate, Antonio Sison, Sheila J. Nayar, Sefanie Knauss, Rachel Wagner, and Jolyon Thomas (2013), "Facing Forward, Looking Back: Religion and Film Studies in the Last Decade," *Journal of Religion and Film*, 17(1): 1–69.
Kierkegaard, Søren (2005), *Fear and Trembling*, Alastair Hanny (trans.), London: Penguin Books.
Kloman, William (1968), "In 2001, Will Love Be a Seven-Letter Word?" *The New York Times*, April 14. Available online: http://www.archiviokubrick.it/english/words/interviews/1968love.html (accessed June 13, 2015).

Konijn, Elly A. (2013), "The Role of Emotion in Media Use and Effects," in Karen E. Dill (ed.), *The Oxford Handbook of Media Psychology*, 1–47, Oxford: Oxford University Press/Oxford Handbooks Online.

Konzett, Matthais (2010), "Sci-Fi Film and Sounds of the Future," in Mathew J. Bartkowiak (ed.), *Sounds of the Future: Essays on Music in Science Fiction Film*, 100–17, Jefferson: McFarland.

Koutsourakis, Angelos (2013), *Politics as Form in Lars von Trier: A Post-Brechtian Reading*, New York: Bloomsbury Publishing USA.

Krahé, Barbara, Ingrid Möller, L. Rowell Huesmann, Lucyna Kirwil, Juliane Felber, and Anja Berger (2011), "Desensitization to Media Violence: Links With Habitual Media Violence Exposure, Aggressive Cognitions, and Aggressive Behavior," *Journal of Personality and Social Psychology*, 100(4): 630–46.

Krämer, Peter (2010), *2001: A Space Odyssey*, London: British Film Institute/Palgrave Macmillan.

Kuberski, Philip (2008), "Kubrick's Odyssey: Myth, Technology, Gnosis," *Arizona Quarterly: A Journal of American Literature, Culture, and Theory*, 64(3): 51–73.

Kürten, Jochen (2011),"Opinion: Lars von Trier Has a Penchant for Provocation," *DW*, May 20. Available online: https://www.dw.com/en/opinion-lars-von-trier-has-a-penchant-for-provocation/a-15092383-0 (accessed July 17, 2019).

Lambie, Ryan (2010), "Gaspar Noé Interview: Enter the Void, Illegal Substances and Life after Death," *Den of Geek*, September 21. Available online: http://www.denofgeek.com/movies/16358/gaspar-no%C3%A9-interview-enter-the-void-illegal-substances-and-life-after-death (accessed June 25, 2015).

Landy, Joshua and Michael Saler (2009), "Introduction: The Varieties of Modern Enchantment," in Joshua Landy and Michael Saler (eds.), *The Re-enchantment of the World: Secular Magic in a Rational Age*, 1–14, Palo Alto: Stanford University Press.

LeBeau, Richard (2011), "Hauntingly Accurate Portrayals of Severe Mental Illness at a Theater Near You," *Psychology in Action*, December 12. Available online: https://www.psychologyinaction.org/psychology-in-action-1/2011/12/12/hauntingly-accurate-portrayals-of-severe-mental-illness-at-a-theater-near-you (accessed July 16, 2019).

LeDrew, Stephen (2018), "Scientism and Utopia: New Atheism as a Fundamentalist Reaction to Relativism," in Mikael Stenmark, Steve Fuller, and Ulf Zackariasson (eds.), *Relativism and Post-Truth in Contemporary Society Possibilities and Challenges*, 143–56, Cham: Palgrave Macmillan.

Ligeti, György and Johnathan W. Bernard (1993), "States, Events, Transformations," *Perspectives of New Music*, 31(1) Winter: 164–71.

Lim, Denis (2010), "Turn On, Tune In to a Trippy Afterlife," *New York Times*, September 17. Available online: http://www.nytimes.com/2010/09/19/movies/19void.html (accessed August 27, 2015).

Little, Jane (2012), "Mayan Apocalypse: End of the World, or a New Beginning?" *BBC News Washington*, December 19. Available online: http://www.bbc.com/news/magazine-20764906 (accessed June 15, 2015).

Lumholdt, Jan (2003), *Lars von Trier: Interviews*, Jackson: University Press of Mississippi.
Lyden, John (2003), *Film as Religion: Myths, Morals, and Rituals*, New York: New York University Press.
MacDonald, Scott (2006), *A Critical Cinema 5: Interviews with Independent Filmmakers*, Berkeley: University of California Press.
Macy, Joanna Rogers (1979), "Dependent Co-Arising: The Distinctiveness of Buddhist Ethics," *The Journal of Religious Ethics*, 7(1) Spring: 38–52.
Mainar, Luis M. García (2000), *Narrative and Stylistic Patterns in the Films of Stanley Kubrick*, New York: Camden House.
Marina, Jacqueline (2007), "Friedrich Schleiermacher and Rudolf Otto," in John Corrigan (ed.), *The Oxford Handbook of Religion and Emotion*, 457–84, Oxford: Oxford University Press.
Marsh, Clive (2009), "Theology and Film," in William L. Blizek (ed.), *The Continuum Companion to Religion and Film*, 59–69, New York: Continuum.
Martin, Joel (1995), "Introduction: Seeing the Sacred on the Screen," in Joel Martin and Conrad E. Ostwalt (eds.), *Screening the Sacred: Religion, Myth, and Ideology in Popular American Film*, 1–12, Boulder: Westview Press.
Martin, Joel and Conrad E. Ostwalt (1995), "Preface," in Joel Martin and Conrad E. Ostwalt (eds.), *Screening the Sacred: Religion, Myth, and Ideology in Popular American Film*, vii–viii, Boulder: Westview Press.
Martin, Thomas M. (1991), *Images and the Imageless: A Study in Religious Consciousness and Film*, Lewisburg: Bucknell University Press.
Maslow, Abraham (1994), *Religions, Values, and Peak-Experiences*, London: Penguin Arkana.
Massumi, Brian (1995), "The Autonomy of Affect," *The Politics of Systems and Environments*, 31(3) Autumn: 83–109.
Matts, Tim and Aidan Tynan (2012), "The Melancholy of Extinction: Lars von Trier's Melancholia as an Environmental Film," *M/C Journal*, 15(3): n.p.
McAleer, Neil (1992), *Arthur C. Clarke: The Authorized Biography*, Raleigh: Contemporary Books.
Melancholia (2011), [Film] Dir. Lars von Trier, Denmark/France/Sweden/Germany/Italy: Zentropa Entertainments.
Menninghaus, Winfried (2003), *Disgust: Theory and History of a Strong Sensation*, New York: State University of New York Press.
Meyers, Gerald E. (1997), "Pragmatism and Introspective Psychology," in Ruth Anna Putnam (ed.), *The Cambridge Companion to William James*, 11–24, Cambridge: Cambridge University Press.
Miles, Margaret Ruth (1996), *Seeing and Believing: Religion and Values in the Movies*, Boston: Beacon Press.
Moreno, Jonathan D. (2016), "Acid Brothers: Henry Beecher, Timothy Leary, and the Psychedelic of the Century," *Perspectives in Biology and Medicine*, 59(1): 107–21.

Mottram, James (2010), "The Shock of the Noé as an Enfant Terrible Returns," *The Independent*, September 10, section 12.
Muss, Lucy (2006), "Slave to Cinema," *The Guardian*, October 20. Available online: https://www.theguardian.com/film/2006/oct/20/londonfilmfestival2006.londonfilmfestival (accessed July 17, 2019).
Nattier, Jan (1997), "Buddhism Comes to Main Street," *The Wilson Quarterly*, 21(2): 72–80.
Nayar, Sheila J. (2012), *The Sacred and the Cinema: Reconfiguring the "Genuinely" Religious Film*, New York: Continuum.
Newberg, A. B. and J. Iversen (2003), "The Neural Basis of the Complex Mental Task of Meditation: Neurotransmitter and Neurochemical Considerations," *Medical Hypotheses*, 61(2) August: 282–91.
Nicodemus, Katja (2005), "I Am an American Woman," *Die Zeit*, November 11. Available online: http://www.signandsight.com/features/465.html (accessed July 17, 2019).
Nicotra, Jodie (2008), "William James in the Borderlands: Psychedelic Science and the 'Accidental Fences' of Self," *Configurations, William James in the Borderlands*, 16(2) Spring: 199–213.
Nietzsche, Friedrich (1974), *The Gay Science: With a Prelude in Rhymes and an Appendix of Songs*, New York: Vintage.
Nietzsche, Friedrich (1999), *Thus Spake Zarathustra*, Thomas Common (trans.), Mineola: Dover Publications.
Nolan, Steve (2009), *Film, Lacan and the Subject of Religion: A Psychoanalytic Approach to Religious Film Analysis*, New York: Continuum.
Nordern, Eric (2001), "Playboy Interview: Stanley Kubrick," in Gene D. Phillips (ed.), *Stanley Kubrick: Interviews*, 47–74, Jackson: University Press of Mississippi.
Nordwall, Owe (1969), "2. György Ligeti," *Tempo*, 88, April: 22–5.
Nymphomaniac I and II (2013), [Film] Dir. Lars von Trier, United Kingdom/Denmark/Belgium/France/Germany: Zentropa Entertainments.
O'Hagan, Sean (2009), "Interview: Lars von Trier," *The Guardian*, July 12. Available online: https://www.theguardian.com/film/2009/jul/12/lars-von-trier-interview (accessed July 17, 2019).
Ogata, Sōhaku (1959), *Zen for the West*, London: Rider, for the Buddhist Society.
Ohnuma, Reiko (2004), "Gender," in Robert E. Buswell Jr. (ed.), *Encyclopaedia of Buddhism*, vols. 1 and 2, 302–6, New York: Macmillan Reference Library/Thompson Gale.
Oldmeadow, Harry (2009), "Rudolf Otto, the East and Religious Inclusivism," in Carole M. Cusack and Christopher Hartney (eds.), *Religion and Retributive Logic: Essays in Honour of Professor Gary W. Trompf*, 229–44, Boston: Brill.
Olson, Carl (2005), "Transcendental Meditation," in Lindsay Jones (ed.), *Encyclopedia of Religion*, 2nd ed., 14: 9289–92, New York: Macmillan Reference USA.
Oppenheim, Janet (1988), *The Other World: Spiritualism and Psychical Research in England, 1850–1914*, Cambridge: Cambridge University Press.

Ostwalt, Conrad E. (1995), "Hollywood and Armageddon," in Joel Martin and Conrad E. Ostwalt (eds.), *Screening the Sacred: Religion, Myth, and Ideology in Popular American Film*, 55–64, Boulder: Westview Press.

Otto, Rudolf (1958), *The Idea of the Holy: An Inquiry into the Non-Rational Factor in the Idea of the Divine and Its Relation to the Rational*, Oxford: Oxford University Press.

Pahl, Jon (2012), "Melancholia," *Journal of Religion and Film*, 16(1) May: Article 10.

Palmer, Michael F. (1997), *Freud and Jung on Religion*, Abingdon: Routledge.

Palmer, R. Barton (2006), "2001: The Critical Reception and the Generation Gap," in Robert Phillip Kolker (ed.), *Stanley Kubrick's 2001: A Space Odyssey: New Essays*, 13–28, Oxford: Oxford University Press.

Palmer, Tim (2006), "Style and Sensation in the Contemporary French Cinema of the Body," *Journal of Film and Video*, 58(3): 22–32.

Park, Jin Y. (2011), *Buddhisms and Deconstructions*, Delhi: Motilal Banarsidass.

Patterson, David W. (2004), "Music, Structure and Metaphor in Stanley Kubrick's 2001: A Space Odyssey," *American Music*, 22(3): 444–74.

Paulus, Irena (2009), "Stanley Kubrick's Revolution in the Usage of Film Music: 2001: A Space Odyssey (1968)," *International Review of the Aesthetics and Sociology of Music*, 40(1): 99–127.

Pezzotta, Elisa (2013), *Stanley Kubrick: Adapting the Sublime*, Jackson: University Press of Mississippi.

Picnic at Hanging Rock (1975), [Film] Dir. Peter Weir, Australia: British Empire Films.

Plate, S. Brent (2008), *Religion and Film: Cinema and the Re-creation of the World*, New York: Wallflower.

Plate, S. Brent (2009), "Mother (Nature) Will Eat You: Lars von Trier's Antichrist," *Religion Dispatches*, October 28. Available online: http://religiondispatches.org/mother-nature-will-eat-you-lars-von-triers-iantichristi/ (accessed July 17, 2019).

Poole, Robert (2001), "2001: A Space Odyssey," *History Today*, 51(1) January: 39–45.

Poynor, Rick (2010), "Critique: A Soul Drifting in Neon Limbo," *Eye: The International Review of Graphic Design; London*, 78 (Winter): 8–9.

Prebish, Charles S. (1999), *Luminous Passage: The Practice and Study of Buddhism in America*, Berkeley: University of California Press.

Prendergast, Mark J. (2000), *The Ambient Century: From Mahler to Moby—The Evolution of Sound in the Electronic Age*, London: Bloomsbury.

Priestley, D. C. (2004), "Psychology," in Robert E. Buswell Jr. (ed.), *Encyclopaedia of Buddhism*, vols. 1 and 2, 678–92, New York: Macmillan Reference Library/Thompson Gale.

Pyysiäinen, Ilkka (2011), "Believing and Doing: How Ritual Action Enhances Religious Belief," in Armin W. Geertz and Jeppe Sinding Jensen (eds.), *Religious Narrative, Cognition and Culture: Image and Word in the Mind of Narrative*, 147–62, Abingdon: Equinox Publishing Limited.

Quandt, James (2011), "Flesh and Blood: Sex and Violence in Recent French Cinema," in Tanya C. Horeck and Tina Kendall (eds.), *The New Extremism in Cinema: From France to Europe*, 18–28, Edinburgh: Edinburgh University Press.

Reed, Barbara E. (2004), "Ethics," in Robert E. Buswell Jr. (ed.), *Encyclopaedia of Buddhism*, vols. 1 and 2, 261–5, New York: Macmillan Reference Library/Thompson Gale.

Rice, Julian (2008), *Kubrick's Hope: Discovering Optimism from 2001 to Eyes Wide Shut*, Lanham: Scarecrow Press.

Rios, Riccardo de los and Robert Davis (2007), "Digital Frames and Visible Grain: Spatial and Material Reintegration in Irreversible," *Film Criticism*, 32(1) October: 95–109.

Rochlin, Nick (2017), "Fake News: Belief in Post-truth," *Library Hi Tech*, 35(3): 386–92.

Rorty, Richard (1997), "Religious Faith, Intellectual Responsibility and Romance," in Ruth Anna Putnam (ed.), *The Cambridge Companion to William James*, 84–103. Cambridge: Cambridge University Press.

Rose, Steve (2010), "Gaspar Noé: 'What's the Problem?'" *The Guardian*, September 17. Available online: https://www.theguardian.com/film/2010/sep/16/gaspar-noe-enter-the-void (accessed June 14, 2015).

Rowe, Carel (2002), "Myth and Symbolism: Blue Velvet," in Jack Hunter (ed.), *Moonchild. The Films of Kenneth Anger: Persistence of Vision Volume 1*, 11–46, London: Creation Books.

Rowe, Christopher (2013), "The Romantic Model of 2001: A Space Odyssey," *Canadian Journal of Film Studies*, 22(2): 41–63.

Salthe, Stanley N. (2013), "Evolution," in Anne L. C. Runehov and Lluis Oviedo (eds.), *Encyclopedia of Sciences and Religions*, 793–8, Dordrecht: Springer Netherlands.

Schaberg, Christopher (2018), *The Work of Literature in an Age of Post-Truth*, New York: Bloomsbury Academic.

Schmidt, Lisa M. (2010), "A Popular Avant-Garde: The Paradoxical Tradition of Electric and Atonal Sounds in Sci-Fi Music Scoring," in Mathew J. Bartkowiak (ed.), *Sounds of the Future: Essays on Music in Science Fiction Film*, 22–43, Jefferson: McFarland.

Schmidt, Stefan (2014), "Opening Up Meditation for Science: The Development of a Meditation Classification System," in Stefan Schmidt and Harald Walach (eds.), *Meditation: Neuroscientific Approaches and Philosophical Implications*, Studies in Neuroscience, Consciousness and Spirituality 2, 137–52, Basel: Springer International Publishing.

Schmidt, Stefan and Harald Walach (2014), "Introduction: Laying Out the Field of Meditation Research," in Stefan Schmidt and Harald Walach (eds.), *Meditation: Neuroscientific Approaches and Philosophical Implications*, Studies in Neuroscience, Consciousness and Spirituality 2, 1–6, Basel: Springer International Publishing.

Schofield Clarke, Lynn (2002), "The 'Protestantization' of Research into Media, Religion and Culture," in Stewart M. Hoover and Lynn Schofield Clark (eds.), *Practicing Religion in the Age of the Media: Explorations in Media, Religion, and Culture*, 7–34, New York: Columbia University Press.

Schrader, Paul (1972), *Transcendental Style in Film: Ozu, Bresson, Dreyer*, Berkeley: University of California Press.

Schrader, Paul (2004), *Schrader on Schrader & Other Writings*, Kevin Jackson (ed.), London: Faber.
Schwam, Stephanie (2010), *The Making of 2001: A Space Odyssey*, New York: Random House Publishing Group.
Schwartz, Susan L. (2000), "I Dream, Therefore I Am: What Dreams May Come," *Journal of Religion and Film*, 4(1): n.p.
Searby, Mike (1997), "Ligeti the Postmodernist?" *Tempo*, 199: 9–14.
Sentes, Bryan and Susan Palmer (2000), "Presumed Immanent: The Raelians, UFO Religions, and the Postmodern Condition," *Nova Religio: The Journal of Alternative and Emergent Religions*, 4(1) October: 86–105.
Shay, Roshani Cari and Henrik Bogdan (2014), "Sex and Gender in the Words and Communes of Osho (nee Bhagwan Shree Rajneesh)," Henrik Bogdan and James R. Lewis (eds.), *Sexuality and New Religious Movements*, 59–88, New York: Palgrave Macmillan.
Sight & Sound (2012), "The 2012 Sight & Sound Directors' Top Ten," 69, September. Available online: http://www.bfi.org.uk/news/sight-sound-2012-directors-top-ten (accessed August 12, 2012).
Sitney, P. Adams (2002), *Visionary Film: The American Avant-Garde, 1943–2000*, New York: Oxford University Press.
Smith, David L. (2005), "Eternal Sunshine of the Spotless Mind and the Question of Transcendence," *The Journal of Religion and Film*, 9(1): n.p.
Stephenson, Hunter (2010), "Gasper Noé's Big Trip," *Interview Magazine*, September 10. Available online: http://www.interviewmagazine.com/film/gaspar-noe-enter-the-void (accessed June 15, 2015).
Stevenson, Jill C. (2013), *Sensational Devotion: Evangelical Performance in Twenty-First Century America*, Ann Arbor: University of Michigan Press.
Strassman, Rick (2000), *DMT: The Spirit Molecule: A Doctor's Revolutionary Research into the Biology of Near-Death and Mystical Experiences*, New York: Simon and Schuster.
Streng, Frederick J. (2005), "Truth," in Lindsay Jones (ed.), *Encyclopedia of Religion*, 9368–77, Detroit: Macmillan.
Sutcliffe, Steven J. (2003), *Children of the New Age: A History of Spiritual Practices*, London: Routledge.
Suzuki, Shunryu (2010), *Zen Mind, Beginner's Mind*, Colorado: Shambhala Publications.
Szendy, Peter (2015), *Apocalypse-Cinema: 2012 and Other Ends of the World*, Will Bishop (trans.), 1–4, New York: Fordham University.
Taves, Ann (2005), "Religious Experience," in Lindsay Jones (ed.), *Encyclopedia of Religion*, Gale Reference Library, 2nd ed., 11: 7736–50, Detroit: Macmillan.
Taves, Ann (2009), *Religious Experience Reconsidered: A Building-Block Approach to the Study of Religion and Other Special Things*, Princeton: Princeton University Press.
Taylor, Charles (2007), *A Secular Age*, Cambridge: Harvard University Press.
The Holy Mountain (1973), [Film] Dir. Alejandro Jodorowsky, Mexico: ABKCO Films.

The Numbers (2017), "Enter the Void: Summary." Available online: https://www.the-numbers.com/movie/Enter-the-Void - tab=summary (accessed January 3, 2017).

The Theosophical Society (2017), "Theosophy and the Theosophical Society." Available online: http://austheos.org.au/about/theosophy-theosophical-society/ (accessed January 4, 2017).

Thepyanmongkol, Phra (2008), *A Study Guide for Samatha Vipassana Meditation Based on the Five Meditation Based on the Five Meditation Techniques*, Bangkok: The National Coordination Center of Provincial Meditation Institute of Thailand.

Thomson-Jones, Katherine (2008), *Aesthetics and Film*, New York: Continuum.

Thorsen, Nils (2014), "Interview: Longing for the End of All," *Melancholia Official Website*. Available online: http://www.melancholiathemovie.com/ - _interview (accessed September 21, 2014).

Trinity-X (2016), "Director Gaspar Noé," Available online: http://www.trinity-x.com/films/enter_the_void/directors_interview (accessed November 9, 2016).

Turnock, Julie A. (2014), *Plastic Reality: Special Effects, Technology, and the Emergence of 1970s Blockbuster Aesthetics*, New York: Columbia University Press.

Twin Peaks (2017), [TV Program] "Gotta Light?" Dir. David Lynch and Robert Frost, Showtime: Season 3, Episode 8.

Ungureanu, Camil (2014), "Religion Against Religion in Lars von Trier," in Costica Bradatan and Camil Ungureanu (eds.), *Religion in Contemporary European Cinema: The Postsecular Constellation*, 126–44, Abingdon: Routledge.

Urban, Hugh B. (2012), *Tantra: Sex, Secrecy, Politics, and Power in the Study of Religion*, Delhi: Motilal Banarsidass.

Versluis, Arthur (1993), *American Transcendentalism and Asian Religions*, Oxford: Oxford University Press.

Versluis, Arthur (2014), *American Gurus: From Transcendentalism to New Age Religion*, Oxford: Oxford University Press.

Walker, Alexander, Sybil Taylor, and Ulrich Ruchti (1999), *Stanley Kubrick, Director: A Visual Analysis*, New York: W. W. Norton and Company.

Weber, Max (2003), *The Protestant Ethic and the Spirit of Capitalism*, Talcott Parsons (trans.), New York: Courier Dover Publications.

Webster, Patrick (2010), *Love and Death in Kubrick: A Critical Study of the Films from Lolita through Eyes Wide Shut*, Jefferson: McFarland.

White, Rob (2012), "Interview with Manuel Alberto Claro," *Film Quarterly*, 65(4) July: 17–20.

Whitehouse, Harvey (1996), "Rites of Terror: Emotion, Metaphor and Memory in Melanesian Initiation Cults," *The Journal of the Royal Anthropological Institute*, 2(4) December: 703–15.

Whitehouse, Harvey (2002), "Religious Reflexivity and Transmissive Frequency," *Social Anthropology, Religious Reflexivity*, 10(1): 91–103.

Whitehouse, Harvey (2004), "Modes of Religiosity and the Cognitive Science of Religion," *Method and Theory in the Study of Religion, Modes of Religiosity*, 16(3): 321–35.

Wonders of the Universe (2011), [TV program] "Destiny," Dir. Chris Holt, BBC2: Season 1, Episode 1.
Wood, Matthew (2007), *Possession, Power and the New Age: Ambiguities of Authority in Neoliberal Societies*, Aldershot: Routledge.
Wright, Melanie J. (2009), "Religion, Film and Cultural Studies," in William L. Blizek (ed.), *The Continuum Companion to Religion and Film*, 101–12, New York: Continuum.
Wuthnow, Robert (1998), *After Heaven: Spirituality in America Since the 1950s*, Berkeley, CA: University of California Press.
Xygalatas, Dimitris, Panagiotis Mitkidis, Ronald Fischer, Paul Reddish, Joshua Skewes, Armin W. Geertz, Andreas Roepstorff, and Joseph Bulbulia (2013), "Extreme Rituals Promote Prosociality," *Psychological Science*, 24(8) August: 1602–5.
Yates, John, Matthew Immergut, and Jeremy Graves (2017), *The Mind Illuminated: A Complete Meditation Guide Integrating Buddhist Wisdom and Brain Science for Greater Mindfulness*, New York: Simon and Schuster.
York, Michael (1999), "The Religious Supermarket: Local Constructions of the New Age Within the World Network," *Social Compass*, 46(2) June: 173–9
Zackariasson, Ulf (2018), "Introduction: Engaging Relativism and Post-Truth," in Mikael Stenmark, Steve Fuller, and Ulf Zackariasson (eds.), *Relativism and Post-Truth in Contemporary Society Possibilities and Challenges*, 1–18, Cham: Palgrave Macmillan.
Zeller, Benjamin E. (2010), *Prophets and Protons: New Religious Movements and Science in Late Twentieth-Century America*, New York: New York University Press.
Zoja, Luigi (1989), *Drugs, Addiction, & Initiation: The Modern Search for Ritual*, Einsiedeln: Daimon.

Internet Movie Database (IMDb)

Reviews Cited

Reviews can be found online at the addresses below where reviews are presented in a running list that can be sorted by date. This research considered all reviews written up until April 9, 2016.

Stanley Kubrick, *2001: A Space Odyssey* (1968), https://www.imdb.com/title/tt0062622/reviews
Gaspar Noé, *Enter the Void* (2009), http://www.imdb.com/title/tt1191111/reviews
Lars von Trier, *Melancholia* (2011), http://www.imdb.com/title/tt1527186/reviews

2001: A Space Odyssey

ackstasis. "Its Origin and Purpose Still a Total Mystery." December 6, 2007.
Alexandre Silvolella. "A True Cinematic Experience." February 12, 2014.

Andariel Halo. "Epic." January 20, 2010.
Andrews Benatar Luque. "It Asks More Questions Through Images, Rather than with Dialogue." October 30, 2013.
anonymous. "Wow. Wow. Wow." March 31, 1999.
anthonymueller. "Creation and Consequences." October 12, 2000.
antonjsw1. "Visual Poetry—A Landmark Achievement." May 9, 2010.
Antti Keisala. "Possibilities." January 10, 2014.
arcadefreak2000. "Worst Movie of the Century." May 10, 2005.
atomicpunks22. "The Longest Two Hours of Your Life." May 6, 2008.
BeardedVillain. "Impressive for Its Time." June 9, 2014.
beetleborgs69. "It's Crap." March 2, 2015.
Ben Harding. "A Journey Through Time and Space." May 12, 2009.
berlioz747. "Art on Screen." November 9, 2008.
bgiamou. "A Mind Numbing Journey into Past and Future." September 29, 2015.
billreynolds. "As Beautiful and Boring as an Actual Space Flight." July 6, 2005.
blakebabe411. "The Movement into Pure Thought." May 3, 2006.
brando647. "Absolutely Epic in Scope, Visually Stunning, and a Bit of a Rough Watch." January 17, 2011.
brenda1028. "Kubrick's Silent Movie." March 31, 2002.
Brendan Sheehan. "Not a Religious Movie in the Conventional Sense." August 26, 2010.
buckdharwin. "Psychedelia and Enlightenment." May 2, 2009.
BUNI. "Kubrick's *2001* Is (so far) THE Great American Film." February 25, 1999.
cameron-lee. "Better Second Time Around." July 9, 2013.
Cantrell sam. "Not Surprised *2001* Doesn't' Ring with the MTV Generation." August 14, 2003.
Celluloid Junkie. "My Favorite Film." August 15, 2002.
cereal 11. "In Defence of My Favorite Film." June 17, 2002.
Chance_Boudreaux19. "The Special Effects Are Better Than CGI in Most Movies Today." April 7, 2016.
Cristian. "Strange, Beautiful and Excellently Made for an Open and Patient Mind." December 23, 2007.
Dalibor Andric. "Masterpiece." October 14, 2013.
dangerhorse. "The Tip of a Very Large, Deep Philosophical Iceberg." August 14, 2002.
Daniel Little. "What was Kubrick Hiding?" February 17, 2003.
David H. Schleicher. "In Space, Everyone Can See You Dream." November 21, 2005.
David Johnson. "Mystery Science Theatre 3000 . . ." June 30, 2006.
dbdumonteil. "Absolute Masterpiece." June 22, 2001.
dead47548. "Breathtaking." January 8, 2008.
DeathFish. "Beauty Is Underestimated." January 2, 2007.
deodatgyorei. "All Time Favorite Movie!!!" April 2, 2016.
donald willy. "Mysterious, Beautiful and Profound!" February 19, 2002.
doveniki. "My Fav Sci-Fi Hands Down." November 21, 2011.

dunmore ego. "Also Sprach Kubrick and Clarke." June 1, 2006.
eddie olsen. "1968: The Year When Sci-Fi Got Interesting." June 8, 2009.
ElMaruecan82. "An Intelligent Masterpiece, Victim of Its Own Greatness." October 4, 2010.
Erik G. "Very Positive (Spoilers)." March 2, 2000.
erniekelvin. "Reminds Me Of . . ." December 28, 2006.
Esteban Esq. "Space Documentary." January 15, 2013.
Evolzzzz. "Science, Religion, Humanity: Philosophy." December 30, 1999.
Ezekiel Zeke Steiner. "Mythological Documentary." November 4, 2005.
fearless3003. "Space Documentary." July 5, 2015.
FilmWiz. "Withstanding the Test of Time ad Holding Strong." January 8, 2003.
Gary. "Not for the Dim, Dull, Sleepy Eyed Bulk." August 20, 2005.
ghosthawk5. "Visual Condensation of Humankind's Evolution Amid the Stars." May 3, 2001.
Gorie Catalin. "This Is More Than a Movie . . ." January 31, 2002.
Graza Shaw. "Once You Realise the Meaning . . . You Will Be Dazzled!" September 29, 2011.
Gross Ryder. "Provocative Poetry in Motion Picture Evokes Questions . . ." May 21, 2012.
grrrr97. "THE GREATEST LEAP FORWARD THE FILM WORLD HAS EVER EXPEREINCED." January 24, 2003.
ikorni. "Mystic Journey." June 26, 2000.
Indy-52. "My Little Insignificant Summary of *2001*." November 1, 2001.
intrepid-s-t-88. "H.A.L. and I.B.M." August 4, 2013.
IPreferEvidence. "A Must See for Fans of Sci-Fi." April 4, 2011.
Jacob-28. "A Strong, Insightful Movie, One of Kubrick's Best." September 5, 1999.
jbirtel. "A Milestone in Storytelling! Often Misunderstood (& Understandably So)!" September 11, 2005.
Jeff (motownmaniax). "Unbelievable . . ." September 14, 2004.
Jeff Hatfield. "How the Solar System Was Won." May 23, 2005.
jimmoir. "Best Film Ever." November 7, 2014.
joebobs. "One of the Boldest Films Ever Made." February 15, 2014.
JoH-2. "I Really Don't Know What to Write Here. Eh . . . It's Great to Watch :-)." December 27, 2000.
john mavety. "Not Just a Movie, a Glimpse of the Sublime." March 12, 2008.
John Novarina. "A Study of Intellectual Evolution." July 30, 1998.
jonathandoe se7en. "Manages to Transcend Words and Become One of the Most Important Films Ever Made!" September 6, 2001.
josephclarkedunning. "Thus Spake Zarathustra Is the Interpretive Key to This Film." November 12, 2012.
Juan Mendoza. "You're Left Confused . . . But Satisfied." September 9, 2013.
jukangliwayway. "A Visceral Cinematic Total Mindfuck Experience," April 16, 2013.
Justin Watson. "A Guideline for what Sci-Fi Movies Should Be." January 22, 2013.

Ken Stephen. "A Masterpiece for All Time." February 17, 2011.
Kieranmc. "Unique Cinema." April 26, 2000.
Lechuguilla. "Cosmic Art." February 6, 2005.
LMAN JINA. "1 to 10 It Is a Negative 5." February 2, 2013.
lost2you2002. "Can We Open Doors and See Through Our Ignorance?" September 13, 2002.
lost2you2002. "Birth . . . Breath . . . Soul . . . Science." June 26, 2003.
Lostman_815. "Beyond Excellence." May 21, 2014.
loufalce. "In a Class By Itself." December 10, 2007.
mameeshkamowskwoz. "A Film That Is Wide in Scope and the Best Word to Describe It: Limitless." December 6, 2012.
Manuel Josh Rivera. "Open the Pod Bay Doors, HAL." March 23, 2014.
Mark Schofield. "How to Appreciate Watching 2001." November 29, 2001.
Maz Murdoch (asda-man). "PhenomenHAL." December 14, 2014.
Metal Angel Ehrler. "Impressive Sight and Sound Show You're Bound to Be Mesmerized By!" August 13, 2009.
mfb138. "Come On People, Evolve." September 27, 2003.
Michael O'Keefe. "Out of This World Tremendous. An Instant Classic." January 1, 2001.
Michael. "Profoundly Prophetic and Philosophical." July 20, 2013.
Michael. "The Coloring Book of Film." February 6, 2016.
mikemacisaac. "Great Film." January 8, 2007.
Monos Z. "Epic." November 5, 2010.
moviedude-72. "A Refreshing, Beautiful Work of Art." September 25, 2006.
Mr. Hulot. "Magnificent and Deliberately Mysterious." August 21, 2002.
Mr. Blockbuster. "The Ultimate Trip." January 1, 2001.
mypharmcon. "Why I Became a Scientist After Watching 2001 Space Odyssey. It Was That Black Screen as the Film Began to Roll!" February 16, 2014.
Nick Formica. "Why It's Great, Clarification for Disbelievers." July 24, 2000.
nowarkfilmstudios. "*2001 A Space Odyssey*, THE Science Fiction Film." June 1, 2011.
onumbersix. "A Wonderful Revisit." January 19, 2012.
oreo1013. "Good Idea . . ." September 8, 2001.
Panapaok. "One Great Achievement!" July 14, 2013.
peter Henderson. "*2001*—A Prophecy About US Foreign Policy and the Need to Change It?" October 2, 2013.
photonutz. "One of the Greatest Films Ever Made." October 9, 1999.
polos are minty. "Great But Aloof Film." April 7, 2010.
ptsportsguy1. "I Love This Movie Dearly." July 19, 2013.
Pulpthatsfiction. "WOW Best Sci-Fi Movie Ever." October 11, 2007.
raymond chandler. "Kubrick's Magnum Opus." July 31, 2001.
rcj5365. "The 40th Anniversary of a Stanley Kubrick Masterpiece. A Landmark Achievement in the Science Fiction Genre." December 18, 2008.
Reggie Santori. "The More You See It, the More You See in It." December 2, 2001.

RFS23. "This Film Comes from the Universe Using Kubrick as It's Middle Man . . . Pure Magik on Film." October 21, 2001.
Richard Pollard (HAL8000). "'I Think It Was Better Than Star Wars' . . . Myself, 1978." October 27, 1999.
Robb 772. "Landmark Cinema." May 25, 2006.
Rob Snyder. "*2001* Can Not Be Spoiled in Words." September 13, 1999.
Rod Davies. "Amazing!" April 6, 1999.
rooprect. "If Only One Film Makes It Off This Planet, It Should Be *2001*." January 25, 2012.
royale_w:cheez44. "A Landmark in Science Fiction That Still Holds Up Today." February 10, 2006.
Sahan Fernando. "A Classic!!!" January 11, 2012.
Sam Bartos. "One of the Best Films of All Time." September 12, 2011.
Sandra. "Daisy, Daisy . . ." November 28, 2008.
scootwhoman. "The Ultimate Trip, Exploring Our Beliefs." May 30, 2006.
seanwilson556. "One Man's Interesting View of Humanity." July 17, 2011.
secondtake. "What Is Greatness—In Movies, Over Time, From Here?" June 14, 2009.
serafinogm. "Thank You Stanley for the July 1969 Moon Landing!" October 7, 2015.
Serata. "All I Have to Say Is . . ." December 4, 2003.
ShibanPD. "*2001*: A Space Odyssey." November 12, 2012.
ShootingShark. "My Mind Is Going." March 15, 2008.
Spleen. "The Only Film in History Worth Seeing for the Special Effects Alone." November 7, 1999.
st-shot. "Magnificent Self Indulgence." June 8, 2014.
StarCastle99. "A Magnificent Epic That's Terribly Misunderstood." May 29, 2002.
Steve Pulaski. "A Film That Will Grow with You." April 23, 2014.
T RajahBalaji. "An Experiential Journey into Fundamental Questions of Our Origin and Destiny." February 20, 2002.
TheArizonian2014. "An Epic Sci-Fi Film." March 7, 2012.
The Centurion. "The Greatest Achievement in Cinema Since 'Citizen Kane.'" January 26, 2009.
The Ebullient One. "A Mirror of Your Own Interpretation." December 14, 2002.
Tomasasaz. "A Masterpiece. I Regret Not Seeing This Movie Before." January 2, 2011.
Tony Mathew. "Unmatched Excellence!" November 19, 2013.
Torgo Approves. "Mesmerizing Experience." August 19, 2006.
tpeterson 1955. "You have to let this film 'happen' to you as a 'right-brained' experience, and then it becomes 'the ultimate trip' as it was originally intended!" February 17, 2012.
tribble-841-35156. "The Movie People Love to Interpret." September 24, 2010.
tvcunningham. "You Have to THINK When You Watch This One. That's It." February 25, 2009.
txk02. "Going Ape Over Things They Don't Understand." May 18, 2008.

vovazhd. "An Unforgettable Experience That Transcends Cinema and Our Imagination." October 1, 2007.
watercrake. "Overwhelmed!" June 20, 2000.
wawain. "A Film for Introspective, Silent Audiences." February 6, 2001.
woodpecker99. "All-Time Great Movie Openings." December 22, 2005.
Wunderwaffe. "What Cinema Is All About." September 30, 2013.
wwe7961. "Wow." August 2, 2010.

Enter the Void

A Different Drummer. "Gaspar Noe Is Crazy . . . Not That That Is a Bad Thing . . ." November 28, 2013.
AMadLane. "Like Requiem for a Dream Married Up to Fantasia—Grim, Overlong but Visually Brilliant." November 11, 2010.
ashleym9000. "It a Work of Art. Genius. Watch with Headphones or Surround Sound." October 1, 2011.
Atavisten. "Stronger Than Acid." February 6, 2011.
awmurshedkar. *"Enter the Void."* June 11, 2012.
Ben Hinman. "A Jarring Mind Trip, A Film Unlike Any Other." January 19, 2015.
bradleybean86. "Examine the 'Agony of Ecstacy.'" November 16, 2012.
Brian Daly. "This Film Will Change Your Life." November 6, 2014.
Cassandra Kelsey. "A Psychedelic Journey Through Consciousness." June 13, 2013.
chaos-rampant. "An Experience to Live Through, but Is It One Worth Living Through?" February 4, 2011.
Charlene Lydon. "Crazy, But Technically Brilliant!" September 14, 2010.
Chris Blachewicz. "Visually Challenging, Yet Disappointing." March 10, 2011.
CinemaPat. "'I Don't Do Drugs, I Am Drugs' Salvador Dali." December 9, 2010.
Colin George. "Enter at Your Own Risk." October 10, 2010.
dallasryan. "Enter the Place You Won't Soon Forget!" March 1, 2012.
DonFishies. "A Unique, Experimental Trip That Is Clearly Not for Everyone." January 23, 2011.
downtek-889-148371. "A Stunning Passion Play That Compels the Recognition of Sin and Suffering." November 5, 2010.
Elsa HOnkemup. "Deeply Morbid While Pretending to Be an Eye-Opener." May 26, 2011.
felipedigre. "Intended to Be Deep but Ending Up Being a Long Torture." September 12, 2015.
Fighterdan6. "Wow What A Head F#@k, I Should Point Out I Dropped Acid Before This Movie." June 28, 2012.
Gino Monaco. "Once in A Lifetime Movie Theatre Experience." August 9, 2012.

gizmomogwai. "You May Enter." April 21, 2014.
Greg Magne. "Stunning . . . In Many Ways." September 15, 2009.
Hardeep Pthak. "Enter the Void Haunts Me and It Shall Be So Throughout My Life!" May 13, 2012.
Hector Asensio. "Obra Maestra." June 15, 2015.
HumanoidOfFlesh. "Entering the Void with Tibetan Book of the Dead." January 15, 2011.
Imaocarrots. "Perhaps the Greatest Film Ever Created," November 16, 2011.
Indyrod. "Amazing Psychedelic Neon Trip Through the Mind." October 18, 2010.
jaredmobarak. "Did They Hear Me? Did I Scream?" September 19, 2009.
jimi99. "The Ultimate Trip." January 28, 2011.
jjanerney. "Euphoric, Toxic, Beautiful, Rancid and Enchanting." April 2, 2016.
John DeSando. "What Clint Eastwood Might Have Done." November 28, 2010.
Jorge Campoverde. "Best Watched with Headphones." March 19, 2011.
Joseph Sylvers. "Out of Your Body and into the Fire." October 6, 2010.
kentuckyfriedpanda42. "Astounding and Infuriating All at the Same Time!" August 23, 2010.
liebeistderweg. "Take a Deep Breath." February 26, 2012.
macocael-353-951088. "A Heady Trip through the Eye of the Camera." June 8, 2012.
makelajanne75. "Some Potential, Wasted by the Director's Self-Indulgence." June 31, 2013.
Matt_Layden. "Where to Begin?" January 23, 2011.
Michael Kenmore. "Good for the First ½ Hour, Then Went Downhill with Pure Indulgence." January 23, 2010.
mwbartko. "Worst Movie I Have Ever Seen." December 7, 2010.
nanthande. "Different . . . Belle . . . . Erstaunlich . . . Bueno . . . Good . . ." June 30, 2013.
Nicholas Lopez. "'Citizen Kane' on Acid and More Stripper Poles." February 16, 2011.
OgierdeBeauseant. "Breakthrough Film." February 17, 2011.
oOgiandujaOo. "Ambitious, Deeply Mystic and Provocative Movie with Earth Shattering FX." October 17, 2009.
otuswerd. "Get Ready . . ." August 13, 2010.
RachyLovesRattys. "An Epic Journey Through Life and Death." September 2, 2013.
radioheadrcm. "Relentlessly Nauseating Modern Art." October 4, 2010.
Radu_A. "The Intellectual's 'Inception'—A 'Now I've Seen It All' Death Trip Back to Life." December 13, 2010.
Richard Alex Jenkins. "This Trip Went on Too Long." January 16, 2014.
robocopssadside-1. "Enter the Void (2009)." January 28, 2011.
Roman James Hoffman. "New French Extremity Turns Metaphysical." July 27, 2014.
rumid. "A Visionary Piece of Cinematic Experimentation, Beautiful and Dark, Dirty and Bright." May 26, 2013.
sabareesh10. "The Most Intense Movie Experience Ever." August 3, 2013.
Siddharth kalkal. "This Is No Movie, It's an Experience of the Ultimate Trip . . . Death." June 27, 2013.

SiilentMiike. "WTF Just Happened?" January 11, 2012.
Simon Kraft. "A Neon Ride into the Grown Up World." November 22, 2009.
Taylor_Gillen. "Transcending Traditional Cinema." January 2, 2016.
TheCultureSlut. "This Is Like A 3 Hour Acid Trip That Starts Out Nice and Then Goes Horribly Wrong." April 15, 2012.
thismango. "Garish Metaphysical Pornography." November 10, 2012.
tieman64. "Jupiter and Beyond the Infinite." February 19, 2011.
Tom Clift. "Enter the Void Is a Cinematic Achievement. It's Just Not One You Should Bother Watching." January 13, 2011.
tom van de Bospoort. "The Film; Not for Your Eyes." September 25, 2010.
uglyzombie. "Gaspar Noe's Masterpiece." January 27, 2011.
vikram-ry123. "New Generation Underground Movie Gets a New Void." February 12, 2011.
w-sky. "A Stirring Story of Love Passion, Cinematography Taken to a Higher Level." September 2, 2010.

Melancholia

(victor7754@hotmail.com). "No Drugs." April 20, 2012.
AMichaelL. "Those Who Are Depressed Act Calmest Under Stress." January 13, 2012.
anna19864. "A Dark, Surreal, Though Captivating and Evocative, Doomsday Film." July 3, 2012.
aurora7. "A Beautiful Meditation of Being and Nothingness." December 2, 2011.
blackvenom-1. "A Movie That Literally Takes Your Breath Away." September 10, 2011.
bluestemz. "Dare I Say It . . . BREATHTAKING." September 26, 2011.
Bones Eijnar. "Welcome to His World." June 27, 2011.
by_all. "What Did You Do to Me von Trier." October 11, 2011.
chaos-rampant. "The Sound of Void Washing Itself Empty." September 20, 2011.
Chris_Docker. "Perhaps One of the Year's Most Important Movies." October 19, 2011.
cowboyandvampire. "*Melancholia* Is Beautiful, Frustrating." October 20, 2012.
CubeRic9000. "The Realism of Suffering, in a Life That's Far from Perfect." December 5, 2011.
David. "Enigmatic Beauty." April 8, 2013.
dr luj. "Not for Everyone." November 19, 2011.
earlytalkie. "Difficult to Warm to, But Definitely Worth It." January 15, 2013.
Echooche. "So Good That It Makes Me Forgive LvT About Antichrist." August 24, 2011.
Emma Diaz-Nicholson. "Acidly Funny, Traumatic, Haunting, Overwhelming—An Experience Not to Be Missed." April 14, 2013.
Golligow. "Beautiful in Form and Content." May 22, 2012.
gradyharp. "Film as an Art Form." May 16, 2012.

Grumpy. "Another Nazi Apology from Everybody's Favorite Apologist." October 19, 2015.
Harley Green. "Crazy/Beautiful 10 Years Later." December 28, 2012.
hazefjord. "A Film About Depression and Helplessness." June 14, 2012.
hedgehog5. "Lars von Trier's Wagnerian Opera of 2011—The Ragnarok of Western Capitalism." October 1, 2011.
jebophos. "I Highly Recommend This Film—But It's Not for Someone Looking for a 'Cheerful Romp.'" August 4, 2012.
jennyhor2004. "Portrayal of Depression as Escape and Freedom from Middle-class Shallowness and Hypocrisy." December 24, 2011.
Jess-K. "A Movie That Gets Under Your Skin." June 29, 2012.
jmillerdp. "Magnificent!" November 22, 2011.
Joe Mason. "Earth Shattering!" September 26, 2011.
jon_orourke45. "A Gem . . . A Sparkling Diamond." February 14, 2012.
junkielee. "Melancholia." December 4, 2011.
Justafilmwatcher. "*2001*: A Space Odyssey Is Its Only Analogue." November 21, 2011.
Karen. "Transform to Lars von Trier for 2 Hours." July 14, 2011.
Khemaluck Deeprawat. "Has Such a Deep and Beautiful Message for Depressive People." January 22, 2015.
KineticSeoul. "Well the Title Explains It All and That Is About It." October 1, 2011.
M. J. Arocena. "A Maddening Work of Art." November 28, 2011.
malull2. "The Beauty of It." November 6, 2011.
manupravda. "Another Powerful LVT Movie." August 4, 2011.
Mario Nicolaou. "Emotionally Bleeding." May 16, 2012.
masoroso. "A Movie That Literally Takes Your Breath Away." September 26, 2011.
Michael Niebuhr. "Visually Spectacular, Beautifully Acted, Compelling Dialogue, Strong Direction." May 20, 2011.
misty 77. "Powerful and Meaningful If You've Been There." February 13, 2012.
olga255. "The Two Faces of Depression." October 4, 2011.
oOgiandujaOo. "Dark Wine." October 4, 2011.
ribeiroworld. "Haunting." November 19, 2011.
Roger Burke. "Hey, Don't Worry, Be Happy—The End Is Always Near, Anyway." June 16, 2012.
Rudd Thijs. "An Intriguing and Memorable Masterpiece." January 5, 2012.
samkan. "Must Let Go When Viewing Lars." November 24, 2011.
Sarah Cupit. "Lars von Trier's Melancgolia Is a Stupendium." December 27, 2011.
sarahmillyhannah. "View in This Movie Will Not Leave You with a Feeling of Melancholia." January 16, 2012.
sarnela. "Sticks to Your Mind . . ." November 9, 2012.
saternbaby. "Eat the Rich (or Don't Let the Dark Night Get You Down; Living Art Will Come Around Again)." May 9, 2012.
sebbastiann. "My Favourite Movie of 2011." January 8, 2012.

secondtake. "An Ambitious Imperfect but Interesting Artistic Effort—Human Emotions vs. the Cosmos." September 23, 2012.

stan Collins. "The Toilet and the Magic Cave." January 13, 2013.

steve_plumber_man. ". . . the very core of my existence was challenged by this movie." July 20, 2014.

Summer Black. "Helplessness." September 12, 2011.

tabuno. "An Amazing Sensory Delight That Misses an Important Human Component." April 1, 2012.

tvspace. "Dizzifying." November 14, 2011.

Uncle Newgod. "The Force of the Nonrepresentational." December 25, 2011.

Vincentiu. "A Special Experience." October 4, 2011.

Vlad Coroama. "A Reflection on the Human Soul, an Invitation to Truthfulness and to Life." November 14, 2011.

William O. Tyler. "A Fantastic (and Fantastical) Study in Depression." January 28, 2016.

Xaaralia. "I Was Apprehensive . . ." November 10, 2011.

zephyryoun. "It's Magical, Terrifying, and Yet so Human." October 28, 2012.

ZombieLittlePony. "Heartbreaking, Mindblowing, Overall Unforgettable." October 16, 2011.

Index

2001: A Space Odyssey (Stanley Kubrick)
  new religious movements and
    alternative spirituality   41–5, 55
  Starchild   51–4, 72–6, 86, 97, 102,
    125–7, 130–1, 153

altered states of consciousness
  dissociative   4, 12, 70, 79, 106, 113–14,
    123, 126–9, 150, 159, 163, 188
  dream states   76, 120, 125, 127, 130,
    139, 142, 146, 163–5
  entheogens   120, 122–3, 140, 143–9,
    181
  sleep deprivation   146–7
alternative spirituality   3, 21–8, 31–7, 48,
  50, 89–90, 116, 124, 181–2, 190–2
American avant-garde   120
apocalyptic   43, 47–8, 163, 169, 171–8, 185
art cinema   18–20, 73–5
atheism   45, 48–52, 121, 176, 180–2, 186
audience (viewing attitude)
  immersion   12, 16–17, 61–5, 77–80,
    84, 87, 97, 102, 108, 130, 134,
    149, 164
  lyrical-associative (Torben Grodal)
    73–5, 98, 103, 139, 147, 160,
    164, 189
  openness   30, 79–80, 89, 136, 147
  preparation   78–80
  repeated film viewing   96–9
audience response, *see* religious
    experience
audience response (visceral)   13, 16,
  61, 65, 85–7, 100–1, 137–8, 141,
  165–6, 179
authority   23–31, 49, 82, 100, 105–7, 109,
  115–6, 181
  nonformative authority (Matthew
    Wood)   31, 115–17

Buddhism
  attachment   47–9, 76–7, 128–9, 145,
    150, 171–4, 183

dependent co-arising   69, 129
Easternization of the West (Colin
  Campbell)   27, 31–5, 59, 190
enlightenment   8, 23, 32, 49, 58,
  69–70, 72, 82, 87, 92, 103–4, 128–9,
  144–50, 171, 185
koan   17, 58, 72–3
lightning-bolt path/tantra   128, 186
meditation   17, 30–5, 43–4, 58–70,
  76–80, 123, 135–6, 140, 146, 181,
  185, 189
mindfulness   19–20, 58
non-discursive state of mind   29,
  57–8, 76, 79, 84, 88–90, 108, 125,
  160, 164–5, 181
no-self   33, 171
The Tibetan Book of the Dead   122,
  135
voidness   33, 171
Western Buddhism   30–5, 68, 76–7, 82
Zen   17–18, 33–5, 58, 146, 174

Clarke, Arthur C.
  2001: A Space Odyssey   39–44, 51
  Childhood's End   38, 43, 144
confronting darkness   5, 113, 172, 178,
  185
consumerism   3, 27–8, 32, 34, 109, 114,
  123, 133, 167–8
cultic milieu (Colin Campbell)   109, 117

deconstruction   2, 4, 35, 48, 50, 52, 54,
  69–70, 112, 129, 169, 171, 185,
  190–1
democratization/individualism   3–4,
  24–5, 27–8, 31–5, 54, 93, 108–10,
  116–17, 168, 180

early twenty-first century media culture
  atomization   107
  desensitization   111–13, 133
  post-truth   109–11
epistemology, *see* truth

faith (Søren Kierkegaard) 183
film technique
  ambiguous 11, 19–20, 39, 72–4, 103–4, 110, 113, 132, 185
  confronting 49, 94–5, 100–4, 111–14, 124, 127–8, 130–1, 134, 139–40, 142, 150, 151–2, 179, 191
  disparity (*Transcendental Style*) 11–12, 66, 68, 70–2, 132, 152, 158–9, 162–3, 189
  the everyday (*Transcendental Style*) 11, 68, 70–1, 132, 152, 158
  existential themes 19, 92–5, 106, 189
  frontality (*Transcendental Style*) 75, 153, 159–60
  meditative 11, 17–18, 20, 30, 57–69, 72–3, 76, 78–9, 128–9, 135–6, 145–7, 150, 183, 185
  repetition/patterns 62, 64, 68–9, 72, 118, 138–40, 161
  sensory overload 16, 69, 77, 87, 103, 108, 120, 131, 133–5, 137, 149–50, 151, 167
  sound techniques 12, 59–65, 68, 70, 131, 133–5, 137–9, 152, 154, 157–8, 160–3, 178
  stasis (*Transcendental Style*) 10, 12, 70, 72, 75–6, 81, 92, 131–2, 142, 157, 163–4, 167, 185, 189
  symmetrical composition 60, 65–9, 75, 145, 154, 159–60, 163
freedom 4, 24, 27–8, 35, 142, 190, 192

God 12, 25–6, 32, 36, 42, 44–53, 77, 85, 87, 91, 122, 176, 183–4

Higher Self 24, 31, 89, 116
Hinduism 27, 30, 33–5, 82, 145

immediatism (Arthur Versluis) 28, 122, 186

Kubrick, Stanley
  subconscious religious impulses 57, 102, 106

Lynch, David 139–40

memory 29, 73–4, 99–102, 106, 117, 132, 138–9, 142, 165–7, 187–8, 190–1

micropolyphony (György Ligeti) 59–60, 69, 138

new extremism (in film) 112–14, 151
Noé, Gaspar
  2001: A Space Odyssey 107, 120–1, 125–6
  cinematic ecstasy/possession 119–21

Picnic at Hanging Rock (Peter Weir) 162–4
pluralism 3–4, 21–2, 50, 105, 107, 113, 115, 122, 168–9, 189–90, 192
possession (Matthew Wood) 48, 104–5, 115–16, 124
potentiality 3–4, 42–4, 53–4, 70, 142, 150, 168, 190–1
psychologizing of religion/sacralization of psychology (Wouter Hanegraaff) 24–6, 45, 172, 184

religion and film studies
  Internet Movie Database 1, 10
  morals/values 9, 14, 16
  narrative 6, 9, 19
  ritual 14–19
  transcendental style 2–3, 7–8, 10–13
religious experience
  aesthetic 13, 16–17, 57, 77–9, 86–7, 188
  agency 26, 49–50, 74, 87, 101–4, 114–17, 124, 142, 145, 166, 182, 188
  ineffability (William James) 81–8, 147–9, 164
  mysterium tremendum et fascinans (Rudolf Otto) 29, 81–2, 85–7, 100, 113, 164, 182
  mystical practice (Jess Hollenback) 30, 59, 97, 145, 189
  noesis (William James) 70, 88–95, 131, 157, 188
  passivity (William James) 99–105, 115, 124, 158–9, 166, 186
  presence 4, 17, 67, 74, 84, 87, 104–6, 142, 172, 182, 184, 188
  transiency (William James) 95–9
ritual 4, 15–19, 95, 99–103, 120, 143, 146, 174–5
Romantic Ethic (Colin Campbell) 27, 32–3, 114, 167–8, 172

seekership 21–2, 74, 105, 107, 110, 114, 122, 133, 186
   guidance 31, 105, 181, 192
subconscious 24–6, 30–31, 41, 43, 57, 66, 74, 82–4, 103–5, 115, 120, 125, 146, 163–6, 188–90

Transcendental Style in Film (Paul Schrader), *see* film technique, disparity; the everyday; frontality; stasis
truth
   disgust (Winfred Menninghaus) 141, 149, 175, 191 (*see also* confronting darkness)
   esoteric/gnostic 23, 45–9, 72, 85, 96, 103, 143
   post-truth 109–11
   pragmatic/relativized 24–7, 31, 69, 105, 121, 124, 189, 190–2
   unmediated 18, 23, 26, 28, 31, 48, 74, 76, 90, 108–11, 115–16, 122, 141–2, 168–9, 181–2, 189, 191–2

unconscious, *see* subconscious

viewer, *see* audience
von Trier, Lars
   religious belief and practice 180–3

www.ingramcontent.com/pod-product-compliance
Lightning Source LLC
Chambersburg PA
CBHW072233290426
44111CB00012B/2069